THE COST
OF FEAR

THE COST

WHY MOST SAFETY ADVICE IS SEXIST AND HOW WE CAN STOP GENDER-BASED VIOLENCE

OF FEAR

MEG STONE

BEACON PRESS, BOSTON

BEACON PRESS
Boston, Massachusetts
www.beacon.org

Beacon Press books
are published under the auspices of
the Unitarian Universalist Association of Congregations.

28 27 26 25   8 7 6 5 4 3 2 1

This book is printed on acid-free paper that meets the uncoated paper
ANSI/NISO specifications for permanence as revised in 1992.

Text design and composition by Kim Arney

The author uses pseudonyms to protect the privacy
of some people who shared their stories.

Author's Note: This is a work of nonfiction. Most interviews were
recorded and transcribed. When recording and transcription was not
possible, I took detailed notes, which included exact quotes. My personal
stories are told from my perspective based on my memory of events.

Library of Congress Cataloging-in-Publication
Data is available for this title.
ISBN: 978-0-8070-1622-0; e-book: 978-0-8070-1623-7;
audiobook: 978-0-8070-1819-4

CONTENTS

SCARED AND POWERFUL

On a dusty mat in a high school gym or in a cramped classroom with desks shoved into a corner, I teach teenage girls to resist sexual coercion. The class is called self-defense, so some of them come in expecting to learn how to fight off a creepy stranger with kicks and punches from an action movie. Instead, we're teaching them to resist a guy they know and like. My co-instructor will portray that guy, the one at the party who invited her to go somewhere quiet. To listen to music, he said. All night he made her feel special, getting her drinks, ignoring other girls' flirtations. But when they get to the upstairs bedroom, all he wants is sex. He's charming the first time she refuses. Telling her she's beautiful, and it's not a big deal, and she doesn't have to worry because he's more experienced than other guys she's dated. When she refuses again, he yells. She shouldn't have come upstairs if she was going to be a tease. He could hook up with any girl at this party, and why did she waste his time. She gets up to leave. He blocks the door.

There's a sprawling debate about situations like this one, and most of the sides people take have nothing to offer her in this moment. For many, the problem is him. He should have been raised to respect her and taught how to get consent. If that fails, a group of well-trained bystanders should rush into the bedroom to stop him. For others, she should have known better. The problem is her poor choices. Or the problem is sexual liberation—if there were tighter rules about young men and women being alone together (and a complete erasure of same-sex intimacy and gender fluidity), she wouldn't be facing the prospect of sexual assault.

I believe we need a deep and specific investigation of where he learned that it was okay for his sexual desires to eclipse her limits, an investigation that would guide us toward the kind of change that will forever eliminate situations like this one. But that's a long-term endeavor with no guarantee of universal success. Meanwhile, a girl is stuck in a bedroom with a guy who doesn't care that she refused sex, and that guy is blocking the door.

We teach her to stand up, move away from him, put her hands in front of her chest, and yell, "Let me leave!" He might move aside, probably calling her a bitch as he does. In that case, she learns to get out fast. Other times he grabs her wrist. We teach her to break the grip, using her whole-body weight against his hand. To strike the head or groin if he doesn't relent. A person who tries to assault her may be larger and have more muscle, but everyone's body has weak points: eyes, head, groin. I'm not training Ultimate Fighting Champions. The goal is to cause enough pain to end the threat, and the surest way to do that is to strike the vulnerable parts of his body.

My co-instructor wears fifty pounds of protective gear, which makes it possible for our students to practice defending themselves by striking as hard as they can. With this level of realism, most people feel scared or angry or immobile in all the ways they would if the situation were real. And because of that, they learn to access their power in the midst of all those feelings.

Some sexual violence can be stopped by ordinary strength. Researchers who analyze the National Crime Victimization Survey, which reaches 150,000 US households per year, consistently find that women who physically or verbally fight back are less likely to experience rape. Most—but not all—of these kinds of studies also show that fighting back does not increase a person's chances of serious injury.[1]

I don't want to put the burden of stopping rape on teenage girls. But options don't have to be burdens. We can give people the skills to protect their bodies without making them responsible for someone else's decision to harm them. And we can do this without diminishing the experiences of survivors for whom fighting back was not an option. My friend and colleague Martha Thompson made the analogy of a hypothetical city in which large numbers of people are drowning. Of course, she says, there should be government-funded lifeguards, and of course, city leaders should work to determine why so many people are falling into the water. "I do not want to eliminate these structural supports for minimizing drowning," she explains, "but I want to add the possibility that people have opportunities to learn how to swim."[2]

With something like drowning, it's easy to accept that working to change the conditions that cause the problem and giving people the skills to save themselves are two necessary parts of the same solution. Each of these efforts would be less effective without the other. But gender-based violence is different.

Gender-based violence is defined by UNICEF as "physical, sexual, mental or economic harm inflicted on a person because of socially ascribed power imbalances between males and females."[3] It includes sexual assault, sexual harassment, street harassment, intimate partner violence, stalking, trafficking, and identity-based hate violence. People of all genders can experience gender-based violence. When it's directed at men, it usually targets them for being too feminine or not masculine enough. When it's directed at nonbinary or gender nonconforming people, it targets them for not conforming to the gender they were assigned at birth.

One of the reasons gender-based violence remains prevalent is that it's woven so tightly into the fabric of our lives that people often experience it as normal or inevitable. Most of this violence is enacted in one of two contexts: close relationships or economic relationships. Close relationships include partners, family members, friends, and acquaintances. Economic relationships include those in the workplace as well as the institutions that prepare us for work, like school or college. Experiencing gender-based violence disrupts our ability to trust, or it disrupts our ability to support ourselves. It persists because laws are inadequate or inconsistently applied, institutions dismiss the problem to avoid accountability, cultural norms about this violence are inconsistent, and some people are capable of abusing. Gender-based violence is a social and political problem, but it's often enacted in the most intimate spheres of our lives. To stop this violence, we need strategies that are just as intimate.

Still, working to prevent gender-based violence by building individual skills requires discernment. Victim blame is rampant. Survivors get messages, blatant or subtle, that if they hadn't gone to that party, worn that skirt, taken that drink. There are two opposing philosophies of how to make people safer, one exacerbates victim blame and the other challenges it. I call them *safety through compliance* and *safety through resistance*.

Safety through compliance puts the burden on women and others who are targeted for gender-based violence. We are assaulted, they say, because we make bad choices. The way to avoid being a victim is to be smarter. But being smarter has nothing to do with reasoning or thinking. The way to be smarter is by following. Safety through compliance gives us life-limiting rules we're supposed to follow if we want to avoid being attacked: Don't undress in front of your bedroom window. Always take the elevator (criminals hide in stairwells). Don't shop alone. These rules are usually made by men who don't provide any good reasons for why we should follow them.

Most women I know have encountered this kind of directive: an unnuanced claim that our daily routines are dangerous. To stay safe we should forego errands and pleasures, we should treat our friends and spouses like chaperones whose job it is to protect us from being in public alone. There is no evidence that constricting our lives in any of these ways makes us safer. Also, these directives are irrelevant to most gender-based violence. Not walking alone at night won't save you from your boss's sexual harassment. Avoiding stairwells does nothing to help the girl in my class get out of that bedroom. Compliance-based safety advice targets women, even when it is presented as gender-neutral. A Google search for "women how to be safe" turns up billions of results, most of them lists of activities we should avoid or do only in groups. But when you search "men how to be safe" most of the top results are articles about what men can do to avoid making women uncomfortable. Only a few articles help men avoid being victims, and almost all of those were published outside the United States.

It's an insidious way to control us. Rather than telling women to retreat from public life, advice like this scares us into diminishing ourselves. It also mis-calibrates our fear. If we listen to it, we feel unsafe in parking lots or stairwells, rather than paying attention to the people who are more likely to harm us—bosses, acquaintances, intimates, religious leaders.

At its core, safety through compliance diverts us from connecting our personal safety with social inequality. It's compelling because the risk of random violence by strangers is greater than zero and the fear many women feel walking alone after dark is real. Decades of research, reviewed by sociologist Fiona Vera-Gray, shows that women are more afraid of crime than men are.[4]

Safety through compliance can make us feel like we're taking control of our lives. But by harping on the small percentage of assaults perpetrated by people we don't know in places we routinely visit, it protects us from hard questions: *I'm falling in love, but can I trust someone who mocks me every time I tell him what my limits are? I love my local church, but leaders in our denomination covered up clergy sexual abuse. Is it safe to stay? Is it ethical?*

Safety through resistance gives people who are targeted for gender-based violence the skills to protect themselves without blaming them for being attacked. Its advocates understand violence as a political and social problem, not as the fault of those who are assaulted. We protect ourselves by challenging restrictive rules, not following them.

Resistance-based self-defense training emerged from social justice movements, most visibly feminist and Black liberation. Sometimes called empowerment self-defense, this approach to personal safety emphasizes choice and agency. Women and nonbinary people make ourselves safer by resisting the conditions of inequity that often show up in our personal lives as coercion and control from people we know, like, and love. Most gender-based violence starts with demands for compliance: an abusive partner who doesn't want you to see your friends, a boss who promises a promotion if you stay late and if you don't complain when he tells sexist jokes (he's just being funny and you should learn to lighten up).

Self-defense skills are taught to individual people because other systems and structures, like laws and community interventions, are not enough to stop assaults in the moment. Safety through resistance gives people practical skills to minimize harm against themselves. But more than that, it helps them experience the power of their bodies and voices. It puts the people who are most likely to experience harassment, abuse, and violence at the center of efforts to stop it.

Safety through resistance presents a range of self-protection strategies and invites people to choose the ones that work for them. The range includes the usual kicks and strikes that people picture when they think of self-defense but also verbal skills and options for physical escape that don't involve hurting the other person. If we're threatened by people we love, or people who have power over us at work, physically striking them might not be viable. Safety through resistance presents options that range from politely refusing unwanted attention to yelling a firm "No!"

Even though most gender-based violence is caused by people we know, safety through resistance recognizes that too many women are diminished by deep, gut-level fear. It surfaces in dark parking lots or empty stairwells or anywhere else we've been told we shouldn't be alone. It's so entrenched in our psyches that no logical argument can dislodge it. Self-defense training gives us an equally visceral experience of our power. When we walk past a group of drunk men or down a poorly lit street, we can imagine protecting our bodies with a kick or strike. This response to a situation we might otherwise experience as threatening keeps us from being diminished by fear. As a result, we may be less likely to avoid places we need or want to go.

Safety through resistance helps us ask hard questions: *How did we learn to disregard our intuition? Why are our working conditions so precarious that we feel we have to endure sexual harassment to earn money? Who told us our bodies were weak or that fighting back was not possible, and who benefits from our lack of confidence in our strength?*

There are two ways that safety through resistance is grounded in evidence. First, it focuses on the types of violence that are statistically common. In most groups of teenage girls that means sexual assault by a friend or intimate; Indigenous women are taught skills to resist abduction (in response to the crisis of missing and murdered Indigenous women) while mostly white groups are taught that abduction is rare compared to abuse from people they know. Second, self-defense programs that are explicit in their social and political analysis of violence have been shown by research to be effective. Research on empowerment self-defense programs in Canada, the US, and Kenya has shown that they reduce sexual assault by 50 to 65 percent.[5]

I come from a family of silences, though we don't fit the profile of people who suppress the truth. We are loud laughter and generous hearts. Holidays with thirty people around a table, ten conversations at once.

But that much joy crowds everything else out. I was in my late twenties before anyone else acknowledged that my father was abusive. There were so many other ways the adults described him—troubled, eccentric, complicated. We had a privileged family's access to doctors who provided a constant stream of diagnoses to explain his hostility. My mother was relentless in her efforts to create a happy family. She built us a world of dance recitals and theater. She swallowed all the hard truths, enduring my father's cruelty alone. There are a hundred ways my life is better for having been protected from the whole story of my family, but the silences left me conflicted about whether I could trust myself. Instead of developing awareness or discernment, I stayed numb.

I didn't feel like I belonged anywhere until I started working at a domestic violence crisis center. In a cramped office near the back door of a YWCA building in Poughkeepsie, New York, I found home. I shared desks and sometimes chairs with other women who talked about rape and abuse like it was any other topic. No averted eyes or changed subjects like I got from my parents when I talked about my work. I became a court advocate, helping survivors get orders of protection. I made sure they were never alone during the hours-long wait to see a judge. I kept up a steady stream of conversation about the fruit bowl paintings on the waiting room walls or the weather or the view of the Mid-Hudson Bridge from the fourth-floor window.

I spent my young adulthood immersed in other women's emergencies because stories of abuse that had details and incidents kept something alive in me. When I couldn't articulate the violations I'd experienced, domestic violence crisis work gave me the next best thing: an intimate connection to abuse that didn't require me to reveal—or even under-stand—anything about myself. When I was in court, my life made sense. Most other times it didn't. I was nineteen the first time I helped a survivor get an order of protection against an abusive partner. Ten years later, the survivor who needed my help was my mother.

But the more emergencies I absorbed, the more disembodied I be-came. I sometimes sat in my car in the courthouse parking lot and slapped my forearms just so I could feel something.

I believed in the law. I had this idea that something important would change if abuse was decisively punished. I wanted judges to tell abusers how wrong they were, and for survivors to feel whole because a man in a position of power said that their partner was wrong. But the "abuse prevention orders" that the court clerks produced almost never lived up to their name.

I wish I could say I made a principled decision to leave the court system. But I left because I could no longer force myself to drive to that building and sit through those hearings. Absorbing other survi-vors' crises without attending to my own trauma became untenable. I realized if I couldn't heal or empower myself, I would never be useful to anyone else. I needed to feel powerful, capable of stopping a person who might try to hurt me. I needed to know I could do something about my father's too-tight hugs and grabs and yelling. So I began learning self-defense.

I learned the beauty of being scared and powerful at the same time. I found the strength in my hips, the power of my arms and legs, the precision of my fingertips. I learned that I didn't need any special athletic talent—only training—to resist sexual violence.

––––––––––––

I am in a rape scenario, lying down on the mat, crying. The instructor, playing the role of an attacker, pins my arms. I have learned not to fight arms with arms; this is not a contest. Instead, I take the tension out of my arms. I know my hips and lower body will throw him off if he gets on top of me, and if he doesn't, there is a limit to how much he can hurt me with so much of his body occupied restraining my arms. The minute he moves, I move. He has to let go of my arms to proceed, and when he does, I will find a vulnerable part of his body to strike.

Before learning self-defense, there were beliefs I'd espoused: *It's OK to say no when you don't want sex. Everyone's body deserves respect.* And there's a way I didn't fully own what I was saying until I had the visceral experience of protecting my body.

The next time my father tried to pull me into an unchosen hug, I put my hands in front of my body and said "No." I didn't consciously decide to do this. Self-defense changed an unconscious part of me—I could protect the integrity of my body even when I didn't have the presence of mind to make a decision.

My tiny moment of resistance helped me understand the role self-defense plays in preventing gender-based violence. Often when people experience or witness acts of abuse, we freeze. This response is a biological reality. The research of neuroscientist Amy Arnsten[6] and others shows that when humans are overwhelmed by stress, the part of our brains that are responsible for reasoning and decision-making are the most compromised. When humans are under stress, we default to our habits. Self-defense training can make resisting a habit. If more people have the tools to keep from being immobilized by our physiological fear responses, then a critical mass of us would be available to challenge a teacher who makes too many comments about a teenager's developing body or to interrupt a person who is dragging a passed-out woman into an upstairs bedroom.

Even with pandemic-related increases, violent crime has declined substantially in the last four decades, but not all declines are equal. A middle-class white college student is much less likely to be mugged by a stranger in New York City than she was decades ago, but she's just as likely to be sexually assaulted on campus by someone she knows. According to the National Crime Victimization Survey, the sharpest decreases over the past thirty years are in crimes committed by strangers against people with the highest incomes.[7]

There are countless ways compliance and resistance, confidence and fear play out in people's lives. There are times we make deliberate choices about our safety and times we don't feel like we can. There are times, too, when the line between agency and coercion is blurrier than it should be. My own experiences of safety through resistance have forever changed me, but no single person's experience can be the whole story. Especially a person like me, who is shaped by race and class privilege. So to get a more complete picture, I interviewed close to one hundred people about their experiences of fear and power or their professional expertise about gender-based violence and ways to prevent it. Some of them chose to be identified by their full names, others by just their first name. Still others chose to use pseudonyms for their first name, their last name, or both to protect their privacy.

Every time we alter our lives to avoid violence, we are making a political statement, whether we intend to or not. Crossing the street to avoid a homeless person says one thing. Not leaving your kid alone with a parish priest in the wake of a clergy sexual abuse crisis says another. There are two kinds of safety choices: those that disrupt power structures and those that leave them unquestioned. Safety decisions that challenge power inequities require more fortitude, but they also lead to real change.

PART I

WHAT HOLDS US BACK

CHAPTER 1

MONUMENTAL, UNSATISFYING VICTORIES

Roxanne's ex was having a good day. The two of them were standing together in the courthouse parking lot when I arrived for the hearing, laughing at each other's jokes. Roxanne's jaw was tight, and her smile looked forced, but there was an ease and familiarity to their conversation. All I knew about this guy was what Roxanne had told me—the times he'd tried to strangle her, the hateful words, the threats. So I found it disconcerting to see him hold up his end of a normal conversation.

That day was the disposition hearing, where Roxanne's ex would respond to the allegations and the judge would decide if the temporary order of protection became permanent. Usually this hearing was when a temporary order's teeth were pulled. While a temporary order said "no contact or communication," the permanent order was full of exceptions—except when he picks up the kids, except when his boss tells him to go to the store where she works, except his back is hurting from sleeping on his mother's couch so he needs to move back home. Judges often see the men who appear before them as fathers who deserve access to their children, not as manipulative people who are looking for covert ways to harass their partner and take advantage of loopholes in the order. Most of our efforts to oppose the exceptions failed.

I'll do whatever you want, Roxanne's ex told her. *Let's get this over with.* I took that as my cue. I was a court advocate, barely twenty, with aspirations of law school. I had a backpack full of pens and a legal pad, and I'd read the order of protection statute more thoroughly than any of my homework assignments. I suggested terms of the permanent order, and for each one, he said, "Sure, whatever she wants." We got him to agree to stay away from her 12-step meetings and to pick up the kids at his mother's so he'd never have to be at her house. When we got into the courtroom, he kept his word, and with everyone in agreement, the judge had no reason not to sign off.

I left court that day feeling like I had made the system work. But when Roxanne came to the YWCA for support group the next week, she looked like a crumpled piece of paper. Her ex had found ways to circumvent even the most specific provisions of the order, and he was still harassing her.

I was heartbroken. I expected so much of the courts. I believed, or I wanted to believe, that the heartbreak of domestic violence could be repaired by strongly worded orders of protection. I wasn't experienced enough to separate my disappointment over the failure of my perfectly crafted order from Roxanne's much more urgent fear and distress. My more skilled coworkers listened and empathized. They invited other women in support group to share how they'd coped with their exes pushing against the boundaries of orders of protection. That didn't feel like enough to me, so I soothed myself with a fantasy: I would become a lawyer, and when I did, I'd have the power to fix the system for Roxanne and everyone else.

In a way, Roxanne even having an order of protection was progress. A woman asking a court to tell her children's father to stop abusing her was unthinkable for most people in her grandmother's generation. Twenty years before that hearing, there were no rape crisis centers or domestic violence shelters in the United States. The prevailing belief in many communities was that what happened in the home was nobody else's business, or worse, that any woman whose husband hit her must have done something to deserve it. The court system getting involved in assaults by intimate partners is a form of social change, defined by sociologists as changes in human interactions, relationships, and social expectations that transform culture and institutions. Social change is accomplished by coordinated efforts to change laws, people's minds, and social norms, which are unwritten rules governing which behaviors are appropriate.

There is no questioning the magnitude of social change on the issue of gender-based violence. Marital rape was legal in my lifetime. When Anita Hill testified before the Senate Judiciary Committee in 1991, it was only five years after the US Supreme Court ruled that sexual harassment violated the Civil Rights Act of 1964. A 2017 Gallup poll found that 69 percent of Americans view sexual harassment as a major problem, up from 50 percent in 1998.[1] Another Gallup poll, from 2013, found that an overwhelming majority of Americans, 82 percent, believe there should be government-funded rape crisis centers.[2] A 2022 Pew Research Center poll found that the number of people who support the #MeToo movement is more than twice the number of those who oppose it.[3]

University of North Carolina political scientists Sarah McAdon and Frank Baumgartner identified promising changes in news media coverage of campus sexual assault. They reviewed articles published in three major outlets, the *Washington Post*, the *New York Times*, and *USA Today*, between 1980 and 2014. Not only did they find an increase in the number of related articles published—from a few dozen in the 1980s and '90s to over four hundred in 2014—they also saw substantive changes in the way sexual violence was framed. In the 1980s and '90s, most articles focused on a single rapist, who was presented as a deviant or an aberration. In contrast, more recent coverage focused on the magnitude of the problem, the experiences of survivors, and institutions' responsibility to prevent sexual assault. Research on media coverage of other social issues, like poverty and the death penalty, shows that news stories that focus on the magnitude of the problem are more likely to sway public opinion than stories about a single person or incident.[4]

Still, there's a complicated relationship between changes in people's beliefs (or the version of beliefs they share with public opinion researchers) and the actual prevalence of gender-based violence. Psychologist Mary Koss found that decades of raising awareness of campus sexual violence have not made women safer. Her 2015 study showed that rates of campus sexual assault were higher than they had been in 1985.[5] At the same time, most federal data sources show sharp declines in violent crime since the 1990s. According to the National Crime Victimization Survey (NCVS), a nationally representative study of 220,000 people in 150,000 households conducted by the US Department of Justice every year, aggravated assault fell 83 percent from 1993 to 2021. Simple assaults, which don't involve weapons or cause serious injury, were down almost 80 percent.[6] But violence linked to social and political inequity is not declining as consistently as other types of crime. Even before the Covid pandemic sparked increases in anti-Asian hate violence, the US Department of Justice found no significant decrease in race-based violence between 2005 and 2019.[7] Rapes and sexual assaults reported to the NCVS have declined since the 1990s, though not as steadily or consistently as other crimes. For example, rapes and sexual assaults reported to the NCVS more than doubled between 2017 and 2018, the first year of the #MeToo movement. That same year there were no stark increases in reports of other violent crimes.[8]

Framing gender-based violence as a crime may not be the best way to capture how prevalent it is. Mary Koss is recognized as the first researcher to uncover the high rates of sexual violence perpetrated by familiar people. She coined the term "acquaintance rape" in the 1980s, when the prevailing belief both inside and outside of academia was that most rapes were committed by strangers. After reviewing some ridiculous research proposals from her male colleagues (one of which had women enter a lab wearing bras of different sizes and then asked male study subjects to rate how "rape-able" they were), Koss saw the need to ask students directly about their experiences of sexual violence.[9]

Koss developed a questionnaire called the Sexual Experiences Survey, which asks participants about behaviors that meet legal definitions of rape or sexual assault but don't use those labels. One question asks if they've had an unwanted sexual encounter because the other person was "using force, for example holding me down with their body weight, pinning my arms or having a weapon." Koss also developed a survey to assess perpetration, with questions like "Have you engaged in sex play (fondling, kissing, or petting, but not intercourse) when she didn't want to because you overwhelmed her with continual arguments and pressure?" (She is working with a team to make the survey more gender-inclusive.) By asking students about behaviors rather than using politically and psychologically charged words like "sexual assault" and "rape," Koss was able to capture the magnitude of the problem. She also captured the disconnect between the behaviors that constitute rape and sexual assault and the labels. In her initial research, only 43 percent of women who responded yes, they had been forced to have intercourse against their will also responded yes to the question that asked if they'd been raped. Mary Koss also found differences in responses based on women's relationships to the person who had raped them: 55 percent of women who had been forced to have sex against their will by strangers considered the experience to be rape compared to only 23 percent of women who had been forced by acquaintances.[10] In Koss's 1985 study, 27 percent of women reported experiencing sexual assault or rape while 7.7 percent of men reported perpetrating sexual assault or rape. When Koss repeated the study in 2015, 33.4 percent of women reported experiencing rape or attempted rape and 12.7 percent of men reported perpetration.[11] A larger study conducted in 2019 by the Association of American Universities found that 23 percent of women experienced some form of sexual assault during college.[12] A wide range of researchers continue to use Koss's Sexual Experiences Survey. Even those who don't use the Sexual Experiences Survey have followed Koss's lead, asking about behaviors rather than labels that are associated with crime.

The US Centers for Disease Control and Prevention (CDC) is the only federal agency that measures the magnitude of gender-based violence by asking about behaviors. Kathleen Basile, deputy associate director for science in the CDC's Division of Violence Prevention, leads the National Intimate Partner and Sexual Violence Survey (NISVS). This survey focuses solely on sexual violence, intimate partner violence, and stalking and asks questions about the impact of this violence on people's health. NISVS was first conducted in 2010, and it is not released annually like the National Crime Victimization Survey. Public health research is under-resourced compared to crime research. The most recent NISVS, conducted in 2016 and 2017, included just over 27,500 people. Earlier surveys reached between 10,000 and 16,000 people, a fraction of the 220,000 the Department of Justice surveys every year about crime.

According to the 2016–17 survey, 26.8 percent of women and 3.8 percent of men experienced attempted or completed rape in their lifetime and 47.6 percent of women and 23 percent of men have experienced other types of unwanted sexual contact. About 8 percent of women reported rape or unwanted sexual contact in the preceding year.[13] Basile says she hopes that over time the NISVS will be able to measure changes in gender-based violence from year to year. The survey has changed significantly each time it was conducted, so year-to-year comparisons are not yet meaningful. She also notes that the CDC attempted to measure perpetration in the first survey, but they stopped because almost nobody was willing to acknowledge that they'd abused. NISVS is administered over the phone, and Basile believes that may help explain the low rates of disclosure.

Research suggests that the way a survey is set up impacts how many people are willing to acknowledge that they forced or coerced someone to have sex. Psychologist RaeAnn Anderson led a systematic review of research on sexual assault perpetration by college men between 2000 and 2017 that looked at seventy-eight studies involving a total of over 25,000 participants. Results were inconsistent, due to how researchers defined perpetration. Also, in studies where participants could answer anonymously, more men reported that they had sexually assaulted than in studies that involved face-to-face interviews. Though estimates varied widely, this review found that an average of 29 percent of college men had perpetrated some form of sexual assault.[14]

We are in a historical moment with unique challenges. The invisibility of sexual assault by familiar people is in the past. But in its place is a disconnect between what people know they're supposed to do and what they do when not enough people are paying attention.

In 2018, Harvey Weinstein was charged with rape and Bill Cosby was convicted of sexual assault. A *New York Times* analysis identified 201 powerful men brought down by the #MeToo movement.[15] With all the news stories about reckoning and accountability, a person might have thought that every major institution had serious plans to root out abusive behavior, if for no other reason than to avoid damning publicity. But Sarah Cardozo Duncan knew better.

A social worker turned career counselor, Sarah noticed a disturbing situation. Women PhD students and postdoctoral fellows in the sciences were experiencing harassment and abuse, and university administrators were doing nothing to help them. Women in the early stages of their careers are navigating a specific power inequity. They work in labs often run by a single scientist, usually a tenured male professor who brings the university millions of dollars in grants. This person has control over whether they graduate, whether their research is published, and whether they get the recommendations they need to get a job. For those who are in the United States on work or student visas, getting fired could even mean having to leave the country. If you're abused in another kind of job, Sarah tells me, you can leave. "But unless you get your PhD," she explains, "you're kind of screwed."

Sarah tells me about a woman whose advisor tried to keep her from graduating because he said he was in love with her. This woman showed university administrators explicit emails he'd sent her, but they did nothing, and he delayed her graduation. Another woman was told tight budgets meant she would have to share a hotel room with her male boss at a conference. Another was fired from her lab for reporting financial impropriety. Women at multiple institutions were given racist nicknames by their coworkers. "The Saudi was called the terrorist in her lab, the Mexican the maid, the Brazilian the nanny," says Sarah.

Sarah's hair and lipstick are bright red. Her face is framed by thick black glasses. She talks about women in science with passion and urgency, using careful and emphatic hand gestures. They go to sleep thinking about science, they wake up thinking about science. It's been that way since someone gave them their first microscope when they were six.

The thought of women being forced to give up their purpose in life to escape bullying and harassment fills Sarah with pain and anger. But if you ask her about Title IX offices, you'll get a rant. Her gestures grow larger and more emphatic as she tells me about egregious conduct that university administrators ignored. Then she gets quiet. *Title IX doesn't work*, she says. *Human resources doesn't work. Trying to pretend it does just causes women more hurt.* Sarah knew she had to do something that didn't involve official channels. So in 2018—when some powerful men were facing consequences for sexual harassment and abuse, but most still weren't—she founded Friends of Sarah.

Friends of Sarah is a support system that helps women scientists get out of toxic labs. Sarah Cardozo Duncan brought together twelve of her friends, women scientists who are tenured professors or corporate executives in the STEM field. They mentor younger women, helping them find a way out of their situations and into a different lab, a biotech company, or a government agency. Anything but out of science.

Before the Covid pandemic, Friends of Sarah met in a first-floor conference room of an institute I've agreed not to name. Sarah kept the lights dim, she tells me. Harsh fluorescents wouldn't have worked. She got the institute's permission to let women attend the meeting without giving their names at the front desk, to make it safer for those worried about anonymity. It was a relief for some to know they were not alone and it wasn't their fault. Sarah acknowledges the power of empathy and connection, but that isn't enough for her. Friends of Sarah couldn't just be a support group. "So I called ten men," she tells me. "And I said, If I send these women to you, I don't want you coaching them. I want you to evaluate their science. And I want you to refer them to your male friends that have jobs."

During Covid, Friends of Sarah went virtual. With only a modest internet presence and a little bit of outreach, their distribution list grew to three hundred people. Most, but not all, were women. Now, Friends of Sarah reaches women all over the world, some of whom get up in the middle of the night to log on. They've added the option of meeting one-on-one with a mentor for those who don't want to share their situation with a group.

Joanne Kamens, a biologist and DEI (diversity, equity, and inclusion) consultant, is one of the mentors. She hasn't given up on changing the system, but she doesn't see it as a viable option for most of the women she helps. "I don't advise them to make a report," she tells me, especially if it's only one student blowing the whistle on a lauded scientist. "Even if someone can put a dent in the system, their chance of thriving after trying to use official channels is very low," she says. "We just want to get these women into a better situation where they find joy in their science again, and they have a potential for a career going forward, hopefully with their doctorate intact."

A big part of the problem, Joanne tells me, is that in academia, powerful professors don't have any real accountability. Their boss is a dean, another professor who, more often than not, isn't trained to investigate harassment. Some deans hold their positions for a few years, begrudgingly taking their turn doing administrative work. "I have not heard a single case where someone has gone to a superior, even a dean that's sympathetic, where anything has been done," Joanne says.

Most of the people I interview have complicated answers when I ask for solutions to the problem of gender-based violence, but for Sarah Cardozo Duncan, it's simple: tell the funders. Tenured professors who are much less professionally vulnerable should report abusive behavior to the government agency that is funding the abusive professor's research, like the National Institutes of Health (NIH) or the National Science Foundation (NSF). In July 2022, Congress strengthened federal agencies' authority to remove abusive scientists from government-funded research. A representative from the NIH confirmed to me that they accept anonymous reports and that they have the authority to investigate claims of harassment and discrimination that are filed anonymously. The representative said in an email that if the results of their investigation warranted it, "NIH can take several actions that could include or result in a change in senior personnel, or remedies for noncompliance, such as suspension or termination of the grant award."[16]

But Sarah Cardozo Duncan isn't hopeful. She tells me about a conversation she had at a cocktail party with a woman scientist, a tenured professor. "And she said, 'Well, Sarah, we shouldn't be arguing about this. We should find solution.'" But when Sarah proposed the solution of telling the funders, she tells me, the woman abruptly ended the conversation.

Friends of Sarah is not the Hollywood movie version of justice. But it works. And it's better than sacrificing women scientists to feed our need to believe in a specific narrative of social change. In a way, Sarah's strategy reflects the progress that has and has not been made in the last four decades. A lot of people know what they are supposed to say about gender-based violence. Rape is wrong. Nobody deserves to be abused. *Law & Order: SVU* is in its millionth season and one study of first-year college students found that those who watched it were less likely to believe in rape myths and more likely to say they would respect their partners' sexual boundaries than students who watched other crime dramas.[17]

Women's bathrooms in hospitals and bars have fliers in the stalls with facts about abuse and information about how to get help. The number of rich and powerful men who face consequences for sexually abusing is greater than zero. Still, according to the CDC, the majority of US women have experienced some form of unwanted sexual contact in their lifetimes, and three-quarters of women who have experienced intimate partner violence were twenty-five or younger when they were first abused.

Sometimes the act of resisting violence does more to keep us safe than depending on the institutions that are supposed to protect us. Esther Lee was on a New York City subway in October 2021 when the man sitting next to her tried to give her a fist bump. When she refused, he yelled at her. He called her a "carrier" and commanded that she suck his dick. Esther is Korean American. She recognized "carrier" as a racist slur blaming Chinese people (or all Asian people) for Covid. He tried to get close to her, maybe to grab her.

Because of a self-defense class she'd taken at work, Esther says, she felt calm. She got up and moved away. She put her hands in front of her body. "Don't come any closer," she told him. She pulled out her phone, hit record, and for fifty-seven seconds, captured him threatening and swearing, grabbing his crotch, yelling the word "carrier" at her. You see her hand in the frame, firm and still, communicating "Stop." "Do you see what he's doing?" she asks the other subway riders, most of whom look away or at their phones. He spits at her. The other riders don't react.

It took a few hours for Esther Lee to realize she'd been the victim of a hate crime. In the moment, her actions felt automatic. She compares her self-defense class to fire drills many of us learned in school—you practice what to do in an emergency enough times that when the emergency happens, you just do what you've learned, without thinking about it. She'd practiced protecting herself from verbal harassment and physical assault in the relative safety of a classroom, so when she faced that threat on the subway, she immediately understood what was happening. "It created a much greater sense of clarity in the moment," she tells me. That understanding gave her a sense of power. "Where the aggressor feels that they have the upper hand," she explains, "you also have the upper hand." Esther believes that her decisive response prevented the man from physically assaulting her.

When the train stopped at Forty-Second Street, Esther Lee moved to a different car. At Fifty-Ninth Street, she got off the subway, somehow remembering the police station there. Her legs shook as she climbed the stairs and walked into the precinct.

From the moment Esther began interacting with the police, she experienced what she describes as "poor bedside manner." The lieutenant asked questions that were as intrusive as they were irrelevant: *Where do you work? Where do you live? Do you have a husband?*

Then, for months, she heard nothing. So she called the NYPD Hate Crime Task Force to check on the status of her report. That was when she learned that the police hadn't classified the incident as a hate crime. She assumed that in the middle of widespread publicity about the rise in anti-Asian hate violence related to Covid, that the term "carrier" would be recognized as a racial slur. She was told to go back to the original precinct and request a copy of her police report and then request it be amended.

There's a form on the NYPD website, but someone told her that nobody reads them. So, in addition to filling out the online form, she printed, notarized, and mailed the application to the precinct with a self-addressed stamped envelope. She did this in October, and in

December, she got a copy of her report. That was when she learned that the officer hadn't documented that the man on the subway had called her a "carrier," which he did several times in the portion of the incident she'd filmed.

Esther Lee is the daughter of immigrants who instilled a deep sense of justice in her. You fight for what's right, and you take that fight as far as you can. So she called her friend, Jo-Ann Yoo, president of the Asian American Federation, who helped her get in touch with Jessica Corey, head of the NYPD Hate Crime Task Force. What followed, Esther describes, was a series of "curbside assessments" from Corey and other officers. Without conducting a thorough investigation, the police gave Esther several explanations for why they weren't treating the incident as hate speech. *You triggered him by filming him. Maybe he was just being friendly and you overreacted. Maybe if he had come at you from across the car it would have been a hate crime, but you sat next to him.*

Esther has a new appreciation for what it means to experience trauma. She had panic attacks for the first time in her life. She once began crying uncontrollably while ironing her clothes. For the most part, it wasn't the incident itself that continued to unsettle her.

"It was the frickin' trauma from dealing with the NYPD. And being told you're crazy, being told it's your fault," she tells me. "Being called a carrier is just as racially charged as being called a chink," she says.

Having to fight to get the police to acknowledge the magnitude of hate and violence directed at Asian Americans was a source of heartbreak. "You leave a conversation feeling deflated. You leave the conversation feeling revictimized. You leave the conversation thinking, oh my God, I can't believe that the head of the Hate Crime Unit is telling me that this was my fault because I filmed him."

Esther Lee has not stopped speaking up. She's intentional about pushing back against stereotypes that cast Asian women as docile and submissive. She spoke at a rally in New York City, and another in Washington, DC. She got the most traction when her friend, local news reporter CeFaan Kim, posted her video on his social media. He then interviewed Mayor Eric Adams, asking him to explain why the NYPD was ignoring anti-Asian hate violence. Shortly after Kim's story aired, the NYPD removed investigator Jessica Corey from her position as the head of the Hate Crime Task Force, calling the move a "routine reshuffling."

Esther and her community put a dent in a system that is notorious for quashing efforts to hold it accountable. She's inspired, she says, by Asian American activists and journalists who post regularly about hate violence on social media. It's impossible to know what's going on inside the NYPD, but she believes that the unrelenting attention is making it harder for politicians and the police to dismiss Asian American activists.

Most people in power begrudge change. Some actively resist it; others stall, hoping that if they run out the clock, activists will get tired or distracted and leave them alone. Still others wage a counterattack of slick brochures and heartfelt messages, trying to appear on board with progress. In 2020, municipal governments across the US posted Black Lives Matter signs in public buildings while they stalled on legislation that would have meaningfully reformed policing. The work of pushing back against all these tactics is tedious and necessary and slow. But the safety of our bodies is immediate.

Activists in feminist and Black liberation movements have long recognized that the institutions that so adamantly resist change can't be trusted to protect us. Self-defense, they have argued, is necessary for the health and wellness of political movements. Journalist and former member of the Student Nonviolent Coordinating Committee Charles E. Cobb Jr. argues that the Black civil rights movement of the 1960s would not have been possible without the armed activists who protected its leaders, even those who, like Martin Luther King Jr., advocated nonviolence.[18] Historian M. Aziz has documented the practice of martial arts and self-defense by Black Power activists from the 1950s through the 1970s. As a strategy for self-determination, self-defense training was pragmatic, enabling activists to protect themselves and each other since they didn't trust the police. Aziz's research also shows that self-defense was embraced by activists who saw that dismantling legal segregation alone did not create political and economic equity. "Feeling a sense of bodily autonomy and power could be accomplished immediately," they note, in contrast to political and economic progress, which was slow and inconsistent.[19] Martial arts and unarmed self-defense skills were taught by members of the Black Panther Party, the Committee for a Unified Newark, and other Black activist groups as a way to increase mental and physical confidence and to give people the spiritual resiliency to stay engaged in activist struggles. Aziz articulates the importance of martial arts and self-defense as "movement arts," which they define as "meditative, healing arts that allow the body to physically release and move through trauma, violence, and cultural and spiritual colonization. In creating such a release, practicing movement arts allows space to open for cultural and bodily autonomy."[20]

The role of self-defense in feminism can be traced back to the women's suffrage movement in the late nineteenth and early twentieth centuries. The research of historian Wendy Rouse shows that both British and American suffragists "consciously trained to use their bodies as physical sites of political struggles" by learning boxing and jiujitsu.[21] While some popular media at the time depicted self-defense as a way to help elite white women stay safe from men of color and poor immigrants as they left the domestic sphere for a bigger role in public life, Rouse shows that feminist activists saw self-defense as a way to upend power structures. Mainstream American suffrage groups initially distanced themselves from more militant British activists who used self-defense to counter police brutality. But that changed after a 1913 parade in Washington, DC, where suffragists were assaulted by the crowd and police did nothing to protect them. As a result, feminists in St. Louis, Washington, Ohio, and elsewhere started training in self-defense. "Just as the female body had long been subjected to violence and abuse," Rouse explains, "these women used their bodies as tools to resist assault and secure for themselves a sense of personal and political empowerment."[22] Around that time, prominent feminists also began calling for women and girls to learn self-defense to protect themselves from abusive partners.

In the 1970s and '80s, feminist martial artists began teaching self-defense as a strategy to stop violence against women. In a 1987 history of the feminist self-defense movement, sociologists Patricia Searles and Ronald Berger noted that while some feminists were responding to sexual and domestic violence by opening crisis centers, others looked to self-defense as a prevention strategy that gave power to women themselves rather than depending on police or other institutions.[23] In a 1997 study of feminist self-defense, sociologist Martha McCaughey articulates the specific role self-defense plays in feminist activism. "The politics of male domination are embodied," she explains, but "[a]s women embrace their power to thwart assaults and interrupt a script of feminine vulnerability and availability, they challenge the invulnerability and entitlement of men and, by extension, the inevitability of men's violence and women's victimization."[24]

Embracing self-defense doesn't mean giving up on legal and political change. What it means is knowing when not to depend on institutions or the law for our immediate safety. The systems we've fought for decades to change are reliable and unreliable. They are so much better than they were for previous generations and they're no different than they've always been. Changing laws and attitudes is essential to preventing gender-based violence but also inadequate. Because gender-based violence is intimate and personal, strategies for stopping this violence need to be intimate and personal too.

CHAPTER 2

THE COST OF FEAR

Elizabeth Graves worked as a scientist at a pharmaceutical company in California. When she went out with coworkers, she had a rule: only one drink, no matter what. She got invited to a basketball game once by the CEO and vice president of research. She's thirty-four, at a place in her career where she needs to find mentors if she wants her ideas to get traction. At the game, the men her age pounded back beers, matching the executives drink for drink. Meanwhile, Elizabeth explains, "I have to be the weirdo that's like, 'I'm good, I don't need another.'"

She's tired of watching her male colleagues shine at events like this one while she drinks a single beer as slowly as she can. At her last job, she tells me, her choices about drinking got more attention than her memos about scientific theories, which were dismissed when she presented them in meetings. Choosing not to socialize with executives the way men do, she says, has affected her professionally: "I'm not one of the crew. I'm outside. I can't engage in these bonding experiences on their terms and suddenly I'm not flexible."

During her PhD program, Elizabeth was raped by a medical student she'd been dating. She didn't trust anyone at the university to help her, so she didn't follow through with the report she'd made. The rape forced Elizabeth to rely on herself. She no longer ignores her intuition. "I realized I needed to protect myself sooner," she explains. "If I don't protect myself sooner, then I'm the one that's going to get hurt." But that kind of self-protection costs her professionally. When we talked, she was between jobs, unsure if she wanted to stay in STEM.

Elizabeth is one of thousands of women making this calculation, which sociologist Fiona Vera-Gray calls "trading freedom for safety." Vera-Gray's research shows that women fear crime more than men, even in cities or countries where men are more likely to be victims.[1] In a 2007 study led by epidemiologist Carol Runyan, women reported altering and constricting their lives to avoid violence. Of the 1,800 women surveyed, 46 percent avoided something they needed to do, like running an errand, and 71 percent avoided something they wanted to do, like going to a party or a bar. When asked what they did to keep themselves safer, almost every woman surveyed said they remained aware of their surroundings and kept their doors locked at home. Additionally, 73 percent said they got someone to accompany them if they left the house after dark, while only 19 percent said they took a martial arts or self-defense class. Women who had experienced violence and knew others who had experienced violence were the most likely to alter their lives. They were one and a half times more likely to own a gun—and two and a half times more likely to have another kind of weapon.[2]

More recent research illuminates gender differences in safety precautions. Through in-depth interviews with college students on a suburban campus, criminologist Shannon Jacobsen found that a majority of the women—and none of the men—avoided certain places or activities in order to be safe. One participant said she decided not to enroll in a class that met at night. Almost all the women but only a third of the men said they had walked around campus in groups to avoid violence. When the research team asked follow-up questions, they discovered that the men walked in groups in order to protect their female friends while women felt safer walking with a man and walked in larger groups when only women were present.[3]

In a 2023 Gallup poll, only 46 percent of Black women reported feeling safe walking alone at night in their neighborhoods compared to 75 percent of Black men and 73 percent of adults of all races and genders. That same poll found that 67 percent of Black women believe they would be treated with respect in an interaction with the police compared to the national average of 86 percent.[4]

"It's hard to see the world as being full of opportunities when you know that you can only do them during lighted hours," says Jaclyn Siegel, a social psychologist. For a month or more, each time I logged onto social media, yet another person in my network was sharing her viral tweet. "Every time I tell a man about all of the personal safety precautions I take, he looks at me like I'm crazy," it read. "Every time I tell a woman, she tells me a horror story and gives me a new safety behavior to add to my list." In an interview, she tells me the tweet was inspired by her research, which involved surveying women about how much psychic energy they devote to avoiding violence.

Before she moved in with her boyfriend, Jaclyn tells me, she maintained a rigorous routine of vigilance. She did theater, and rehearsals ended after dark. The shortest route to her apartment was through a poorly lit park, so she never walked directly home. She varied her route, too, to keep people from following her home. During that time in her life, the harassment and abuse she experienced in public was unrelenting. She was catcalled. She was flashed in public by a man who jumped out of the bushes, an experience she describes as almost laughably stereotypical. In the stacks of the library, a man came up behind her, trapped her, and said, "I need to take you on a date, I need to take you out." Another man pointed a knife at her and tried to get her to go with him. She's been doxed and harassed online for her outspoken feminist Twitter feed. Someone went as far as to make pornographic deepfakes of her.

She got her landlord to put bars on her windows and later moved upstairs after she saw a man masturbating outside her window and another banging on her window insisting she let him in. She looks over her shoulder when she walks around, and she doesn't go out alone after dark. She confines herself to well-lit areas and walks the other way if she sees a group of men congregating on the street. She doesn't go running at night. She claws her keys between her fingers when she walks. She knows the statistics—women are much more likely to be sexually assaulted by someone they know—but the amount of harassment she's experienced from people she doesn't know has left her in a constant state of vigilance. "The fear of experiencing sexual violence is very, very real. I don't go to clubs. I don't go to bars by myself. There are lots of things that I don't do," she tells me.

Jaclyn Siegel is a feminist. She's committed to holding men accountable for everything from egregious abuse to everyday sexism, so when she experiences harassment, it's hard to walk away without addressing it. But she doesn't feel like she has any other choice. "Standing up for myself might put me in more danger," she says. "If you're in a dark area by yourself, what's to stop the person? If there's no other people around, if it's too dark for security cameras to see what's going on," she explains.

I ask Jaclyn why she believes that resisting the men who harass her would make things worse. She is quiet for a while, maybe surprised by the question. As if women's vulnerability is a fact of life. It's a question I get from students all the time: Won't fighting back just make the attacker more angry? The body of research that answers this question is small, but the findings are consistent. A 2018 meta-analysis by criminologists Jennifer Wong and Samantha Balemba analyzed three decades of National Crime Victimization Survey (NCVS) data. They discovered that women who physically and verbally resisted attacks were less likely to experience rape.[5] There's some disagreement in the field about whether fighting back increases women's chances of sustaining other injuries. But one careful analysis by Jongyeon Tark and Gary Kleck found that resisting sexual assaults did not increase women's chances of being seriously hurt.[6] The NCVS asks people who have experienced an incident to answer detailed questions about it. Tark and Kleck thoroughly analyzed those reports and found that women who resisted did not sustain injuries after fighting back. Their research also found that multiple types of resistance were effective at reducing rape—forceful physical self-defense, yelling, and running away. The only strategy not associated with reduced rates of rape was arguing, reasoning, pleading, or cooperating. Research on resistance has been around since the 1980s, but it isn't reflected in the advice most of us get. Where I live, it's not uncommon for a news story about a woman who fights off an attacker to be followed by a statement from the police telling us to stay inside after dark. According to a systematic analysis of safety advice on university websites by Nicole Bedera and Kristjane Nord-meyer, the overwhelming majority of this advice is directed at women. Safety tips instructed women to be vigilant while walking, driving, or at home. Other common tips discouraged women from being alone or trusting anyone.[7]

Jaclyn Siegel feels safer in the world now that she lives with a man. Other men leave her alone when she's with him. But she also notices that everyone from servers at restaurants to a mechanic who was fixing her car talk to him instead of her. He's like "a shield and an invisibility cloak," she tells me, protecting her from unwanted attention but also seen as the person in charge. "I have felt so uncomfortable by how much bigger my world feels when I'm standing next to a man. And that's not because of some internalized beliefs I have about the value of women and the importance of being in relationships," she says. She's somewhere between amused and appalled when she realizes how much safer the world feels for him. He'll suggest going out for ice cream at night as if it's just a thing that people do. Much as Jaclyn loves her partner, thinking about how much safer she feels when she's with him makes her uneasy. She could imagine a woman staying in a relationship that is otherwise unfulfilling because the presence of a man keeps other men away.

Sometimes constant fear and vigilance is passed down through generations. Jenna was only twelve when her mother got mad at her for being alone with a male teacher and a couple of boys in her class. They were on a school field trip and had split into smaller groups for a short time before rejoining the rest of the class. In Jenna's mind, a teacher was an authority figure, which meant she was safe with him, unlike the strangers her mother had told her to fear. She didn't understand why her mother was so upset that she was the only girl in the group.

Jenna doesn't know why her mom is so fearful. She suspects it was her upbringing in a high-income suburb, where her family always drove and never walked. As a child, Jenna heard her mother condemn business owners whose racism was overt. Her mother's family had refused to eat in restaurants with signs saying "No Blacks or Jews." But Jenna sees a subtle racism that informs her mother's fears. "Good" neighborhoods are quiet and wealthy and full of white people. "Bad" neighborhoods are to be avoided.

Jenna thinks critically about her mother's beliefs, but she still feels the gut-level fear her mother instilled in her. She avoids being out alone after dark. When she lived in New York, she took a cab to visit her friend rather than walk through Central Park. Jenna sometimes lies to her mother when she thinks she hasn't been careful enough. They'll be on the phone and Jenna will mention a party she attended, and if she took the bus home, she'll lie and say she took a cab. For a time, Jenna wouldn't tell her mother she was taking Lyfts because there was something on the news about Lyft drivers kidnapping their passengers.

It hasn't been all bad. Jenna met the woman who is now her wife because she was out after dark and needed someone to walk her home. But she also once wound up on an awkward date with a man—he thought she was interested in him because she asked him to walk her to her car.

Other times, past experiences of abuse leave survivors feeling afraid of everything. For Elicia, every minute is a calculation. She tries to go to the grocery store when her five-year-old son is in school so she doesn't have to keep track of a child and her shopping bags while scanning the parking lot for predators. If she can't avoid shopping with her son, she parks near the cart return and limits what she buys so she won't have more than two bags. She won't park near a white van, or any other car that is large or has blacked out windows. She keeps her keys between her fingers and a knife in her purse. No matter how careful she is, there's always something else to be afraid of. She describes the complicated thought process that went into picking up dinner a few days before we talked. "Do I park near the restaurant, even though it's going to be harder to find parking because it's dark outside?" she thought. "Or do I park farther out under a light?" She takes her son to parks that are surrounded on all sides by grass or trees, never cars. If someone tries to take him, she figures, it will be harder for them to get away. She dresses him in bright colors, too, so he doesn't blend in.

It's been more than ten years since Elicia spent weekends at clubs with her friends, but she's quick to rattle off the rules they lived by: *Dudes only buy us drinks if we watch them made. Nobody goes to the bathroom alone. If someone decides to go to a man's car, someone else goes with. Everyone leaves at the same time and no one goes off alone.* If one of her friends gave her what she calls "the look," Elicia would step in and protect her. Elicia is an experienced martial artist. She began training at age six and earned her black belt by twelve, so she trusted her ability to fight off a guy paying the wrong kind of attention to a friend. But her martial arts training was a source of deep and confusing violations. The harm she experienced from instructors she thought of as family is the reason she's still so afraid.

Elicia was an accomplished fighter. She won sparring matches from the time she was eleven. But as one of the only girls in her martial arts school, she was subjected to a specific type of abuse. She was berated for her mistakes and blamed for other people's. Her teachers yelled and criticized her in front of her male peers, then told her that they were being hard on her because she was part of the family. When she got older, the abuse turned sexual.

"The man that had been my coach for five or six years at this point, decided to start having sex with me," she says. "I was sixteen, he was twenty-four." He owned the martial arts school, and he made her a lot of promises. They would get married, have babies, and open martial arts schools together. "He was feeding me all the lines that every young athlete wants to hear from their coach," she says. "I love you. You're amazing. You're so mature for your age. And then when it was all said and done, and I did give him my virginity, I told him, 'OK, I gave you what you asked. Now it's time to make this relationship real.'" In response, he withdrew. He told her she was too young, that she had to keep the relationship a secret. She had complied, but he never kept his promises. By the time she was seventeen, everyone in her martial arts community was calling her a home-wrecker and a slut.

Elicia lets out a sarcastic laugh when she talks about the disconnect between who she was taught to fear and who was actually harming her. She described a self-defense lesson she got from one of the most toxic martial arts teachers. "The instructor would turn his belt around and put a backwards hat on. And he would practice being a stranger like, 'Hey, little girl, you want to come see my puppy?' and we would practice telling the stranger 'No.'" As Elicia got older, the scenarios focused on dating. But it was always about saying no to a creepy guy who wanted to date her, not a trusted mentor who got sex by lying to her about their future.

Elicia grew up hearing constant messages about "stranger danger." She can't exactly place where the messages came from, but she has internalized them: "You trust the people that care about you. And then you fear the people you don't know." Even after all the abuse she endured from people she knew and trusted, she still feels a visceral fear of strangers. And the vigilance, Elicia tells me, is exhausting. It takes away from everything she's trying to enjoy about her life. But she believes she'll be blamed if something happens to her. Even more so if she doesn't take every imaginable precaution, if she lets her guard down just enough to park far away from the entrance to a building or go running after dark.

We know the cost of rape. A Centers for Disease Control and Prevention study found that the estimated lifetime cost of rape in the US was $122,000 per survivor in lost work, criminal justice proceedings, and health care expenses. The study also found that a third of these costs are borne by states and the federal government, an estimated $1.1 trillion.[8] We've invested considerably less effort in determining the cost of fear. If we added up the costs of turning down late shifts, taking rideshares to avoid the bus at night, and buying whistles, guns, and guard dogs, how many trillions of dollars would that be? If we add up the promotions women don't get because they have only one drink and leave the basketball game early, how many trillions more?

The cost of rape is borne by governments and employers, but the cost of fear is borne by women. There is an invisible trail of missed opportunities, of extra labor we perform. Vigilance about safety costs women in every realm of life—work, home, public space, and political power. It keeps us occupied with an impossible question: *How much we need to restrict our lives to avoid being blamed for someone else's decision to hurt us?*

Then there are the costs that aren't financial. How do we measure the mental energy it takes to avoid white vans or get errands done before dark? How much calmer and more creative would women and others targeted for gender-based violence be if our minds weren't occupied with the prospect of violence?

One of the most devastating costs of fear is the way it inhibits activism. Amanda Pauley used to get along with her neighbors. She lives in a small rural town in Pike County, Pennsylvania, where she could go to the grocery store or her kids' school and know almost everyone she saw. She lives near the compound owned by Rod of Iron, a religious cult related to the Moonies that believes in owning and using AR15s to enact God's will on earth. The first sign of trouble was in 2018. Rod of Iron held a gun salute the weekend after the mass shooting in Parkland, Florida. The event attracted people from all over the country.

It got worse in 2020. The pandemic brought even more right-wing extremism to Amanda's community. She watched, heartbroken, as her neighbors got sucked into conspiracy theories. The ranks of the Proud Boys, Moms for Liberty, and a few local extremist groups swelled. In response, Amanda got involved with Red Wine and Blue, a national organization that supports local activism led by suburban and rural women in swing states. She started speaking up at school board meetings at the height of the pandemic. Her daughter has asthma, serious enough to put her in the hospital a few times a year, so Amanda fought as hard as she could to make sure teachers and other kids wore masks. She stayed politically active, pushing back as her neighbors descended into vitriol over critical race theory, book banning, and whether the school should allow transgender kids to be themselves. "We were able to stop book bans in my really conservative community even though we lost the masks," she says. But even when they won, Amanda and her allies were always outnumbered. "It would be like a hundred of them," she tells me, "and only ten of us."

During school board meetings, members of the Proud Boys and other extremist groups would get physically close to Amanda and her supporters, yelling in their faces. They would stand at the exits, too, and try to block them from leaving. The school board promised to put more cops in the parking lots to see that everyone got to their cars safely, but that only lasted for one meeting. Amanda and her group tried to stick together, to always leave meetings in pairs, but they were so outnumbered it was easy to get separated. "That time for me was the most scary," Amanda says, "because they were making threats to find us."

It was one thing to be called a pedophile and a groomer in the middle of a school board meeting, but it was much worse when Amanda was with her children. She starts crying as she tells me about the time her son met her at a school board meeting because he needed a ride home. They called him an asshole for wearing a mask. Another time she was at Walgreens with her daughter. One member of Moms for Liberty began following her around the store, yelling, "The pedo queen is here!" There was a long line at the register. Her town is in the Poconos, and in the summer it fills up with New Yorkers who have vacation homes there. Amanda's daughter, who was eleven at the time, ran to the next aisle. "And while I was looking for my daughter," Amanda says, "I could hear her telling customers to keep their children away from me, that I was a pedophile, and a groomer. And I shouldn't be in the store."

What happened in the store was embarrassing but not as painful as having to answer her daughter's questions. "The hardest thing for me," Amanda says, "was when she got in the car, and she said, 'Mom, why did they say that about you?'" Amanda was at a loss for what to say. "How do you explain their weird connection with the LGBTQ community and pedophilia? I never wanted my daughter to connect them."

When you don't live in a small town, Amanda Pauley tells me, extremism like this is something you read about. But it's tearing her community apart. "These are people that I know. Our kids were friends prior to this nightmare," she explains. "I know these people, and I just think they're being fed a lot of misinformation. And my job is to correct that." But she hates that taking on that responsibility means having to think about her safety all the time, and she hates even more that her daughter is afraid. A few weeks before we talked, Amanda asked her daughter to run into a store so she didn't have to get out of the car. "What if one of them is in there?" her daughter asked.

Fear of harassment is costing Amanda her activism: "I was losing my voice because I didn't want my kids to reap the repercussions. And I knew that I had to take a step back because I didn't want it to affect them." So she stopped going to school board meetings in her own town. She stayed involved behind the scenes and went to meetings in other towns, but the impact was deep. "It just felt like they had silenced me," she says. "When you lead in organizing it's really hard to tell everyone how afraid you are because you don't want them to stop. So I felt really isolated." Her group once organized through a public Facebook page but they've gone underground—they use encrypted messages instead. "It's hard to talk about this with our members," Amanda tells me. "Because I always want them to feel safe and secure." Their numbers have gotten smaller. She doesn't fault anyone for being afraid, but losing people is demoralizing.

After facing harassment, Amanda Pauley and her allies got more strategic. She lives in what she describes as a 70/30 community—70 percent of residents oppose her beliefs while only 30 percent agree—so they kept their focus narrow, prioritizing issues they could influence. They also changed their approach to the school board. "They want a show," Amanda says. So her group doesn't give them one. They sign up to speak first and leave before the meeting is over.

Even after curtailing her activism, Amanda no longer feels safe in her hometown. Her husband travels a lot for work, so she didn't go to her daughter's parent-teacher conference because she was afraid to go to the school alone. She's been called a groomer at her kids' concerts and games. After her daughter introduced her to the school librarian at an event in town, Amanda noticed a member of an extremist group filming their conversation. Amanda used to wear sports jerseys with her son's number on them. She doesn't do that anymore. Her kids made the honor roll, but she didn't put the stickers on her car. She's afraid when she goes to the grocery store. She's noticed, too, that her kids don't want to go to town events. They didn't want to go to a beautiful skating rink in the park last winter, and it broke her heart.

Still, Amanda is not without hope. She participated in a virtual self-defense class for organizers, and she's put what she learned into practice. One day, when she was picking up lunch, she ran into a man who called her a "Fauci fucker" for wearing a mask. She turned around, put her hands in front of her chest, and yelled, "Stop it now!" And he did. "I will not let them silence us," she tells me. She's worked all over the state and seen local activists win fights to save their schools. "No one works harder than rural organizers," she says. Even if they can't unseat the extremists on their school boards, she tells me, they can sway a house seat or statewide election by increasing voter turnout by 1 percent. Occasionally she gets the vacation homeowners to understand how terrible the political climate is, and a few have found ways to help.

The impact of threats and harassment is also felt in supposedly liberal cities, particularly for those who are part of the most hated communities. Thomas Sennett is a transgender person who works in the psychology field. He wants to fight for trans youth so they have access to gender-affirming care, but he holds back. He's experienced the vitriol of anti-trans hate groups. A Nazi website (he no longer calls them neo-Nazi) published his roommate's name and a picture of their house. Knowing that members of hate groups can find where he lives makes him feel like a target. When he gets into his car or goes to the subway or goes outside to get his mail, he wonders if someone is watching. "It messes you up, like you never really feel safe anywhere. And that's why they do it," he says.

Thomas struggles with the line between protecting himself and his responsibility to his community, particularly children and teens, who are more vulnerable than adults. "I do have some privilege," he tells me, "but I'm also a member of this community and I am vulnerable." He wants to speak out. He wants to use his research and counseling expertise to challenge misinformation in the media, but he's afraid to sign his name to an op-ed.

Thomas lives and works in a liberal city where he's part of a community of health care providers he describes as thoughtful and nuanced in their approach to caring for trans and gender nonconforming youth. He describes how deeply relaxed and joyful he feels in his colleagues' presence because they are kind and empathic and never let outside noise keep them from doing what's best for the young people in their care. But even in a city that paints rainbows on its crosswalks every June, gender-affirming care providers face death threats. Sometimes hate groups show up outside the hospital. "I don't think it's an accident," Thomas says. "I think they do it on purpose to make us feel scared, even though they know they can't necessarily win here, they can always remind us that we can never be completely safe from them." Anti-trans hate groups have no shame lying. And because trans people are so stigmatized, the most ridiculous statements can get traction. Some propaganda Thomas has heard accuses his colleagues of cutting off children's genitals. "I guess trans people are seen as so 'other' and so monstrous that people are able to put them in a category of people who would do terrible things," he tells me. "That's the point of these tactics," he says. "It's effectively making providers afraid to provide care."

Thomas wants to correct the record. He shares facts about the history and science of gender-affirming care with an ease that is only possible when your expertise is deep. He can cite examples of trans people getting the care they needed in the early twentieth century and empirical data to debunk the panic. I want people who think they have never met a trans person to read Thomas's words, instead of the baseless, hateful memes their uncle keeps posting on Facebook. But Thomas is not willing to talk to the media. "The quote could be chopped in half and misquoted later and then it'll be my fault if something happens," he says.

Sometimes Thomas feels angry, but mostly, he's just sad to be living with so much fear, and to know that so many trans people are much less safe than he is. "I never feel like I'm doing enough to meet my responsibilities towards people who are suffering, but I also never feel like I'm doing enough to protect myself," he says. "I wonder how much trying to protect myself could make me sick."

Thomas is ambivalent when he suggests that people who are not trans should speak up more. He doesn't want more privileged people to get all the recognition when trans people have been fighting for safe and affirming care for decades. But he acknowledges that cisgender people are at less risk for bodily harm.

Florida is in the news for enacting legislation that restricts teachers' ability to talk about gay and trans people. A lot of us in blue states think we're above all that. But on a freezing cold Saturday morning in February, a group of LGBTQ+ community leaders have assembled for a self-defense class. It's been a couple months since the drag story hour they sponsored at a public library in a small city south of Boston was invaded by white supremacists, but for most people in the room, the fear is raw. Members of the hate group covered their faces. They sat among the parents and children, threatening them. One person remembers blowing bubbles to keep the kids calm. Another sat close to the drag queen to make sure she was protected. As the group of leaders practices physical and verbal skills, the mood is heavy. *They know who we are*, one participant says. *They saw our faces, but they kept theirs hidden.* When she goes to the grocery store or out to dinner, she looks at people to try to figure out if they were at the library. It unsettles her to know that people who hate her live in her community, and even more that she doesn't know who they are. The Pride parade is months in the future, but people are worried. Organizers have even less control on a public street than in a library.

A month later, we're back. The room is packed, and heavy with fear and trauma and urgency. One man imagines himself being attacked on his way out of a bar. He asks my co-instructor for racist and homophobic hate speech so he can practice responding to it. His posture is strong. His hands are shaking but steady in front of his body as he yells "Stop!" and "Leave me alone!" Another person who works with youth wants to know what she should do if members of the hate group show up at her information table at the Pride festival. She asks my co-instructor to accuse her of sexually grooming children. She practices responding to him in a calm voice, telling the young people to go to a tent where it's safer. We teach her to use the table as a barrier to keep him from touching her. She stands firm, telling him to leave.

I feel a deep heartbreak thinking about how vivid and specific people's fears are. It's disconcerting how quickly my mind can turn a table into a barrier, rainbow swag into a weapon. But the alternative is too little celebration and not enough activism.

People who hate us and want to keep us powerless use violence intermittently. The unpredictability is the hardest part. One story hour is overrun by white supremacists and the next one goes just fine. Then, when they don't show up, we feel ridiculous for having worried. It's Massachusetts after all, the first state to legalize same-sex marriage. But then we get too comfortable and feel too safe, and we are completely shocked when they show up outside Boston Children's Hospital to threaten doctors who provide gender-affirming care.[9] The cost of fear is change that comes slower than it needs to and change agents who are exhausted from constant vigilance.

CHAPTER 3

HOW NOT TO GET STRANGLED BY YOUR PONYTAIL

I t felt good to hit something.

I was in my early twenties, taking a women's self-defense class taught by two police officers. They held worn leather boxing pads in front of our faces and commanded us to punch. I felt a rush of joy when my fist clapped against the pad. It was the first time I'd ever felt strong. When I was growing up, the only attention I gave my body was anger that it wasn't thin enough. In college I wore baggy clothes to hide the weight I'd gained after rejecting the beauty standards I'd once gone hungry to achieve. Kicking and punching gave me a way to end the war I'd waged against my body, an experience of power and delight that would forever change me.

But in between rounds of punching we got lectures about all the stupid things women do. We leave our valuables unattended or we walk around wearing headphones. We go out alone at night or we drink too much. We wear high heels, tight skirts, and flashy jewelry, dressing like a target. In making these bad choices, the officers explained, we bring crime on ourselves.

The authoritative tone in their voices shut down my critical thinking. It felt like the only way to be smart was to do what they said. I was a feminist. I had a sharp analysis of every TV show I watched, and I was never quiet when the men in my family sat at the dining room table expecting women to clean up after them. But violent crime felt like an emergency. Questioning the police felt indulgent and privileged.

I was grateful to the officers for helping me find the power in my body and my gratitude made me want to please them. I wanted to prove I was different from the dumb women who failed to park their cars in well-lit areas. Then, maybe, I could live up to their ill-defined standard of "street smart," and if I did that, I could avoid being a victim of an equally ill-defined crime.

I worked in a domestic violence crisis center. I didn't know anybody who'd been assaulted by a stranger in a parking lot, but I knew dozens of women who'd been raped by friends or exes, or sexually abused by family members. The officers didn't explain how any of the punches could be used against a person we knew. They didn't offer ways we could protect ourselves if we were assaulted by someone we weren't willing to punch. Still, held up against their stern warnings, my own experience felt less valid.

Stern voices no longer shut down my critical thinking, but the mix of kindness and victim blame I experienced in that class persists. I see it most often from men who are police officers or martial artists or who served in the military. They offer self-defense training or personal safety advice targeted at women. Nobody does it for the money. Most volunteer their time or charge modest fees. They're compassionate and sincere, but underneath the kindness is an expectation that we do what they say. Even if they can't give us a good reason why.

Missing from this type of advice is an understanding of how political inequalities affect women's decisions. In his book *The Power of Awareness,* former military operative Dan Schilling introduces us to Ashley, a single woman who made bad choices.[1] According to Schilling, Ashley lived in a gated apartment complex in California. One day a man came up behind her and asked her to hold the gate. He was there, he told her, to visit a friend. He looked "clean-cut," she said, and "not your typical problem-type beach drifter," so she agreed, even though he gave her a look she described as "creepy." Ashley was in the laundry room later that night when the man came in and tried to rape her. Schilling described how fiercely Ashley fought back, how she yelled for help until neighbors arrived and stopped the assault. But none of that is the point he is using Ashley's story to illustrate. Schilling instead focuses on how wrong she was not to trust her intuition. He offers no analysis of why she, like many women, might not have felt she was entitled to refuse him. Schilling quotes Ashley as having said, "I didn't want to be a bitch and I thought it would be kind of ridiculous."[2] But what follows is not discussion of how she got the message that saying no makes you a "bitch." Or how she learned to discount her feelings or why she convinced herself she was overreacting. Schilling's point is that Ashley was wrong not to trust her intuition and, because of her mistake, she was almost raped.

The idea that women become "easy targets" for attackers because we make bad decisions is a common characteristic of this kind of safety advice. Harry Glick, a retired prosecutor and private practice lawyer, owns the website selfdefenseforsmartwomen.com. When we meet on Zoom, the wall behind him is covered with framed diplomas he's earned over five decades studying martial arts. His website includes a page of safety advice with vague warnings like "Don't be a target," as well as more specific directives about how women should restrict our lives. "Don't wear a ponytail on the street, especially at night," the site reads. "A ponytail gives an attacker something easy to grab so he can readily pull you away."

I ask him what evidence supports this advice.

"It really depends on how old you are," he says. "I have grandchildren with ponytails and I'm not going to tell them not to wear them." But, he explains, that ponytails should be avoided because "an assailant can easily just grab onto a ponytail and pull you anywhere." He doesn't stop there. "You can easily be strangled with a ponytail as well." There's no epidemic of ponytail strangulations. Of all the things I could be vigilant about, there's no good reason to choose my hairstyle. But as soon as I've formed that thought, he's changed the subject: "To me, nowadays one of the worst things to wear are headphones. Get rid of them."

"But your website says ponytails," I push.

"It's just one of the many things I can tell you—ponytails are one of them," he responds. But then he's right back to women on their phones, deflecting the question again. "I saw this even today," he tells me. "Women on their phones, they're talking while they're walking in the street, and they're listening to music, and have no clue what's going on around them. That's dangerous."

He tells me he does a lot of research, that he reads the FBI website every day. Yet he steers our conversation away from every direct question I ask about the evidence that supports the advice he gives women. Other pages on his site reference credible sources, from the US Department of Justice to the Pew Research Center, which only makes their absence on the safety advice page more glaring. In addition to advising women not to wear ponytails, Harry says that they should yell "Fire!" if they're attacked. He doesn't remember where he got that one, probably a medical or psychological professional.

I can argue with his advice, but not the sincerity of his intentions. Before he retired, Harry Glick was the go-to self-defense teacher in the suburban county where he practiced law. Hundreds of women lawyers came to his classes. Others he trained one at a time in the privacy of their offices or homes. "It was another kind of attorney-client privilege," he explains, for women didn't want their colleagues to know they were afraid.

I interviewed one of Harry's students, a lawyer who first met him when he taught a class at the Women's Bar Foundation. She's grateful to Harry for helping her feel less afraid. "You never know. You get out of a meeting late at night and you're walking in the streets," she explains when I asked what drew her to self-defense. "You want to feel that you can take care of yourself."

Harry Glick isn't the only person telling women our ponytails are dangerous. The sheriff's department in Ripley County, Indiana, has a page of its website devoted to telling women that ponytails make them easy targets. The article titled "Through a Rapist's Eyes" has no author and cites no sources. It claims to be based on interviews with "a group of rapists and date rapists in prison" about "what they look for in a potential victim." I've seen it before. It's been floating around the internet for decades and it shows up in my inbox every few years like a cold that keeps coming back.

"The first thing men look for in a potential victim is hairstyle," the unnamed author claims. "They are most likely to go after a woman with a ponytail, bun, braid, or other hairstyles that can easily be grabbed. They are also likely to go after a woman with long hair. Women with short hair are not common targets." Rapists also carry scissors, the article claims, so we should avoid clothing that is easy to cut. But fear not. Not everything we do makes us more vulnerable. All you have to do to deter a rapist is carry an umbrella, one that's large enough that the rapist can see it from a distance.

Sheriff Jeff Cumberworth is fifty-eight days from retirement when we talk. I ask him why the department chose this article. "I can't tell you how it got there," he tells me. "There should be a better answer than that." He's served as sheriff for almost eight years, and he can't remember if he's read the article. He tells me I'm the first person who has asked about it. They get comments about the other public safety tips on their website, the ones that alert people to common internet scams or help them fortify their homes against burglars.

It's a rural county, he explains. People still read newspapers and the department only has twelve road deputies. In his time as sheriff, he's only had one rape case. And even that one wasn't really local. The people involved were at a rest stop on the interstate, he says, and the allegations turned out to be bogus.

The problem that people in Ripley County will acknowledge is drugs. The state of Indiana, he tells me, devotes almost no funding to programs for people who struggle with substance use. And the few programs with government support are part of the probation department. "A mom calls us and says she's worried about her son's drug use," the sheriff says. "And we have to say to her 'I'm sorry, he has to get in trouble with the law before there's anything we can do.'" Because of this, he's much more aware of the drug and alcohol resources on the sheriff's department website.

But when it comes to rape, he's not saying it doesn't happen, just that his department doesn't see it.

"I mean there's some domestics," he explains. "Some he did and I didn't want to, or some girlfriend-boyfriend situations where they get in an argument and they want us to sort it out."

"So, rape within marriage?" I clarify.

"Well, I guess it is if she doesn't want to," he says.

Jeff Cumberworth is warm and affable. He's not defensive but not quite apologetic when I read him portions of the rapist article and ask why his department endorsed it.

"It's telling you something to be aware of," he says.

I keep pressing. "So, the advice says that rapists target women with ponytails and long hair and clothing that is easy to remove. What am I supposed to do with that? Should I shave my head and dress in coveralls?"

He seems surprised by the question, as if giving the advice doesn't involve thinking about what it would mean to take it. I doubt the sheriff's department is trying to turn the women of Ripley County into umbrella-wielding skinheads. But these appeals to "raising awareness" or "giving people something to think about" are a way of abdicating responsibility. This is an official government website, funded by taxpayers. More than that, it's the website of a law enforcement agency, a source a lot of people trust for information about crime. There is no county health department in the US telling people, for example, not to eat vegetables indoors because they won't absorb as many vitamins. Most of us would consider that advice ridiculous. Most of us would agree that disseminating it on an official government website is irresponsible. But when it comes to law enforcement agencies telling women how to avoid crime, the same standards don't seem to apply.

At the end of our interview, I ask if there's anything we've discussed that he doesn't want me to write about. He says he wants me to make it clear that he's not speaking for the state police. They handle serious crimes, he tells me, and probably a lot more rape cases.

At least Jeff Cumberworth will talk to me. The DeSoto County sheriff's department in Florida responds to my interview requests with curt emails from a public information officer. On one page of their website, "Tips for Women on Staying Safe!" the sheriff tells them to "avoid shopping alone. Try to shop with a friend or relative." When shopping at night, the sheriff's department advises, women should ask a security guard to walk them to their cars, but they should not approach just anyone in a uniform because a lot of criminals pose as security guards.

I ask if DeSoto County has high rates of crimes against women in shopping centers or in hotel rooms, where the sheriff's department advises them to be vigilant. "The information on our website informs our community and increases awareness of their surroundings during day-to-day activities," the public information officer responds. "This information is not a reflection of criminal activity in DeSoto County but is for educational purposes."

These efforts to sidestep my questions don't seem like efforts at all. It's like I'm a fly that evades the swatter or a two-year-old kid whose response to every statement an adult makes is "Why?" Women should just restrict ourselves. We should be scared or vigilant, or maybe a little less scared because we've picked something to be vigilant about. Shopping centers, hotel rooms, ponytails.

There's a trust some communities place in the police. An expectation that people whose job is stopping crime know a lot about crime, so the advice they give is based on actual crime. Baseless safety advice betrays that trust, but it does so in ways that make the betrayal feel like help. I've been in rooms full of mostly white women who nod emphatically at every directive an officer gives. I've felt those nods in my own body in the years before I knew which questions to ask.

The most pervasive source of this kind of advice is Rape Aggression Defense (RAD), the largest police-led self-defense program in the United States. Founded in 1989 by retired marine and police officer Lawrence Nadeau, RAD has over eleven thousand teachers, most of them college and municipal police officers.

After weeks of calls and emails to RAD headquarters, I speak on the phone with Kathy Wright, a retired police officer who is the director of women's programs. She's warm and respectful. Right away she acknowledges that most sexual assaults are perpetrated by familiar people and that a lot of women "get worn down" by friends and coworkers who constantly erode their boundaries. She wants to give women a sense of self-worth so they can speak up when someone crosses a line. She also tells me she's committed to running her classes in a way that respects every woman's choice about how much she participates. "No one touches you without your permission," she says, and that applies to her and every other RAD teacher.

It's hard to reconcile what Kathy Wright is telling me with the manual RAD distributes to women who take their classes. It advises them to "draw the drapes and pull the shades. If the drapes are thin or worn, you may want to consider investing in a heavier fabric to prevent silhouetting." It also tells them to "replace and/or trim large shrubs and bushes close to doorways and windows. It is recommended that bushes under windows be kept at least 6 inches below the ledge." Women are also advised to "be careful about how your name is listed on a mailbox or how it is listed in the telephone directory, consider using initials" and to "try to avoid displaying a vehicle license plate with your name or feminine labels. This could make you an easy target for stalking type behavior."

The first time I ask for the evidence that supports the advice RAD gives women, she says it comes from the US Department of Justice. But when I reach out to the Justice Department after our conversation, they tell me they have no data to support the claims that heavy drapes, well-trimmed hedges, or gender-ambiguous mailboxes make women safer.

When I repeat my question about where the advice comes from, the answers get more vague. "It's a popular crime prevention strategy," she says once. Another time, she says it comes from McGruff, the cartoon dog from the 1980s who encouraged children to "take a bite out of crime." But the more I persist, the more reflective she gets. At the end of a self-defense class, women are motivated and vulnerable, she tells me. She wants to give them something they can do right away. She's taught them punches and kicks they may never use, but most of her students could buy new drapes, or at least close the ones they have.

I understand her desire to make self-defense training immediately useful, but she doesn't have to do it by telling women to take arbitrary precautions. She could instead encourage them to communicate their boundaries and pay attention to how the other person reacts. The week after my first self-defense class, I set boundaries with everyone from a pushy salesperson to my family. I felt more attuned to situations where someone was trying to coerce me and more emboldened to tell them no. But those ways of putting self-defense into practice are disruptive to people who have power and who may feel entitled to get what they want. Getting new drapes can make women feel like they're taking control without rocking any of those boats.

My coworker, Alicia Ortiz, who became a certified RAD instructor after taking the class in college, found similar problems with the RAD messages. "During RAD trainings, I remember instructors advising us not to have any obviously feminizing characteristics in or on our car, such as leaving a pair of high heels visible in the back seat, or having a glittery personalized license plate, so that it wouldn't be obvious that a woman is driving," she says. That message of achieving safety by expressing yourself less was frustrating and undercut the strength she got from learning to defend herself.

Krista is a social worker and domestic violence advocate in Texas. Her experience of a RAD class convinced her not to recommend self-defense to the survivors she supports. She acknowledges the good intentions of the police officers who taught the class, but she was frustrated by their defensiveness. Krista helps survivors make safety plans for a range of volatile situations involving current and former intimate partners. So she was frustrated that every scenario they presented was of "some stranger coming out of the bushes." They didn't, in her experience, welcome her questions. They shut down nuanced conversations about how hard it is to stay safe when the person who harms you is your kids' father, and if you fight back, you could be charged with family violence. She's seen this happen to her clients.

"They weren't giving people tools," she explains. "They were telling people what to do." She felt pressured to practice the physical scenarios in a way that didn't feel comfortable. They showed a strangulation, and Krista decided she didn't want anyone touching her neck. When she stated that boundary, the instructor tried to overrule her, telling her that women get strangled all the time so it would be irresponsible not to practice fighting back.

Police captain Carl MacDermott invites us to sit in a circle on the turf. His voice is commanding. It can easily be heard over the noise that emanates from all directions of the athletic complex. Behind him are nine people in martial arts uniforms, all men except for one. They've volunteered their time to teach a self-defense class sponsored by the police department in Bridgewater, a town about an hour south of Boston. Carl McDermott is thick bodied with a gray crew cut and an angled nose. His stance is solid—shoulders, feet, and jaw clenched.

He motions for us to move closer. There are children in martial arts uniforms on the other side of the turf and I imagine he doesn't want them to hear what he's about to tell us.

It was the night before Thanksgiving. Carl MacDermott was a brand-new police officer just out of the academy. His shift was almost over, and he thought he was heading home when he got a call about a young woman. A man had convinced her to get into his car, then drove her to an isolated area, took off her clothes, forced her to perform oral sex, and left her naked in a gravel parking lot.

I'm expecting him to tell us everything she did wrong, but he doesn't. He talks instead of how brave and resourceful she was. She saw lights in the distance, and started walking toward them, because where there are lights there are people. She found a suburban cul-de-sac. She tried a few doorbells and got no answers, then came to the house of a couple who was watching Johnny Carson on TV. The wife told the husband to answer the door. They took her in and called the police.

I feel his compassion, for that long-ago woman and for all of us. Months later, he tells us, she got up on the witness stand in the courtroom and identified her attacker. He tells us she did a better job of testifying than he could have. He beams with pride as if she were his daughter.

Carl MacDermott tells the class more stories about violent crimes with specific details of where they occurred—street names and athletic fields, restaurants and a bar where a woman agreed to get in a man's car because he'd acted like a gentleman all night long. She never saw his two accomplices who jumped into the back seat as soon as he closed the door. All three men, he tells us, took turns sexually assaulting her.

"Wow, I know that street," one woman says. "I drive past that field all the time," says another, as if it's familiar landmarks that make it possible for violent crime to happen to them.

"Don't be a victim," he tells us.

In an interview the week after the class, I ask Carl MacDermott what he hopes women will get from those stories. "See how easy it is to become a victim?" he responds. It's a point he sometimes illustrates by asking if anyone planned to be in a car accident that day. Of course not. "It doesn't matter if you're good; crime happens to good people," he tells me. "What I try to get them to understand is you can easily become a victim." He has a soft spot in his heart for women, children, the elderly, animals, all vulnerable groups. "I could lose my job over that very easily by sticking up for someone, you know what I'm saying? I guess that's why I went to the self-defense side, so I could get all that out."

After the stories we practice physical skills. I get paired up with one of the assistants. He's well over six feet tall with a gray beard and kind eyes.

"I'm a bricklayer," he says. "So, I won't grab you too hard."

"No," I tell him. "I want you to really grab me." I tell him I teach self-defense and I want a challenge.

The officers have just shown us a complicated move to free your wrist from a person who has grabbed it. You're supposed to roll your arm around the person's fingers, twist your wrist, and then grab onto the attacker's sleeve. The bricklayer grabs my wrist tight. His muscular fingers reach easily around my not-delicate wrist. I use the technique I know, the one I teach. I grab onto the arm he's got with my other hand, which is free. I find the spot where the fingers meet the thumb, the weak point of any grip. I yank my wrist out through that weak point, stepping back as I yank so it's my body weight against his hand. Even if his grip is stronger than my arm, it's not stronger than my whole body.

"That's not it," he says.

"But I got out," I say.

"But you're too far away from me," he says.

Don't I want to be far away from a person who just grabbed me?

I keep the question to myself. I've come to experience this class, not derail it.

He insists I try again, that I do it the way he showed me. I twist and roll my arm, trying to imitate the technique. I can't get out. He grabs me again, this time so light that my arm practically falls out of his hand. With no resistance, I can get my arm out. But even then, I still did it wrong because I didn't finish the move by grabbing his sleeve. A flash of frustration crosses my face. He assumes I'm demoralized because I couldn't do the move. He tells me not to give up. I'll get it right eventually.

We move on to an exercise in which he is attacking me in different ways, and it's my job to fight back. The officers have told us that the way to avoid being a victim is by not giving up. The bricklayer holds his hand up, simulating a slap or punch. I duck and protect my head. He grabs my wrist tight with two hands, challenging me, I assume, to do the rolling motion I was never able to learn. His groin is open, so I simulate a knee strike. If he blocks his groin, he leaves his eyes vulnerable and only one of my arms is stuck, so I use the fingers of my other hand to simulate a strike to the eyes.

I usually delight in exercises like this one, taking the fear and emotional charge out of an assault, treating it instead like a puzzle. I love, too, the kinds of debates self-defense teachers have, hashing out techniques, arguing for or against their effectiveness the way serious Jewish scholars might argue over passages of the Talmud. Everyone recognizing there is no one right way, everyone willing to subject their conclusions to scrutiny. I once had a two-hour debate with a friend over whether a snap kick to the groin is a good self-defense technique. *It is,* she said, *because you can do damage to the groin without getting too close to the attacker. It's not,* I said, *because that move is not going to be powerful enough unless you are strong and quick and have good balance. You could lose your balance on your own, or the attacker could grab your foot. Still,* she said, *it's better to keep your head as far away from the attacker as you can.*

I love testing my ideas against those of another smart person. Whether or not my opinion changes, debates like these help me make sure I have a clear rationale for anything I teach.

But he doesn't see my ideas as anything other than wrong. Getting me to do it his way seems more important than the purpose of what he's trying to teach me. There's a deep rigidity underneath the kindness. The officers' and their assistants' faces are fixed in compassionate expressions, hearts so firmly planted in the right place. But to get their help, you have to be empty. Don't ask hard questions. Don't tell them there's a way that works better for you.

By deflecting challenges and dismissing questions, these men show women concern but not respect. It's a claim I'm sure they would dispute. But respect is treating your students like smart people who need to be convinced. Respect is earned by presenting evidence that is compelling enough to survive the scrutiny of critical thinking.

As a teacher, I understand how hard it is to see someone reject a technique or strategy I love. I feel a rush of defensiveness when it happens, a knee-jerk need to protect my authority. But I work hard to guard against that impulse. Honoring students' choices about what safety strategies work for them is crucial. Speaking up and advocating for yourself when something feels wrong is at the core of what it takes to protect yourself from gender-based violence. It's more important for me to give someone a positive experience of challenging a person in authority than it is for me to leave class affirmed that my way to break a wrist grab is superior.

Keeping ourselves safer requires critical thinking. *Is this person acting friendly because they're trying to coerce me or are they truly kind? Is this neighborhood really dangerous or am I uncomfortable because of stereotypes about race and poverty that live in my subconscious?* One of the most important things I can do as a teacher is help students develop their critical thinking skills.

Critical thinking is so central to feminist approaches to self-defense that it's addressed explicitly in a code of ethics used by most people and organizations that teach what is often called empowerment self-defense (ESD). "The purpose of ESD is to help people live full lives that are not diminished by violence or abuse and to trust one's own judgment," the code says. "ESD practitioners teach skills and strategies that expand people's choices, not limit them. ESD programs encourage students to make choices that are right for their lives, rather than insisting they follow rigid rules."[3]

Alyssa Wright was intent on being independent. She'd watched generations of women in her family compromise themselves and their beliefs because they were financially dependent on men. She wanted a clean break from the conservative Christianity she was raised to believe, from having to rely anyone. She had her own apartment. She paid her rent and college tuition without help from her family. She stayed out of debt because she wanted to be an entrepreneur and knew she couldn't do that if she had to spend half of her adulthood paying back student loans. "I got to live my values," she says, "because I wasn't relying on anyone to pay my bills." Alyssa maintained her independence by working full-time at Starbucks, taking shifts that started at five in the morning. She went to class in the afternoon and bartended at night, earning most of her money between eight and midnight.

When her college offered a self-defense class, she thought it would be smart to take it. She'd been afraid opening the coffee shop alone some mornings and leaving the bar after dark. Most of the women in her class had had some experience of violence. They'd grown up in abusive homes, or they'd been assaulted on campus. Alyssa remembers that she loved connecting with other people and getting to have real and raw conversations about the enormity of gender-based violence. It felt good to yell too.

The instructors gave them a booklet full of directions about what they shouldn't do. Alyssa remembers the complicated feelings it brought up: "I started to feel like, oh, my gosh, I need to make my life very small if I'm going to avoid being harmed." Alyssa is an extrovert with a big personality. She remembers sitting in that class feeling pressured to be less herself. "I gotta be mindful of my personality," she remembers thinking. "And how big I let myself be." Alyssa remembers the male instructor giving a description of a typical victim. She's coming out of a club, she's wearing a new outfit, she's a party girl trying to have a good time. But she's not aware of her surroundings so she makes a perfect target. "It scared me from having a social life," she tells me. The message she got was clear: *Go back in the box.* Be careful, be vigilant, be small.

It wasn't just Alyssa's big personality that was at odds with this compliance-based vision of safety. It was her livelihood. "I remember having this visceral reaction," she says. "I make the majority of my money to pay my rent and buy my school books when I bartend between 8 p.m. and midnight. It made me feel like my livelihood might be in jeopardy."

The physical scenarios the instructors described felt extreme—"a big muscly man with tattoos coming at me with a knife in an alleyway late at night." It didn't leave her prepared for situations she actually faced. Most of her friends who had experienced sexual assault had been harmed by men they knew who were friendly at first and subtle in their coercion. Nothing she learned in that class felt relevant. She doesn't remember learning any practical strategies for how to be safer alone at night or ways to assess what types of interactions were actually threatening.

Sometimes when I talk to men who are passionate about telling women how to be safe, I can see the vulnerable boys they were. I imagine them distancing themselves from weakness by learning to fight—in boxing gyms or martial arts schools, the military or the police. There's a sense of control that comes from never letting your guard down. And there's a way some people feel powerful or validated when they convince other people to be as vigilant they are, even when they can't produce evidence about why a particular type of vigilance is a good use of energy. For the police officers, I imagine the trauma of witnessing decades of murder, assault, and rape. I can see how it makes them insistent. Be nice to the wrong person and you could wind up naked in a gravel parking lot, your fate in the hands of a wife who may or may not tell her husband to answer the door.

As I reread interview transcripts, I find myself digging for that story. I ask Carl MacDermott if the trauma he witnessed over four decades of police work motivates him to teach self-defense. He doesn't answer the question. He tells me instead that he's glad to be helping people. I keep asking the question in different ways. Getting the answer I want will give me a hook to hang my empathy on. It will make me like him more or make me feel better about how much I like him. I'm afraid that his kindness will shut down my critical thinking the way stern warnings did decades ago. This paternal love, visited on me as an adult, still does its disarming job. I get tears in my eyes when he tells me his father raised him to respect women. "You don't talk back to your mother," he says. "I'm not gonna say my father beat us. But if you said something wise to my mother, you get a smack for that."

There's a visceral empathy I feel as I listen to Carl MacDermott share this story. The respect and compassion he has toward women feels as true for him as anything I believe is for me. I notice I'm trying to construct a similar story about Harry Glick. He tells me that as a kid he studied the fights in his neighborhood. He was never the biggest or fastest, so he stayed safe by being the most vigilant. He spent hours in a boxing gym trying to figure out why some strikes and kicks caused more damage than others. I suspect that Harry's fascination with self-protection comes from a defining experience of vulnerability. But my assumption remains unconfirmed. Every time I ask Harry what motivates him, the answer is about women.

Only one of the men I interviewed acknowledged any personal history of abuse. Michael Loftus, owner of the website crime-safety-security.com, grew up watching his father beat his mother. His older brother tried to rescue her. But Michael tells me his father was a serious brawler and his brother was just a kid. Sometimes they'd run to a neighbor and call the police, who would take his dad away, but only for a night.

"It became very important to be alert and learn how to fight," he says. He studied boxing and eventually began teaching women to defend themselves. Our conversation meanders for close to two hours as I try to pin down his rationale for the safety advice on his website, which is a tangle of dense, wordy pages. He tells me he's spent between twenty-five and fifty thousand hours updating the site. He gets his material from local media stories about crime that are delivered to his inbox by a news aggregator. On one page he tells women to walk down the middle of the driveway in a parking garage so we don't get grabbed by a predator who is hiding behind a car. On another, there's the familiar directive never to wear headphones in public.

At some points in our conversation, Michael readily acknowledges the connection between his childhood and his obsession with safety but other times seems surprised when I ask about it. "I really can't connect the dots," he tells me the first time I ask. "I don't remember that kind of connection, although subconsciously [I do] and what do I know?" Then, the next time I raise the question, he says, "I guess my mother, if she would have learned to defend herself, she would have been better off."

Men like Michael did not become their fathers, but they have not completely abandoned the urge to control women. It is instead transformed into instruction that is generous with everything except the space to form your own opinions. I wonder if men had more space to acknowledge and heal from their trauma, would the result be a more thoughtful relationship to safety?

The more time I spend with men who tell women how to be safe—and the women like Kathy Wright who collaborate with them—the more unwelcome thoughts I have. In a parking garage, I think about the concrete walls of the stairwell and how surely they would muffle my screams. I decide to do all my grocery shopping in one trip, but then I hear a disembodied voice telling me I'm stupid for allowing myself to be weighed down by so many bags. I resent how natural it feels to be afraid of my daily routine.

There was one question I asked in all of my interviews: *As a woman, how am I supposed to follow all this advice without making myself so small and fearful that I barely have a life?* No one had an answer. To a person, everyone evaded the question. The subject was changed so quickly that it sometimes took me a minute to remember what I'd asked. Carl Mac-Dermott said that women should get out of their comfort zones and learn new things. Jeff Cumberworth leaned back into "It's just something to think about." I couldn't help feeling that my freedom had no value, that giving it up was such a nonevent that it didn't warrant being mentioned. I don't know if the evasion was intentional, or even conscious, but it made me realize how easy it is for paternalistic concern to become a form of coercive control.

CHAPTER 4

BAD PEOPLE DO BAD THINGS

Years ago, I taught self-defense to a group of middle school students in a church outside Boston. The mother who organized the class did so with an urgency I didn't understand, emailing constantly, insisting on the soonest possible date. When I got to the church, she pulled me into a stairwell. She told me she'd been checking the registry and found a convicted sex offender in her town. She was scared for her children, but more than that, she was indignant that anyone would let him live so close to her family.

In between pronouncements that anyone who would sexually abuse a child was the worst, most disgusting kind of person, she told me how important I was. She thanked me for my work, treating me like a firefighter who'd arrived just in time to contain the blaze in her neighbor's house and keep it from spreading to hers. Her gratitude and relief made me feel validated. It's hard to admit how much I craved that kind of affirmation. I was passionate about preventing abuse and getting other people to care as much as I did felt like a constant struggle. So, when I found someone as outraged as I was, I affirmed her indignation without thinking carefully about where she was directing it. A mother's impulse to protect her children felt sacred and untouchable, so I did nothing but nod along.

The mother's anger should have surprised me. We were in a Catholic church. It was the mid-2000s, the height of the sexual abuse crisis in the Boston archdiocese. Statistically, her kids were much more likely to be abused by a priest or other trusted adult than by a stranger whose picture and home address were available to anyone with internet access. The vast majority of child sexual abuse is perpetrated by someone the child or their parents know and trust. The Centers for Disease Control and Prevention puts that number at 91 percent.[1]

Still, I imagine a lot of Catholic parents felt stuck. News coverage of the abuse crisis was unrelenting. Almost every day there were new revelations of the sheer number of children some priests abused, of the audacity of the cardinals and bishops who buried abuse reports and moved priests to new congregations without warning parishioners. For those who loved their church and weren't willing to leave, I imagine it felt impossible to trust that they were doing enough to protect their children. Parents' fear and anger had to go somewhere, and a stranger convicted of a horrifying crime was a clean target.

On our way out of the stairwell, the mother told me about a church-sponsored program that taught kids to recognize sexual abuse. She told me how great the program was, with a level of enthusiasm that may only be possible when you're trying to convince yourself.

During our class, the middle school students were guarded and mortified. We tried to get them to use loud voices, but most of them wouldn't speak at all. They spent most of class looking at each other or the floor, anywhere but at us. It's not uncommon for parents to be more enthusiastic about our programs than their children, but in more than two decades of teaching, I can't remember a group that was less engaged.

We asked them for examples of situations in which they wanted to say no to someone they knew. We want young people to learn to pay attention when they feel uncomfortable or unsafe and to communicate their boundaries. Our classes help them develop the skills to refuse unwanted attention and the awareness to notice how people respond. *Does your friend stop playing with your hair when you tell them you don't like it, or do they keep touching you and make fun of you for telling them to stop?* Noticing how someone reacts when we communicate our boundaries is one way to assess how trustworthy they are. In a typical middle school class, students give us scenarios, like a friend pressuring them to go to a party where kids are drinking or a boy who tries to kiss them when they just want to be friends. Students practice saying no and communicating what they want and need. An instructor plays the role of a friend or sibling—pushing back, making fun of them, or really listening and agreeing to be more respectful. The students learn to stay focused and speak up for themselves, even when someone else gets defensive.

We also give them strategies for situations when the person crossing their boundaries is an adult. We teach them to identify safe adults—a safe adult is a person who can help you when you have a problem, doesn't tell you to keep secrets, respects your boundaries, never makes you feel afraid or uncomfortable, and listens to you. We help them assess whether it's possible to say no to an adult who is crossing a boundary, or if they need to get help from a safe adult. Most people who sexually abuse children work to gain their trust while at the same time eroding their boundaries and dismissing them if they say they're uncomfortable. It is always the responsibility of adults to keep children safe, but giving children the skills and awareness to get help early can interrupt these situations before they escalate to overt abuse.

This group shut down even further when we talked about familiar people. One girl told us she wanted to say no to her parents when they expected her to wash the dishes, and nobody else volunteered anything more compelling.

I've thought about that mom often over the years, wishing I could go back to that stairwell. What if I'd had the courage and clarity to ask why she was angrier about one registered sex offender than the leaders of a powerful institution responsible for the sexual abuse of thousands of children? It makes sense to want to have uncomplicated anger toward people who sexually abuse. But demonizing strangers whose names and pictures appear on a sex offender registry, just like following compliance-based safety advice, protects us from asking harder questions. By pinning the problem on that one sex offender, the mother avoided having to grapple with the immoral behavior of religious leaders who claimed to be experts on morality. She didn't have to decide whether it was ethical to support an institution that caused so much harm or what it would mean to give up everything that mattered to her about being part of the church.

One reason I didn't have the courage to challenge that mother is because I've made similar choices. In college, I loved the student feminist organization as much as I imagine that mother loved her church. I also worked at the local domestic violence crisis center, so I felt qualified to scrutinize the boyfriends of my straight women friends, pointing out every sexist comment or miniscule act of control. Imagining myself as some sort of one-woman rescue squad, I was quick to remind people that most intimate violence starts with the abuser isolating his partner from their friends. So, I would ask *Is that why you didn't come out with us last weekend?* Only years later did I realize what I couldn't acknowledge at the time: the two women who led the student group with me were a couple, and one was abusing to the other. I explained away how scared and inhibited one partner was. I worked even harder to justify the unpredictable, rageful behaviors of the other. She'd been through a lot, I told myself. I was too privileged to understand how hard it was for her to be in college while her family struggled. I knew better than to describe their relationship as "tumultuous" or "high drama," but I did anyway. And because I was being so vigilant about men, I did all of this while still believing I was the kind of friend who would never let someone I loved endure abuse alone.

People's capacity to dismiss facts that contradict our beliefs has been the subject of decades of research in multiple academic fields. Psychologists call it *belief perseverance*, defined as the tendency to hold on to our existing beliefs even after we learn evidence that contradicts them. Political science examines how difficult it is to change people's minds about issues even when their opinions are based on statements that are provably false. Political scientist Brendan Nyhan has shown that fact-checking people's beliefs on issues like climate change or vaccination does have the potential to change their minds. However, these shifts are often temporary, especially when leaders they trust continue to espouse false information. Nyhan's research found that when Barack Obama released his birth certificate, there was an immediate decrease in the number of people who believed he was born outside the US. However, false statements made by so-called birthers persisted. A year later, the number of people who believed Obama was not American returned to its previous levels.[2]

Neuroscientist Jonas Kaplan conducted brain scans on people while they read political statements that contradicted their beliefs. He found the brain activity was similar to what it would be if the person were facing imminent physical danger.[3] His colleague Drew Westen measured people's brain activity while they read both political and nonpolitical statements. Political statements seemed to activate the parts of the brain that process and regulate fear, while nonpolitical statements activated the parts that govern reason and thought.[4] Neuroscientists have found similar results measuring people's brain activity when they read statements about religion.[5] I ask Jonas Kaplan why people might react more viscerally and less logically to political and religious statements. "The brain is not built to search for truth," he tells me. "The brain is built to survive and make sure our offspring survive." In an article that synthesized neuroscience research on why facts and evidence don't change people minds, Kaplan explains, "our most sophisticated reasoning abilities are still grounded in our most ancient biology, and that what we believe is tied to who and what the brain considers worth protecting." So, while ancient humans would not have survived if they hadn't protected themselves from predatory animals and rancid food, modern human brains are just as protective of the beliefs most closely tied to our identities.

Cognitive scientists Hugo Mercier and Dan Sperber have reached similar conclusions. They argue that people's refusal to accept evidence that challenges their beliefs does more than just affirm a sense of self. Humans' biggest evolutionary advantage, they explain, was to organize themselves into groups. Our hunter-gatherer ancestors were safer and less likely to starve if they could work together to provide food and protection. Our ability to think and reason evolved to affirm our place in the groups that we depend on for nurturing and protection.[6]

There are no published studies of what happens in people's brains when they learn that someone they love has experienced sexual abuse. We also don't know if the powerful, visceral defensiveness observed in brain scans of people reading political and religious statements would be different if the abuser was a beloved family member or revered leader versus a stranger or member of a stigmatized group. But if powerful leaders and strong group identification can shape people's opinions about issues that are less intimate and immediately threatening, then it's worth investigating how our psychology and biology impedes our ability to keep our communities safe. If powerful leaders can influence people's beliefs about Barack Obama's birthplace or vaccines causing autism, then it makes sense that the mother was unwilling—or maybe unable—to take an unflinching look at her church. Even those of us who tell ourselves that we're committed to believing facts and supporting survivors are vulnerable to dismissing evidence when it implicates people or communities we love. I want to believe I am braver and more astute now than I was in college, but I can't be sure that's true.

At the same time, I can't let compassion or understanding obscure the reality that it's people like this mother who create political will for ineffective public policy. There is little or no evidence that sex offender registries prevent sexual abuse, yet they remain politically popular. In 2021, the twenty-fifth anniversary of the federal law that requires every state to have a sex offender registry, criminologists Kristen Zgoba and Meghan Mitchell published a meta-analysis of research that measured the effectiveness of these laws.[7] Sex offender registration and notification (SORN) laws require states to maintain information about people convicted of sex crimes and to create publicly available websites, commonly known as registries, with names, pictures, home and work addresses, and descriptions of crimes. The original law was named for Jacob Wetterling, a Minnesota boy who was raped and murdered by a stranger in 1989 and whose case remained unsolved until 2016. The original intent of the Wetterling Act was to help the police solve crimes against children by creating a searchable database of people who had committed similar crimes. Under the original Wetterling Act, people convicted of sex offenses had to verify their home addresses with the police. Police had the discretion to share the information when they deemed it necessary.

Two years later, Congress passed an amendment to the Wetterling Act requiring states to make information about registered sex offenders available to the public. The amendment was the result of political advocacy led by the parents of Megan Kanka, a seven-year-old girl who was raped and murdered by a neighbor previously convicted of crimes against children. Making the case that they would not have allowed their daughter to interact with the man if they had known about his crimes, Kanka's parents successfully lobbied to amend the Wetterling Act. States must now share the names and addresses of convicted sex offenders publicly.[8] Jacob Wetterling's mother, Patty, has remained active in child advocacy since her son's murder. Yet since she first lobbied for the registration and notification laws that are named after her son, she has reversed her position. Persuaded by research that shows these laws to be ineffective, she has made numerous public statements opposing lifetime registration for an increasing number of crimes, some of which are not violent.[9]

States have additional SORN laws. Some prohibit registered sex offenders from living near schools, playgrounds, or other places where children congregate. Others restrict the types of employment they can have, while still others prohibit them from leaving their homes on Halloween.

Zgoba and Mitchell reviewed eighteen large studies that included nearly 475,000 people convicted of sex offenses. Most of these studies compared the recidivism rates of registered sex offenders with the recidivism of people convicted of similar crimes before the Wetterling Act went into effect. In an interview, Meghan Mitchell tells me this is the most viable way to study the effectiveness of the law, since state governments can't and wouldn't randomly assign people released from prison to either register or not register. The results of the individual studies were mixed. Some showed that recidivism increased after the enactment of SORN laws, others showed decreases, and still others showed no statistically significant changes. The authors acknowledge that peer reviewed academic journals often don't publish studies that produce negative or null results, so it's notable that they could find published research with all three outcomes.

The studies Zgoba and Mitchell reviewed were consistent enough that they could do a true meta-analysis, meaning they could analyze all the data together to draw one conclusion. They found that sex offender registration and notification laws have had no effect on recidivism. It's also worth noting that the majority of published studies—eleven out of eighteen—used arrest as a measure of recidivism. Only three used conviction. When I ask Meghan Mitchell if arrest is a meaningful measure, her answer is unequivocal: "No." She explained that arrest is often used in research as a measure of recidivism because it's easier to track than other outcomes.

Criminal trials can take years, she explains, and when a person moves through the legal system, they are often transferred between different government agencies, from the police to the district attorney to the department of corrections. Some state governments give each person a unique number that enables researchers to follow their case through multiple departments, but others do not. So in some jurisdictions, arrest is the only outcome that can be reliably measured. And with a population like registered sex offenders, the police have a readily available suspect pool, so using arrest as a measure of recidivism may be especially meaningless. Meghan Mitchell acknowledges the urgency that many people feel about stopping crimes as horrific as child sexual abuse, but she is clear that the current system of registration and notification isn't working. "What we're currently doing is a facade of safety," she explains. "It's this facade of getting tough on crime, it's this facade of really punishing people long term. But the facade doesn't translate into tangible practices of safer neighborhoods, communities, schools, family units."

There's a deep disconnect between the evidence and public opinion. According to a review of opinion research by David Patrick Connor and Richard Tewksbury, the vast majority of Americans support sex offender registration and notification laws. In one study, as many as 97 percent of participants agreed that sex offenders' identities and information about their crimes should be available to the public. In another study, 80 percent of participants rated sex offender registration laws as "very important." Other research found that between 80 and 90 percent of participants believe these laws are effective at stopping crime.[10]

Connor and Tewksbury also reviewed research that surveyed police officers, elected officials, and other professionals who play a role criminalizing people who sexually abuse. While these studies were smaller and less generalizable, they illustrate the complicated relationship between these professionals' actions and their beliefs. In one national study, only 55 percent of state legislators who had sponsored or publicly endorsed sex offender registration laws believed they worked. Lawmakers were also less likely than the public to acknowledge the negative consequences of being on a sex offender registry. A survey of police officers found that only 38 percent believed that sex offender registries were effective at deterring future crimes. Still, 63 percent said they believed convicted sex offenders should have to register.[11]

As part of a national survey of the public's perspectives on political issues, criminologists Andrew Harris and Kelly Socia randomly assigned two groups to receive a series of questions about "sex offenders" and "juvenile sex offenders" or questions that used more neutral terms like "people who have committed crimes of a sexual nature." The statements were otherwise identical, and the survey reached a large sample that was demographically representative of the US population. Harris and Socia found a statistically significant difference between the two groups. Those who received the survey with the term "sex offender" expressed more support for laws that restricted them from living near schools or prohibited them from using social media. That said, the majority of both groups supported these policies—76 percent of the group that saw the survey with the term "sex offender" and 71 percent of those who saw the survey with the more neutral language agreed that the home addresses of people who had sexually abused should be available on the internet. Also, 85 percent of people who saw the "sex offender" survey and 81 percent who saw the more neutral language survey agreed that convicted sex offenders should be prohibited from living near schools or playgrounds. By contrast, Harris and Socia found no significant difference between the two groups' opinions about whether someone who had been convicted of sexually abusing could receive treatment, be rehabilitated, and learn to live a violence-free life. Less than a third of both groups agreed that this was possible.[12]

Some research shows that hostile public opinion influences sentencing. Criminologist Joshua Cochran led a study that reviewed all felony cases in Florida between 1995 and 2011. His team reviewed 1.87 million records and found that sentencing for sex offenses increased in severity over the sixteen-year period while punishment for other felonies remained relatively constant. They also found no increase in the severity of sexual abuse crimes during this period; however, the steeper sentences coincided with increases in media coverage of "sexual predators."[13]

I ask Meghan Mitchell why she thinks there is such a deep disconnect between the evidence and public opinion. She says it's not uncommon for legislation to be out of step with solid criminal justice research. It takes years to build coalitions and relationships with elected officials. And most universities make decisions about tenure and promotions based on the academic articles researchers publish or the grants they get, not on their efforts to advocate for evidence-based public policy.

Even the federal agency charged with implementing sex offender registration laws has at times acknowledged that registration alone doesn't prevent people convicted of sex crimes from reoffending. In 2015, the US Department of Justice Office of Sex Offender Sentencing, Monitoring, Apprehending, Registering, and Tracking (SMART) published a research brief detailing the state of the evidence.[14] No research supports the effectiveness of sex offender registration policies that are solely focused on punishment, but when supervision from the criminal legal system is combined with intensive, skilled therapeutic treatment, several studies have shown decreases in recidivism. One program, Circles of Support and Accountability, matches people convicted of sex offenses with a team of trained volunteers who provide support and hold the person accountable to a personalized plan designed to keep them from abusing again. While funding for research on this model is limited, the available evidence shows that it is effective. Meanwhile, other popular strategies like polygraph tests, GPS monitoring, and commitment to psychiatric hospitals have not been proven effective.

Based on the data, the research brief's author, Christopher Lobanov-Rostovsky, advocates for victim-centered, evidence-informed management strategies led by qualified treatment professionals. Yet he acknowledges that evidence does not always guide public policy. "Despite the intuitive value of using science to guide decision-making, laws and policies designed to combat sexual offending are often introduced and enacted in the absence of empirical support," he says. "However there is little question that both public safety and the efficient use of public resources would be enhanced if sex offender management strategies were based on evidence of effectiveness rather than other factors."

Sex offender registries create a class of abusers that we're willing to throw away. We don't care if they can't keep a job or if they become homeless because they can't find an apartment that is the required number of feet away from every playground or school. We can hate them. And by hating them we can demonstrate how serious we are about protecting children. That we're not soft or easily fooled. We know better than to trust them when they tell us they can change. This kind of harsh, simple justice takes away our agency, and maybe some part of us wants our agency gone. Applying nuance to something as horrendous as child sexual abuse is scary. There are too many possible wrong decisions. There's not enough evidence to show us what works, and even when we have good evidence, no guarantee that we can stop everyone. There are reasons why locking someone up for a decade or more and then branding them for life has widespread support. But for every registered sex offender, there are dozens, maybe hundreds, of other people who have sexually abused—people no district attorney will ever try, no judge or jury will ever convict, people who maintain their positions as respected religious leaders, or talented athletes, or beloved fathers and uncles. Survivors struggle with the heartbreak of seeing the threats their abusers made come true: *If you tell, no one will believe you.* According to a 2019 National Institutes of Justice report, less than 20 percent of sexual abuse reports went to trial, and of those, only half resulted in a conviction or guilty plea. An older study found that only 12 percent of child sexual abuse cases were reported to law enforcement.[15]

Most people who sexually abuse children are loved, liked, trusted, or respected. The thought of subjecting them to a lifetime of stigma by labeling them as a sex offender can feel impossible. Instead we pretend we don't notice the lines they cross, and we call their survivors "crazy" or "dramatic" so we don't have to take them seriously. When we do this, we compound the trauma of the original abuse.

We also miss the opportunity to better understand what it takes to stop this abuse. Preventing sexual abuse means having the discernment and courage to notice the behaviors that are often its precursors, like eroding a child's physical boundaries, touching or tickling a child in ways they don't like, creating inappropriate reasons to be alone with a child, or offering a child gifts or privileges in exchange for keeping secrets. Speaking up when we see these precursors is risky, especially when it means challenging people in authority.

It's not just adults who are subjected to punitive and questionably effective consequences for being convicted of sex crimes. In 2013, Human Rights Watch released a report about children on sex offender registries.[16] The report's author, lawyer and activist Nicole Pittman, investigated 517 cases across twenty states, some of which involved children as young as nine. She conducted 296 interviews with children on the registry, their families, and adults in their thirties, forties, and fifties, who were still facing hardships for crimes adjudicated when they were children. Most of the people Pittman interviewed were tried as juveniles—only 5 percent were convicted in adult criminal courts—yet they were required, sometimes for life, to have their pictures and home addresses listed on public registries. As a result, 52 percent had experienced threats or violence.

When SORN laws were initially enacted in the mid-1990s, Pittman notes, they neither required nor prohibited states from including children. However, as these laws proliferated, most states began requiring children to register as sex offenders, even for cases adjudicated in juvenile courts. Then, in 2006, changes to federal guidelines under the Adam Walsh Child Protection and Safety Act not only mandated that children register as sex offenders but made failure to register a crime punishable by prison. This law also mandated that states eliminate the use of risk assessment tools to determine whether a young person is likely to reoffend, resulting in adjudication and punishment that cannot be tailored to individual situations.

Human Rights Watch found that children were placed on sex offender registries for a wide range of behaviors. Some had seriously harmed others, usually younger children in their families or communities. But others were branded as sex offenders for sexual exploration and experimentation or for things like urinating in public or running around naked at a football game. A fifteen-year-old was convicted of child pornography for taking naked pictures of herself and posting them on the internet.

Pittman interviewed a thirty-five-year-old man who had to register as a sex offender for having consensual sex with his girlfriend when he was eighteen and she was fifteen. The couple have two children but are not allowed to live together because he is still on the registry and the law considers her his victim. In addition to being separated from his family, he has lost seventeen jobs. A twenty-eight-year-old woman Pittman interviewed was convicted of a sex offense for flashing and simulating sex with her younger stepbrothers when she was ten years old. She completed treatment while in juvenile detention, but when she turned eighteen, she was added to the sex offender registry. She was then fired from her job. Angry messages were taped to the door of her college dorm room. Another person Pittman interviewed was placed on the registry when he was fourteen for consensual sex with his thirteen-year-old girlfriend. He now has a daughter of his own. She can't have birthday parties or invite friends to their house because he is not allowed to be around other children.

It's been more than a decade since Human Rights Watch published that report, but not enough has changed, according to Vic Wiener, a staff attorney at Juvenile Law Center. The center's work includes litigation, legislative advocacy, and lawyer referrals on a range of criminal justice issues affecting young people. Ending the practice of putting children on sex offender registries is one of the organization's priorities. Vic sounds more heartbroken than authoritative when they tell me about the research: children on sex offender registries have higher rates of suicide, they're more likely to be victims of physical and sexual violence, and only 2.75 percent of adjudicated youth will reoffend. That number comes from a meta-analysis by psychologist Michael Caldwell that included over one hundred studies of youth recidivism, a combined total of more than 33,000 cases. The studies Caldwell analyzed had an average follow-up period of four to five years.[17] After we talk, Vic sends me a twenty-one-page research index, single-spaced, small font, thick with citations that document the damage these registries cause and the reality that no credible scientist can demonstrate that they improve public safety. One of Juvenile Law Center's few wins on this issue occurred in 2014 when the state of Pennsylvania declared the practice of child sex offender registration unconstitutional. Now, with a few exceptions, children in Pennsylvania no longer have to register. Vic notes that the state did not see an uptick in children committing sex crimes after registration laws were struck down.

But with deep resignation, Vic tells me how little the evidence matters to people who are in a position to change these laws. They tell me about a time Juvenile Law Center brought academic experts to meet with a politician. "The response was quite literally 'I don't care what the research says,'" Vic explains. "That's not going to pass, that's not going to go over well with my constituents." The California legislature, Vic tells me, enacted modest reforms to its sex offender registration laws in 2020. Elected officials were inundated by rageful constituents who falsely declared that they had legalized pedophilia.[18]

The problem with youth registration, Vic explains, is that too few people oppose it. Many conservatives support putting children on registries because it's a way to be tough on crime. But even some of Vic's liberal and progressive friends have a hard time supporting Juvenile Law Center's work. Stiff consequences, for some, is a way for governments to show that they take sexual abuse seriously. When it comes to holding people accountable, Vic explains, "the tools we have been given in our society are criminalization and incarceration, registration and monitoring."

Juvenile Law Center runs a helpline, and a couple days a week, Vic takes calls from people who are struggling with the impact of being permanently marked by a mistake they made when they were ten or twelve or fifteen: A parent who can't go to his kids' basketball games because being in a school could send him to prison. Or someone who lost their job or whose kids are being bullied. Or a person living in Pennsylvania, where they aren't required to register but aren't sure how to comply with federal sex offender registration and notification laws. Sometimes parents of a child on the registry call because they're trying to figure out where their kid can live—they can't be in the same house as other children, or the family happens to live within one thousand feet of a playground and they can't just move. Vic described one call from an adult whose name had been removed from the registry but was still showing up on private websites that download information from public registries. Some states have laws that require the owners of these private sites to remove people once they are taken off public registries. But the laws are inconsistent, and there are few mechanisms and even less political will to enforce them. Some people, Vic tells me, remain on registries even after they're dead.

For Vic Wiener, working to end youth sex offender registration doesn't mean dismissing the harm young people cause when they sexually abuse. While some youth wind up on registries for consensual sex or for using their phones or the internet in ways that turn out to qualify as child pornography, others have seriously hurt people. From their past work in youth development, Vic understands that young people's motivations for sexually abusing are complicated. They don't get boundaries. They act impulsively. They don't have better ways of coping with their own trauma. "How many of the youth are themselves survivors of sexual violence?" Vic asks. "How many of them are experimenting and just really need to understand boundaries?" Too often, though, when young people try go get help, they end up getting criminalized. "A lot of times if a kid has concerning sexual behaviors, getting charged with a crime is probably their fastest route into treatment," Vic says.

It's hard to stay motivated when you advocate for people who are reviled. Vic Wiener does so by envisioning what it would look like if we lived in a country that was truly committed to ending adolescent sexual violence. If teens had access to quality sex education, if they could learn about their bodies and boundaries and consent, if those who had sexual behavior problems could get effective therapy without having to be charged with a crime. "When you do have a young person who really needs an intervention," Vic wonders, "how do we lower every single barrier to ensure that that kid can get the support that they need?"

Harsh punishment has strong popular support, but some evidence shows that the majority of people who have been victimized are more interested in rehabilitation than retribution. In 2022, the Alliance for Safety and Justice conducted a national survey of just over 1,500 people who had been victims of crimes.[19] Survey respondents were demographically representative of the US population and included people with diverse political beliefs. When asked how they thought public criminal justice funding should be invested, 60 percent supported expanding mental health and substance use treatment and 40 percent supported violence prevention and youth programs compared to only 20 percent who wanted more police officers and 10 percent who wanted more prisons and jails. Support for rehabilitation was slightly higher among survivors of violent crimes than those who experienced nonviolent property crimes.

The survey found differences based on political affiliation: 89 percent of Democrats and 78 percent of independents said they believe governments should invest more in schools and education than punishment and prisons. Still, even the majority of Republican crime survivors—62 percent—favored public spending on education over punishment. Additionally, 60 percent of Republican crime survivors favor investment in mental health treatment over prisons and jails.

The survey also found that 42 percent of crime survivors did not report to the police, and most of those who made reports did not get help or support. Only 12 percent said they got help navigating the justice system and just 8 percent rated the system as "very helpful." The Alliance for Safety and Justice began surveying crime survivors in 2016 because no other organization had done so. The federal government has invested in large-scale national surveys of crime victimization since the early 1990s. Yet, the alliance notes, the National Crime Victimization Survey doesn't ask survivors if they were satisfied with their interactions with the police or for their opinions about crime prevention policy.

The alliance is not the only organization questioning the effectiveness of harsh punishment. A growing movement of grassroots groups and thought leaders are envisioning new approaches to justice. Feminist psychiatrist Judith Herman is a widely recognized innovator in the field of trauma and abuse. In the 1970s, her research and clinical work was instrumental in pushing the psychiatry profession to acknowledge the magnitude of sexual abuse in families. At the time, many doctors still believed that child sexual abuse was rare. Herman also demonstrated that it wasn't only Vietnam War veterans who suffered from post-traumatic stress disorder but women who were raped and abused in their homes.

After decades of supporting the healing of thousands of survivors, Herman began grappling with the question of justice. Her 2023 book, *Truth and Repair*, includes interviews with survivors of abuse and trauma about what justice means to them.[20] The people Herman interviewed were clear and consistent in how they envisioned justice. They wanted the people who abused them to admit to what they'd done, to be held accountable publicly, to understand the lasting impact of their abusive behavior, to offer an explanation of why they abused, to feel genuine remorse, to work toward rehabilitation, and to give some form of restitution.

Survivors Herman interviewed also identified numerous ways in which healing and repair were incompatible with criminal processes. Even those who'd had experiences with the legal system that could be described as "successful"—a perpetrator was caught, convicted, sentenced, and incarcerated—found the experience of prosecuting their abusers unsatisfying and even retraumatizing. One survivor participated in the prosecution of the man who had raped her, but the experience of seeing him go to prison did not give her the closure that these proceedings sometimes promise. She had to relive the rape every time she testified, and as a result, she dropped out of college. What this survivor actually wanted was the opportunity to ask the man who raped her a single question: *Why did you do this?*[21] But criminal trials are adversarial. Defendants have every incentive to admit to as little as possible.

Herman and her interview participants note that the fundamental structure of criminal proceedings, for some, contributes to the trauma. In the US, the injured party in a criminal case is the state, or "the people." This puts the survivor in a subordinate role, literally a "witness" to a crime against the government. One of the defining characteristics of abuse is that it robs survivors of their agency. Not having control over how a criminal trial proceeds can replicate that harm. "When the state assumes the role of injured party," Herman explains, "crime victims are reduced to the status of peripheral actors in the high-conflict drama of prosecution versus defense and subjected to hostile interrogation when they testify as witnesses to their own experiences."[22]

I remember this kind of heartbreak from my work as a domestic violence advocate. I once went to court with a survivor who had petitioned a judge to get her ex to make the kids do their homework when they were with him. She understood that not enforcing homework rules was an attempt to undermine her and make her afraid that her kids would fall behind in school. As clear as it was to her that this was a form of emotional abuse, the judge not only didn't see it but became angry that she'd asked the court for help. *These petty squabbles are a waste of this court's time*, he had told her in a stern and scolding tone. Most survivors I worked with experienced the emotional abuse as more devastating than physical abuse. The slaps and kicks left marks that people could see, but the personally tailored insults, or worse, the pretend compliments, would make them feel just as scared. But when they tried to explain how sending flowers was a threat—and not just any flowers but the same roses and lilies she carried down the aisle on their wedding day—nobody got it. Judges and police officers dismissed their concerns. Survivors left feeling angry, or worse, crazy or stupid for hoping a judge could help them.

Some survivors have made even bolder critiques of punishment and criminalization as strategies to stop abuse. The transformative justice movement, led largely by people of color, seeks to build safety and accountability through community-led processes. The goal of transformative justice is to take a deep, critical look at the social and political conditions that made an act of harm possible and to mobilize communities to change those conditions. Transformative justice, by definition, does not involve police or prisons. Many of its advocates support the abolition of the criminal legal system in the ways that previous generations fought to abolish slavery. In their anthology *Beyond Survival: Stories from the Transformative Justice Movement*, activists Leah Lakshmi Piepzna-Samarasinha and Ejeris Dixon uplift the wisdom from marginalized communities about how to hold people accountable for abusing without the criminal legal system.[23] A practical guide that reflects equally on successes and struggles, *Beyond Survival* explores strategies that range from grassroots groups providing security at bars as an alternative to calling the police to friend groups working to hold someone they love accountable for sexually abusing a child.

Organizer and anthology coeditor Ejeris Dixon sees transformative justice as a series of "small, bold experiments" undertaken by people who understand that the criminal system will not make them safer.[24] After a decade of involvement in efforts to envision what it would take for members of the most targeted communities to be safe, Dixon reflects on the importance of community: "Violence and oppression break community ties and breed fear and distrust. At its core, the work to create safety is to build meaningful, accountable relationships within our neighborhoods and communities." Part of building these relationships, Dixon says, is understanding what motivates people to call the police and what they wish they could have done instead: "if we create a culture in which people feel comfortable sharing stories about when they called emergency services but didn't want to, we actually learn about crucial needs for community safety projects."

Amita Swadhin, a contributor to *Beyond Survival*, is the founder of Mirror Memoirs, an oral history and organizing project by and for queer and transgender people of color who are child sexual abuse survivors. Mirror Memoirs has an abolitionist political analysis, which is partly about challenging the notion that police and prisons will stop violence. But, for Amita, it's more focused on creating new models of safety. "Abolition is not just about tearing things down and critiquing what we don't want; we have to be able to start dreaming together and then trying to practice those dreams, of what safety really is, of what pleasure really is, of what mutual care and interdependence really is," they tell me. "It's about giving ourselves permission to unmake everything. In an ideal abolitionist practice, eight billion people would be asking themselves that question and then working towards that answer." Mirror Memoirs produced an audio archive of interviews with sixty survivors who are LGBTQ+ people of color, each of whom were asked to envision healing and ending child sexual abuse. "No one person has the answer to what that looks like," Amita says, "but many of us have pieces of that answer and the more we work to build it the more ethical and visionary our world can be."

Amita, like everyone in the leadership of Mirror Memoirs, is a survivor of child sexual abuse. When they were thirteen years old, their family was reported to child protective authorities. What Amita remembers wanting most at that time was to get their father out of the house. Child protective services forced him to leave. But state involvement was harmful in other ways, some of which have taken decades to fully understand. Amita's South Asian immigrant family was subjected to the authority of the police and child protective workers, who threatened to incarcerate their mother if she didn't comply with their plan. They were required, too, to attend a support group with other teens who were involved in the child protective system. They remember one girl who was taken from her family and placed in an institution where she was sexually abused by a worker. "She ended up taking her own life while inside the institution," Amita tells me. "So that was my experience with state, quote unquote, *support for survivors*. Were we all in that group separated from the people who were directly raping us in our homes? Yes. And that was not by any stretch the end of violence in our lives. And in fact, the state responses made it worse and brought different kinds of violence into our lives."

In their early twenties, Amita began working as a youth organizer in New York City schools. Students were mostly Black and Brown, mostly poor. There were police and military recruiters all over the school, and students cycling in and out of incarceration. Amita was close to the students' age, and one of the only adults who spoke openly about their own experience of child sexual abuse. As a result, a lot of the teenagers confided in Amita. "We had a lot of boys coming back from Rikers into school," they tell me. "And these were boys who would come into my office and curl up in the fetal position and talk about the various kinds of trauma that had happened to them at Rikers." Seeing that incarceration resulted in more violence and more trauma made Amita progressively less willing to understand it as a solution to child sexual abuse.

As an organizer, Amita worked with coalitions and collaborators who saw connections between a range of issues—from military recruitment in impoverished schools to environmental racism and gentrification. But even the most astute activists struggled to see child sexual abuse as a systemic injustice worthy of political organizing. "Most of my comrades, even the ones who were very supportive and caring, treated it like that was an individual issue," they tell me. "Go to therapy, maybe talk to your friends about it. But that's very separate from us organizing to end the war on terror, organizing to get cops out of schools, and they weren't making the connections."

In this void, the most visible political activism around child sexual abuse was focused on the criminal legal system: stiffer criminal penalties for sexually abusing a child, education to help judges and prosecutors understand trauma so they could do a better job working with crime victims. Amita had tried that route, working with national organizations that advocated for reforming police and judicial responses to gender-based violence. But they experienced racism from white leaders and a persistent feeling that locking people up wasn't the solution. On the most fundamental level, knowing that rape is ubiquitous in prisons, how could anyone see putting people in prison as a strategy to stop rape? "There has to be some community-based response rooted in relationship that interrupts that violence," Amita explains.

Years after their family was reported to child protective services, Amita's father told them that he had been sexually abused as a child. That stuck with Amita. Most sexual abuse survivors don't go on to harm others, but hearing this revelation made Amita curious. "Why do certain survivors have a break from their humanity?" Research is limited, but available evidence shows that people with histories of child sexual abuse are overrepresented among sexual abusers. A meta-analysis led by psychologist Ashley Jespersen found that people who sexually abused children were three times more likely to have been sexually abused as kids than those who did not sexually abuse children.[25] These associations were not seen for sexual, or physical, abuse of adults. Authors note that these associations do not prove a causal link between sexual abuse history and later perpetration, but they recommend that these findings should inform prevention efforts.

Evidence like this motivates Amita to challenge prevailing beliefs. "So if our endgame is to end rape, what logical sense does it make to shove people who are already raped as kids and suffering and disconnected from their own humanity and needing connection and needing a healing of their deep shame and their deep wounds, what sense does it make to put them in a cage in which they are very certain to, at the very least, witness more rape happening, perhaps experience more rape themselves, and perhaps go on to rape more people while in that cage?" Amita asks. "[And] because you don't get a life sentence for raping a child, release them back on the streets of our society? Do you want to live in that society? I don't. That does not make me feel safer."

These are crucial questions. Weighing them takes more bravery, compassion, discernment, and risk tolerance than most of us have. But if we don't struggle with them, we're going to keep taking a subset of people who sexually abuse and declaring them irredeemably evil. Then, we're going to subject them to the most humiliating forms of exclusion and shaming, disregarding overwhelming evidence that these efforts don't prevent future abuse. "Nobody changes behavior from feeling ashamed," Amita tells me. "Because shame is an isolating response. It is an othering response. It is like, You're a monster, you go over there. Being shamed in a way that strips people of humanity is always wrong."

Even when people are willing to be accountable for sexually abusing, public opinion undermines them. Joan Tabachnick is the former executive director of the Massachusetts Society for a World Free of Sexual Harm by Youth. She spent decades bridging the sometimes bitter rifts between survivor advocates and therapists who work with people convicted of sex offenses. In the 1990s and 2000s, she organized a series of public dialogues between sexual abuse survivors and people who have sexually abused. Carefully curating her roster of speakers, she worked to find people who were willing to speak publicly about why they abused and how they've changed and whom she could trust not to exploit the attention of an audience.

Joan tells me about a series of public presentations she gave with a grandfather who'd been incarcerated for sexually abusing his grandchildren. The abuse began when the girls' mother was in the middle of a divorce and the kids were spending more time at their grandparents' house. The grandmother noticed changes in the girls—they were depressed, withdrawn, fearful. But she assumed it was the stress of the divorce. Then, the oldest granddaughter disclosed sexual abuse.

Joan explains what happened next in quick succession. Each event feels like a gut punch but none is the point of the story: the grandmother talked to the other two girls and learned that they had also been sexually abused, the family reported the abuse, the grandfather went to prison, and soon after his release, he attempted suicide.

The grandmother leaned into her faith. That gave her the courage and grace to see that her husband was more than the horrible things he had done, but also that he needed to be accountable for how much he'd hurt the girls. She didn't want the girls to stop visiting her, nor did she want them to lose the family traditions that were anchored in her home. So whenever they came over, he had to leave. She made it clear that the kids would not be pressured to see him, and that they were the priority. For Christmas and Thanksgiving, the girls and their mother came to the house, and her husband spent the holidays with members of the church community. The grandmother's faith helped her maintain her priorities. She didn't agonize over whether to forgive him. "God has to decide," Joan explains. "That's not her role. Her role on this earth was about ensuring her family was safe."

Both grandparents honored their commitment to following the girls' lead. A big part of the grandfather's commitment to being accountable for his actions was not putting any pressure on the girls to see him. Eventually, the oldest granddaughter was ready to see him, but the younger two were not. "So again," Joan tells me, "they made sure that the granddaughters made that decision."

The whole family continued with therapy. They lost some friends but stayed together. Also, they stayed vigilant. The grandmother continued to hold her husband accountable. "Even though he personally is committed to never doing this again," Joan explains, "he wants to make sure that everybody around him is watching his actions."

But when Joan Tabachnick and this family spoke publicly, most audiences responded with anger. And the focus of their rage was the grandmother. *How could she not notice her husband sexually abusing the girls? Or how could she stay married to a child molester?* "There doesn't seem to be any understanding," Joan tells me, "that we as a community are safer because of this grandmother's decision."

The girls didn't have to lose a beloved family member nor were they pressured to pretend that the abuse hadn't affected them. They weren't coerced into accepting their grandfather's apology or hurried to get over it because he's a good man who loves them. He wasn't pitched in a dumpster like so many others who share the label "convicted sex offender." The grandfather was not defined by the worst choice he'd ever made. Nor was he allowed to avoid taking responsibility for the enduring trauma he'd caused. This family was able to hold a heartbreaking truth in a way that most of us couldn't imagine. And they believed enough in the choices they'd made that they were willing to endure the ridicule of strangers. This is one family. We don't know how common their experience is because most people in similar situations would not share their story publicly.

Joan Tabachnick is unrelenting in her commitment to hope. After nearly forty years of trying to convince people that humanizing, support-ing, and therapeutically treating people who sexually abuse makes all of us safer, she celebrates all progress, no matter how incremental. When I ask her for examples of hope, she points to a Massachusetts law, enacted in 2019, that prohibits the criminalization of all children under twelve.[26] It also prohibits school-based police officers from getting involved in routine discipline, a practice that was shown by research to disproportionately affect young people of color and disabled youth. This means that young kids won't wind up on sex offender registries and, Joan Tabachnick hopes, will face fewer barriers to the treatment they need. Currently, twenty-four US states prohibit the criminalization of children.[27]

Compliance-based approaches to personal safety do more to promote fear and stigma than prevent violence. Misguided outrage does the same for public policy. Rigid, evidence-poor laws give us the illusion of taking abuse seriously while doing nothing to make anybody safer. Some people who sexually abuse face severe consequences while the most powerful abusers—and the institutions that enable them—too often face none. This kind of rigidity is understandable. It comes from a sense of outrage about abuse and urgency to protect children. But if we stay committed to punishment that is harsh and ineffective, we will never develop the courage to make real change.

CHAPTER 5

COMPLIANCE BREEDS ABUSE

Mandy Meloon never got to compete in the Olympics. She was supposed to go to Beijing in 2008 but was dropped from the team after refusing to recant sexual abuse allegations she'd made against her coach. Dozens of news stories have since detailed the rapes that Mandy and other women taekwondo athletes survived. She was first raped as a teenager living at the Olympic Training Center in Colorado Springs, then later when she lived in Sugar Land, Texas, training at the taekwondo school of then Olympic coach Jean Lopez and his brother Steven, also an accomplished athlete.[1]

Long before gymnast survivors made national news, sexual abuse was rampant in taekwondo and other elite sports. When she lived at the Olympic Training Center, Mandy was supposed to go to school. An older teammate insisted she give him oral sex in exchange for rides to and from school. He later raped her, then came to her dorm room the next morning to declare that she was his girlfriend and the sex was consensual. She didn't trust that she could tell anyone because of a comment from her coach on her first day at the center. "He looked at me and he's like, 'Don't have sex and don't get pregnant.' So when I was assaulted, in my mind, I was like, 'Oh, I'm in trouble,'" Mandy tells me. She was seventeen the first time Jean Lopez sexually abused her. He came into a hotel room she was sharing with another teenage athlete at the 1997 World Cup competition in Cairo. Alone in a foreign country with no idea how to get help, Mandy pretended to be asleep as her body endured the assault. At eighteen, she was coerced into dating Steven Lopez, then in his twenties. He was physically, sexually, and verbally abusive, and he cheated on her with other athletes as a way to stoke divisions between them. Mandy spent most of her teens and early twenties away from her family. Her dad was in the military. Her mom worked low wage jobs to help pay for her training. They couldn't afford to travel with her to competitions, so she was often alone with her coaches and teammates. Mandy's parents trusted the system. It was the Olympics, after all.

There are stories that have been fact-checked by journalists, testified to under oath at a depositions, and shared with investigators who acted like they would hold abusive coaches and the administrators who enabled them accountable.[2] But underlying the overt abuse was an organizational culture that made it possible. And a key component of that culture is compliance. "Your coach was God," Mandy says. With thousands of people vying for just a few spots on the Olympic team, the pressure to please both coaches and administrators was intense. When Mandy lived in Sugar Land, she wasn't allowed to have friends outside the training center. When she tried to date someone outside of taekwondo, her coach prohibited it. She was in her early twenties, no longer a minor, but her life was not her own. "You're literally together 24/7, away from friends and family," Mandy says. "They never wanted us to go home for holidays." The team was expected to spend Christmas and Thanksgiving with Jean and Steven Lopez's parents. They were pressured, too, to get tattoos with the name of the school. Mandy describes it as being branded like cattle. Mandy barely saw her family for the seven years she lived at Sugar Land. They also controlled her money so she couldn't just leave.

"Your life revolved around training," Mandy explains. The physical training was brutal, and she was expected to subordinate her body to her coach. "I couldn't rest, I couldn't say no, I wasn't allowed to have feelings," she says. She won the vast majority of her competitions—thirty-four registered wins and only twelve losses—but when she lost, she was berated and shunned. She also had to train when she was injured. She describes going to a doctor after a particularly brutal competition. "From ankles to shoulders, every inch of my body was covered in bruises," she tells me. The skin was ripped off her legs. Her injuries were so severe, the doctor had a hard time believing they resulted from a sport.

Even with ripped skin and a bruised body, Mandy was expected to train. She remembers Jean Lopez screaming at her to kick, and she protested, saying the doctor had told her it wasn't safe. Jean Lopez then ordered Mandy into a private office with him. Mandy walked out and reported Jean to Olympic administrators.

In response to a sexual abuse report Mandy had previously made to USA Taekwondo, the national governing body of the Olympic sport, administrators had prohibited Jean Lopez from being alone with her. It was the only consequence he faced after Mandy and other athletes had complained to Olympic authorities. But after Mandy refused to be alone with him, Jean Lopez penalized her for refusing to train and she was removed from the team. Later, she was told she could be reinstated and go to the Olympics, but only if she took back the allegations she'd made against her coach. "They told me if you sign a contract, and you say that you're mentally ill, you lied about everything, and you're getting counseling, you can go to the Olympics," she tells me. "I said no."

Mandy struggled when she left the sport. She never stopped fighting to hold the people who abused her accountable. But every step of the process was traumatizing. In 2015, she participated in an independent investigation launched by USA Taekwondo. Having to relive the most terrifying moments of her life took a toll on her health—she couldn't eat, sleep, or work and was repeatedly hospitalized for PTSD. After the sixth hospitalization, Mandy lost her home. Desperate for a place to sleep one night, she went to a bar with three men. But she didn't have an ID so the bouncer wouldn't let her in. Trying to get the men's attention, she pushed past the bouncer, who threatened to call the police.

The next thing she remembers is a man grabbing her from behind. Reflexively she hit him, not realizing he was an off-duty police officer. She spent the next two years in prison for assault. Mandy doesn't glorify incarceration, but she does believe it saved her from a lot of worse fates: "I remember when they put me in that cell it was a relief. It was clean.

I had a shower, I had food, and I could sleep, and nobody was gonna bother me."

When she finally started therapy and healing, Mandy realized the people she related to most were those coming out of cults.

Training for the Olympics takes extraordinary discipline. Athletes adhere to strict regiments proscribed by their coaches, pushing through fatigue, sometimes injuries. But what Mandy experienced was not rigorous training. It was what I call toxic compliance. Toxic compliance occurs when one person or a small group of people insist that their directions be followed at all costs. It's not safe to question or challenge them, or even bring up issues they don't want discussed. Everyone is expected to subordinate not only their opinions but their bodies. While some compliance is necessary in most teams and organizations, it becomes toxic when maintaining the leader's authority is more important than the group's purpose, and when all critical thinking is quashed.

Toxic compliance is a defining characteristic of organizations with widespread sexual abuse crises. The Catholic Church has a sexual abuse crisis; the Unitarian Church does not. The US military has a sexual abuse crisis; the US Park Service does not. Any type of organization can have one, or a few, abuse incidents. But abuse thrives in institutions that demand strict compliance and make it unsafe for people to challenge their leaders. According to reporting by the *New Yorker* and the *New York Times*, for example, employees of the Weinstein Group were required to sign a document that prohibited them from criticizing serial sexual abuser Harvey Weinstein or other company leaders.[3] It's not uncommon for corporations to have agreements that protect the confidentiality of the work product, but the Weinstein agreements are different because their purpose was to silence dissent.

One of the earliest and most thorough explorations of the relationship between compliance and abuse came from disability rights advocate Dave Hingsburger. Starting in the 1980s and '90s, he challenged toxic compliance in social service organizations for people with intellectual disabilities, a population we now know is seven times more likely to experience sexual abuse than people without disabilities. He argued that being constantly expected to comply with the wishes of people without disabilities—usually family members or paid caregivers—puts people with disabilities at risk.[4]

In some group homes and day programs, people with disabilities don't get to make basic choices about their lives. Hingsburger writes about one man who was told he had to eat cereal for breakfast though he preferred toast. He was disciplined for refusing a breakfast he didn't like. Others were told what to wear or compelled to participate in activities they didn't enjoy. People who needed help with bathing or dressing were touched in ways they didn't choose and expected to use the bathroom with the door open, which undermined their ability to understand privacy or believe they deserved it. People with intellectual disabilities have challenges with learning, reasoning, and problem solving. They may also have difficulty understanding the nuances of social and interpersonal interactions. If they are touched without their consent by caregivers, many advocates argue, they may not believe they can do anything to stop abusive touch. Hingsburger argues that organizational cultures that take away people's choices are teaching them to endure sexual abuse. If you can't say no to peas for dinner, Hingsburger reasons, then how can you say no to sexual abuse?[5]

In 2011, Wisconsin's Violence Against Women with Disabilities and Deaf Women Project released a report that examined the expectation of compliance that is prevalent in the disability service system.[6] Amy Judy, the report's lead author, began by posing a critical challenge: *People with disabilities are supervised more than most other people on earth, so why are they also the most abused?*[7]

Judy argues that the compliance culture that exists in disability service agencies and group homes contributes to high rates of abuse. "Getting people to do what you want them to do is part of the job. However, working to get those who receive support to master the lessons of compliance can make a person more vulnerable. The person who learns to comply is more likely when someone says *get in the car*—to get in the car. A person who is taught to be compliant is already partially groomed for a perpetrator. When people don't understand healthy relationships, they might not recognize mistreatment or abuse. The culture of compliance makes people more vulnerable and less safe."[8]

The report includes case examples of disability service agencies that take even the most basic choices away from their clients. Some of these organizations use words like "empowerment" and "self-determination" in their mission statements. Yet when Judy asked caregivers what these terms meant, their responses reflected how few real choices their clients get. One caregiver responded that the adults who live in the group home where she works get to choose juice or water at snack time. They don't get to decide when snack time is. In some group homes, residents are not allowed to go into the kitchen when they're hungry, because the agency management decided that being in the kitchen without supervision would be unsafe. In their own homes, the report notes, adults with intellectual disabilities did not have access to cupboards or the refrigerator. They ate when paid caregivers told them to eat.

The report emphasizes stark differences between the level of autonomy that most nondisabled adults expect and the level of compliance the disability service system demands: "A person receiving support wants more coffee. At your house that would probably mean you get up and get it. This person has learned that she has to ask for permission and did. The caregiver said *you've had enough.* If the person asking for more coffee has mastered the lesson of compliance, that will be the end of it."[9]

Also, according to the report, people who assert desires that are different from staff or management's wishes are labeled as "difficult" or "behavioral." "In the culture of compliance," Judy explains, "we assume the following: I'm fine, the environment (she is in) is fine, the activity is fine and our methods are fine because our intention is to help. The problem is her. She needs to change. We believe that we have the right and the responsibility to change her."[10]

Judy and the other authors acknowledge that most caregivers are not motivated by malice. They are sincere in their commitment to helping people, often for low pay. But the service systems that prize compliance create the conditions in which abuse thrives. "Support workers often say they took a job because they wanted to have relationships with people while supporting them to live full lives," Judy notes. "They learn quickly that they are supposed to get people to do things they might not want to do. They have to get people to follow schedules and engage in activities whether the person is interested or not. They have to tell people when to shower and eat and go to bed . . . For many, the job of support person becomes that of enforcer, often unwelcome enforcer, rather than supporter."[11]

Dave Hingsburger has argued that "the ability to non-comply" is essential to equipping people with intellectual disabilities to resist abuse. "Teaching clients how to stick up for themselves is mandatory," he writes. "If they are ever going to be able to clearly say 'No' when 'No' is imperative." Noncompliance, Hingsburger explains, is a skill that needs to be taught. To illustrate his point, he challenges disability service workers to "think of someone you support. Now imagine yourself standing next to them at a stove with a hot burner. Imagine telling them to touch it," he says. "If you believe that your client would touch it, you have a problem. If you believe that your client wouldn't touch it but that it would be a difficult decision for them to defy you, you have a problem."[12] Being directed by a caregiver to touch a hot stove may be an overstated example, but it invites people who work in the disability service system to examine how often they pressure the people they support to do things that are painful, uncomfortable, or just not fun.

Dave Hingsburger sounded the alarm about compliance culture decades before investigative journalists uncovered the magnitude of abuse in the disability service system. *New York Times* reporters Russ Buettner and Danny Hakim's 2011 investigation revealed a crisis of physical abuse, sexual abuse, and neglect in group homes run by New York State.[13] Though agencies are required to report serious abuse incidents to law enforcement, Buettner and Hakim found thirteen thousand reports of abuse and neglect, only 5 percent of which were reported. They also uncovered a pattern of incidents in which workers who had physically and sexually abused residents were moved to other group homes rather than fired. Six years later, *New York Times* writer Dan Barry investigated a thirty-year operation in Atalissa, Iowa, in which men with intellectual disabilities were warehoused in barely livable conditions, abused and neglected, and forced to gut birds for a local turkey processing plant for only $65 per week.[14]

It was disability rights activists who first named the culture of compliance, yet it's also prevalent in other organizations that have widespread abuse crises, like the Catholic Church. Catholicism restricts many of the most intimate decisions people can make about their bodies from sexuality to contraception and abortion. The strict hierarchies within the institution make it almost impossible to hold leaders accountable.

Sociologist Tricia Bruce has studied the Catholic Church for decades. Her book *Faithful Revolution* is about the founding of Voice of the Faithful, a parishioner-led organization formed in 2002 in response to the first *Boston Globe* stories about rampant sexual abuse.[15] Voice of the Faithful advocates for abuse survivors and for parishioners to have a bigger say in the running of the church. And, unlike other advocacy groups formed by and for survivors of priest abuse, Voice of the Faithful is committed to being part of the institution and working with church leadership to create change. Still, as Tricia Bruce's research has shown, the church institution has remained opposed to shared leadership.

Even in the immediate aftermath of the first *Boston Globe* story, the Catholic hierarchy demanded compliance rather than acknowledging the harm they'd caused and finding ways to be accountable to laypeople. At the first Voice of the Faithful convention in the fall of 2002, over four thousand Catholics gathered to work for change, but no parish priest would say mass because the archbishop forbade it. When Voice of the Faithful raised funds to support the church's charitable projects after donations to the cardinal's appeal dropped sharply in the wake of the abuse crisis, the archbishop compelled Catholic Charities to refuse the donations. Tricia Bruce followed Voice of the Faithful chapters in seven cities; most were prohibited by priests from meeting in church buildings.

Tricia Bruce's research includes everything from interviews with priests about burnout to the nuances in everyday Catholics' beliefs about abortion. When we talk, she encourages me to understand that moment in its historical context. The church was in crisis, and some of the decisions leaders made were more rushed than thoughtful. In her research, she has interviewed priests who are still affected by that moment. At the same time, the toxic compliance that church leaders demanded at that time was not out of character. She explains how the institution's strict hierarchy "creates these structural environments in which some people are invited into the room and others are not. And so right there, you begin to create systems of secrecy and privacy." Bishops have inordinate power and, while they are technically accountable to the pope, there is no real oversight of their decisions.

But what's more devastating for survivors, Tricia Bruce notes, is being abused by someone who is seen as an extension of God. "Ordained men are the only people who can bridge the connection between you and the divine, so to be abused by someone in that position," she explains, is uniquely traumatic. Bruce notes the frustration of lay people who love the church and are committed to making the institution safer, but they struggle with the reality that the church makes no space for the power or leadership of anyone other than ordained men.

Patterns of toxic compliance and widespread sexual abuse also exist in the US military. In a 2021 study funded by the US Department of Defense, the RAND Corporation found that 1 in 4 women and 1 in 16 men experience sexual harassment in the military, and 1 in 16 women and 1 in 143 men experience sexual assault.[16] RAND also found that sexual harassment and assault of women was increasing and that the majority of servicemembers who experienced sexual harassment and assault did not make official reports, citing fear of social and professional retaliation.

The study also found that Equal Opportunity Advisors, civilian employees whose job is to counsel commanders on issues related to equity and discrimination, often do not feel free to make official sexual harassment and assault reports when their commander does not want those reports made. Among the recommendations RAND made was to remove these advisors from the chain of command, so that officers with superior military rank cannot quash efforts to document the prevalence of abuse.

At her first duty station as a lieutenant in the US Army, Lindsey Knapp was given a vibrator by her supervisor. He was concerned, he told her, that she wasn't having enough sex. "Okay," she thought, "this is the price that I have to pay for deciding to serve." She took it on the chin, she says. She couldn't have imagined reporting him.

Motivated by the September 11, 2001, attacks to join ROTC in college, Lindsey served in the second Gulf War. Her unit set up telecommunication infrastructure in the desert. While she was on active duty, she attended more funerals of service members who died by suicide than of those who were were killed in Iraq. She resented having to work twice as hard as men, but sometimes she did it anyway. When she was growing up, her father had treated his son and daughters as equals, so what she experienced in the military was a bucket of cold water.

When she was pregnant, Lindsey was exempt from certain requirements like being around toxic jet fuel in the motor pool. But sometimes she pushed past these limits because she wanted to prove herself. She could have been exempt from taking a test to prove she could use her weapon, but her commanding officer wanted a 100 percent pass rate. So she put on her flak vest, helmet, and "full battle rattle," and passed on her first try. "On my stomach on top of my kid, with a weapon, around all these toxins you're not supposed to be around," she tells me. Lindsey watched as her male counterparts went through the line three or four times before they qualified. Also, she tells me, she beat her only female mentor, a woman who had jumped out of airplanes when she was pregnant.

Lindsey got support from a handful of men, experienced warrant officers who told her when to disregard questionable or suspicious orders. She believes the only reason she wasn't sexually assaulted was because they kept her from being alone with the wrong people.

When she left active duty, Lindsey was recruited to serve as a victim advocate by Special Operations Command, a division of the US Department of Defense that ensures coordination between branches of the military. She was stationed at Fort Bragg, which is now Fort Liberty, in Fayetteville, North Carolina. She saw herself as the perfect person for the job. Not only was she a veteran, but she had experience helping sexual assault survivors, including her sisters. As a teenager, Lindsey had accompanied one sister to court hearings. In college, she had volunteered to educate her peers about sexual assault, and she worked for a rape crisis center after she left the military.

The magnitude of sexual violence in the military was already public knowledge. Lindsey convinced herself she was the right person to fix the problem. "Who better than me," she thought, "to come in and really just shake things up for them." She believed that if she read the regulations carefully enough, she would find what she needed to force the hands of anyone who hesitated to do the right thing. She was also in law school. After work most nights, she drove two hours from Fayetteville to Durham to get to her classes.

But when she tried to advocate for survivors in ways that challenged people in power, she got the same response: *That's not how we do things here.* Lindsey describes herself as "spicy," not afraid to push back when she felt her integrity was at stake. A commander at Fort Bragg came under investigation for what Lindsey described as a "sexually related offense." She went to the brigade commander, who supervised both her and the commander, requesting that he be removed from his position during the investigation. "We're not saying he's guilty," she told her commander. "We're not saying he's innocent, but he needs to be moved." People were being sent on mission all the time, so Lindsey reasoned that this man could be moved in a way that would look like routine military orders. The brigade commander did give the man a new assignment: as Lindsey's boss.

"If you're my boss, I have to brief you on all the open sexual assault cases every month," Lindsey explains. "So now I'm having to brief somebody who is under investigation for a sexually related offense about his own sexually related offense." In response, she says, she "raised holy hell." She reported it to the commanding general, who gave her the same line: *That's not how we do things here.* Lindsey walked an untenable line. Her clients trusted her. None of them knew that her direct supervisor was under investigation. So every time she had to brief her supervisor, all she said was, "I have no updates at this time." Lindsey imagines how she could have compromised survivors' safety if she'd loved her military career too much or had fewer safety nets.

The allegations against this man were substantiated. They were bad enough that he was removed from the military. But, Lindsey tells me, they retaliated against the woman who reported him. She doesn't want to give me details of a confidential investigation, so she speaks in general terms about what often happens to women who speak up. They "command refer" them to behavioral health. Command referrals, authorized by Department of Defense Directive 6490.04, give superior officers the power to compel people below them in the chain of command to be evaluated by a mental health provider.[17] This means that military police show up at someone's door and bring them to an inpatient psychiatric facility run by the military. A mental health provider employed by the military does a psychological evaluation. "They're going to take away your weapon," Lindsey explains. "They're going to take away your security clearance." The outcome of the psychological evaluation is then determined by the military. "They may commit you, they may not commit you, but just the idea that they had to do it is going to have a significant negative impact on your mental health, but also on your military career," Lindsey explains. "What better way to discredit the victim?"

In 2022, *Rolling Stone* published an article about Lindsey's attempt to blow the whistle on a rape case.[18] Cristobal Vallejo, a Delta Force operative, was accused of raping a junior officer. Because the assault was perpetrated off post, the Fayetteville police and Cumberland County district attorney took the case. Delta Force is an elite unit. Lindsey describes them as untouchable. In a military town, they're like celebrities; politicians and corporate executives try to rub elbows with them. When the civilian district attorney attempted to interview witnesses, Fort Bragg refused. Then, with no warning, the military took over the case, court-martialed Vallejo, and acquitted him in a classified trial. The trial did not have to be secret, Lindsey maintains; there was no classified information involved. Lindsey wrote a letter to the commanding general of Special Operations, outlining all the ways the case had gone wrong. She still believed that all she had to do was make a strong enough case. After she did this, she was accused of sending classified information over an unclassified server and placed on administrative leave. Lindsey had a security clearance but was never involved in any secret meetings, so she didn't think she had access to classified information. She kept asking to be debriefed, so she could learn from the error, but nobody responded. Two years later, Lindsey Knapp was fired.

Toxic compliance underlies the military's efforts to discredit survivors. Service members give up control over their bodies and lives in ways that would be unthinkable outside the military. "When you're in military, you can't just quit, right? So like, if you have a toxic boss, or toxic leader," Lindsey explains, "you can't just not show up to work, right? Like you literally can go to jail for that." Beyond that, there are mandatory dental cleanings, physicals, and eye exams. Lindsey describes being lined up like cattle and given injections, having no ability to refuse them. "You wouldn't even know what they were sticking you with."

Also, Lindsey explains, you can't just wake up with a cold and decide not to go to work. Maybe you're not sick-sick, but it would not be the best day to march twelve miles with fifty pounds on your back. Lindsey explains that in order to take a sick day she needed to get permission from a doctor and be put "on quarters." Lindsey gets migraines. Her migraines are exacerbated by strenuous exercise. There were days she could do an 80 percent workout but not 100 percent, when she could have run three miles but she was ordered to run six. She was throwing up and sensitive to light, but she couldn't set limits without a doctor's authorization. Not being allowed to take care of herself was one reason she left active duty.

Lindsey sees a direct relationship between toxic compliance and the egregious way the US military handles most sexual violence. "If you experience sexual harassment and you report it, and they tell you to shut up," Lindsey says, "you're probably just like, 'OK, I guess I have to shut up.'" Lindsey saw a lot of service members respond by taking it out on themselves. She saw survivors start gaining weight—consciously or not. The military has weight requirements and if service members get too heavy, Lindsey explains, "they'll do what they call flagging you because you're not going to be in compliance with the regulations any-more." Service members who don't meet the military's weight and fitness requirements can be discharged. Lindsey wonders if some women used weight gain as a protective strategy, either as a way out of the military or a way to become less conventionally attractive so that men would leave them alone. But even that can backfire. She has clients who were required to do extra physical training to get their weight or fitness into compliance. In the worst cases, that training was overseen by the person who harassed or assaulted them.

"Service members' rights are taken away to such a degree that they cannot hold military accountable in the same way that their civilian counterparts can," Lindsey says. As a result of *US v. Farris*, a Supreme Court case that was decided the 1950s, service members can't bring civil suits against the military or their superior officers. Lindsey describes the court decision as well-meaning. It was intended to protect commanding officers from facing legal consequences for decisions they'd made in the heat of battle. But today it creates yet another barrier for survivors.

Lindsey is trying to find ways to work around that barrier. She founded Combat Sexual Assault, a nonprofit organization that fights for military survivors using their limited legal options. She started the organization during her administrative leave. She laughs about the fact that the military paid her for two years to figure out how to fight them. Combat Sexual Assault lawyers represent service members who have been retaliated against or discharged from the military for reporting abuse. She applies for corrections to their military records that "upgrade" their discharges so they have access to more veteran benefits. Some of her clients were accused of making false statements. Others left their posts after assaults and didn't feel safe coming back, so they got dishonorably discharged for going AWOL. Lindsey fights to change their discharge status. Some of her clients are in the Guard Reserve with few legal options. In these cases, Lindsey says, "I just yell like crazy." That means calling the Pentagon, talking to the media, shining light on how ill-equipped the new federal laws about military sexual assault are when held up against the intractable toxic compliance culture of the US military.

Decades of advocacy and political pressure have resulted in some change. In July 2023, President Joe Biden issued an executive order that changed the Uniform Code of Military Justice. Under the new order, military commanders no longer have authority to decide whether cases of sexual assault, domestic violence, and murder are prosecuted. These reports will now be referred to special prosecutors who are outside the chain of command. Some advocates lauded this change, but Lindsey describes it as a "band-aid on a bullet wound," insufficient to address the deep structural problems.

There are real and hard questions about how to instill the discipline to function in a war zone without creating a culture of toxic compliance. But at the same time, if discipline was really the goal, commanding officers should be able to discipline service members not to sexually abuse. If we understand toxic compliance as a defining characteristic of organizations that have intractable abuse crises, then we can create prevention strategies that address it. But that takes more political will than we have. Even the incremental reforms implemented in 2023 faced years of opposition from the Pentagon.

When Lindsey Knapp founded Combat Sexual Assault, she knew she needed to do more than sue the military. So in addition to bringing legal challenges, the organization's work includes empowerment protocols, which are healing practices designed to help survivors recover from the trauma they experienced in the military. For Lindsey, healing is neces-sary in order to hold the military accountable. "One of the reasons why we have not been able to get as much progress on this issue," Lindsey explains, "is because we have too many unhealed humans out there." She draws the analogy of a soldier who has been shot. No matter how badly they want to stay on the battlefield, they're only helpful if they are taking care of themselves. "You want to go back in and you want to go fight next to your brothers and sisters in arms to make sure they don't get shot. But you have to heal that bullet wound first."

Empowerment protocols fortify military survivors so they can be focused and strategic as they fight for justice. Combat Sexual Assault is intentional about its focus on body-oriented healing. "Talk therapy will only get you so far," Lindsey explains. "And then at some point, you need to process that trauma through the body." There is solid science to support the effectiveness of body-oriented healing, but Lindsey sees it as especially necessary for military survivors, many of whom live with debilitating pain. "You're gonna hold trauma in your body in different ways. Maybe your shoulders are hunched over, maybe you have chronic pain in an area of your body that you have never had an injury," Lindsey says. "We see that a lot in the veteran population, their knee hurts, their back hurts their whatever hurts, but they don't actually know why. And they go to the doctor, they get these MRIs, they get the CT scans, and there is no injury there. So then they feel even more crazy, right?" she says. "What may be hard to understand is that that's some bottled up emotion into your body."

Empowerment protocols are designed to meet the unique needs of each survivor. They include everything from dance and art therapy to yoga. Nobody gets pressured into doing anything that makes them feel worse and nobody has to justify their decisions. Lindsey has a personal understanding of what it's like when a popular healing practice doesn't work. Though she teaches yoga now, she couldn't always tolerate slow, meditative physical activity. "I hated yoga. The first time I did it, I was like, you want me to sit by myself on a yoga mat for sixty minutes with my own mind? Fuck that noise." She found that she could get some of the benefits of yoga by doing a more dynamic workout that was a better fit for what she was feeling at the time. "If you are angry you cannot sit," she tells me. "You have to be moving."

Combat Sexual Assault staff get creative, offering military survivors ways to heal their bodies that are unique to each person. If someone is afraid to leave their house, or in too much pain for dance therapy, can they clean out their garage? Can they garden? It's like a puzzle, figuring out which healing protocol works for each person.

As Lindsey Knapp describes this, I see a purposeful commitment to body autonomy that is a blatant contrast to all the ways she was expected to give up control over her body when she was on active duty. Healing protocols are not as dramatic as the sweeping change and accountability most advocates want. But giving survivors the experience of refusing or changing physical activity based on their own needs is a powerful antidote to toxic compliance.

PART 2

WHAT WORKS

CHAPTER 6

NOT OVERREACTING

There's a kind of liberation that comes from having experienced the power of your body. You look at a man who is hostile or condescending and what you see is eyeballs, a throat, and a groin. Parts of his body that are weak. You tune out his disparaging comments about the mandatory sexual harassment training your employer made you take. Or his not-funny joke about the sex life of a woman who just got promoted. *If he tries to hurt me,* you think, *I know what to do.* You don't think he would physically attack you in the middle of an office but there's a way he is trying to diminish you. By focusing on the weak parts of his body, you remind yourself that just because he's a large, muscular man doesn't mean he's indestructible. His body, like everyone's body, is a complicated mess of strength and vulnerability.

Gender-based violence creeps into the small spaces of our lives. Too often we second-guess ourselves. *Am I overreacting? I mean it's not a big deal, all he did was take a file box out of my hands when I told him I could carry it myself. And yes, his hands lingered over mine when he took the box and my stomach turned. But it was just my hands he touched, not other parts of my body. You hear so many horror stories.* But after learning self-defense, you see it differently. You said what you wanted and what you didn't, and he disregarded it.

Not everybody who dismisses you when you tell them "no" or touches you without your permission is capable of abusing, but most people who abuse start with subtler violations. By choosing to be subtle, he puts you in a tenuous position. You feel uncomfortable, but you know that if you go to HR and tell them someone carried a box for you when you said you didn't need help, you would sound ridiculous. Subtle violations like this one put us at odds with ourselves. They drive a wedge between our gut-level understanding that something is wrong and the reportable facts that may sound petty when we say them out loud. But, as you learned in that self-defense class, subtle intrusions test the water. They show someone who is capable of abusing what happens when lines are crossed. Are people too afraid or embarrassed to challenge them? Does anyone feel safe speaking up?

There's a way to be vigilant without diminishing yourself. And there's power in feeling entitled to get out of tight spots. When he tries to corner you at a work party, you move around a cocktail table. By putting a piece of furniture between your body and his, you deny him quick access to your shoulders and forearms, parts of your body he has touched before. Now, if he wants to touch you, he has to reach across the table and it would be near impossible for him to make it look accidental.

Part of the reason you feel calm and powerful is the physical skills. You've practiced breaking out of grabs enough times that you trust your body. You think back to the satisfying clap of your hand striking a punching bag the size of him, and it makes you feel less stuck. Being small or disabled or having arthritis in both hips doesn't make you defenseless. You learned how to use strong parts of your body against weak parts of his.

The skills you learned went beyond kicking and punching, which means you could use them in situations where hitting someone would make you less safe. You learned to communicate assertively, to say "No" and "Stop" and "I'm not a hugger" and "I don't need your help, thanks," and to refuse attention in a million other ways that you could actually use at work. You learned to use desks and tables as barriers, moving around a room so you feel less stuck. You learned to pay attention when your whole body cringes in response to a look or comment or unchosen touch. You learned that your well-being is important, and you don't have to suppress it.

You almost didn't ask the question that was on your mind, but something emboldened you. *Isn't all this moving around desks and breaking out of grabs just another way of putting extra labor on women? Why can't my company just do their job so I don't have to give up my weekends?* You expected to be told you were wrong. Instead, your anger at the unfairness was respected. *As much as I love teaching these skills,* one instructor said in response to your question, *no one should have to learn them.*

You didn't think much about signing up for a self-defense class. Your friend sent you the link; you thought it could be fun. Maybe you'd learn a few kicks and punches to have in your back pocket if a creepy guy followed you to the subway. You didn't think it would change anything at work, because you couldn't imagine that anything was changeable. You never doubted that you were equal to any man, but it didn't occur to you that you could stop the intrusions.

You see more clearly now how political inequities show up in the most mundane interactions. *How many more times have women been asked to get coffee for a meeting than their male colleagues? How many people of color are presumed to be the waitstaff at company functions?* But you don't just notice these power imbalances; you have a set of skills you can use to shift them or at least mitigate their impact on you. Your voice and body might be more effective than official channels. If you try to report him, you could be sacrificed to an institution protecting itself. The National Women's Law Center and the Time's Up Legal Defense Fund discovered that 72 percent of women who reported sexual harassment to their employers faced retaliation.[1] Law professor Blair Druhan Bullock analyzed reports made to the Equal Employment Opportunity Commission (EEOC). She found that 70 percent of sexual harassment claims included a report of retaliation, and that sexual harassment reports were 90 percent more likely to include a retaliation claim than any other type of discrimination reported to the EEOC.[2]

It wasn't physical and verbal skills alone that gave you confidence. It was being told repeatedly that you are not the problem. There is no different way you could have carried that file box, nothing you did to encourage the lingering touch. But just because you didn't cause it doesn't mean you can't do something to interrupt it.

The benefits of feminist self-defense have been studied for decades. They include increased confidence, improved coping skills, and reduced stress, what sociologist Martha Thompson calls "embodied confidence."[3] They also include increased awareness of gender and other inequities and in some cases increased solidarity with other women.

———————

Hind Essayegh was in the car pool lane at her daughter's school the day after Donald Trump was declared the winner of the 2016 presidential election. She'd lived in the US for almost a decade, but the anti-Muslim, anti-immigrant hatred that Trump unleashed made her question whether it was safe to stay. She'd begun serious conversations with her husband about whether the United States was the right place to raise their daughter. As she inched closer to the front door of the school, a teacher came to her car window. "I want you to know that you are welcome here," the teacher said. "And I cried," Hind tells me. "I cried because I was on the verge." Her immediate impulse was to feel a sense of gratitude, but later Hind thought more carefully about what the teacher had said. "What do you mean I am 'welcome here'? You should say I 'belong here.' Because I am American, just like you. I have a blue passport. So you should not tell me that I am welcome here as if I'm an outsider and you own the place."

Soon after, Hind took a self-defense course for Muslim women sponsored by Malikah, an organization founded by Muslim activist Rana Abdelhamid. It was the experience of belonging that Hind found to be the most healing. "I'm going to be among people who will understand what I'm going through," she thought. "And probably they are feeling the same way." Hind's sense of belonging had been deeply disrupted by the election, so when it came to her safety she didn't want to risk being misunderstood.

After the workshop, Hind began training with DC-based Defend Yourself. She has taught self-defense both internationally and in the

Washington, DC, area since 2017. When asked about the impact of self-defense on her life, she says she uses it every day, to communicate assertively with people she knows and to stay calm in escalated situations. One time when she was visiting Morocco, she saw a group of men sexually harassing two teenage girls. Before learning self-defense skills, she tells me, she would have hesitated to speak up, but in that situation, she felt emboldened. She told her husband to watch the men while she approached the girls to see if they needed help. They asked Hind and her husband to walk with them. Soon after, the men walked away. "I was proud of myself," Hind says, "because I did something I always wished someone would have done for me, because I also was in that same position many times before."

One of the reasons self-defense felt possible to Hind was how she learned it—from someone who shares her life experience. She is the only Muslim self-defense teacher in her predominantly white networks, and that can be a barrier. "The way to make it more accessible," Hind says, "is to have, like, a thousand of me."

Emma was a high school senior when she took self-defense. She was headed to college and concerned about sexual assault, so she wanted some physical skills to make her feel safer on campus. Toward the end of the school year, she started dating a new guy. He was twenty, she was eighteen. They had only been on three dates when she was invited to a party at a friend's house. She was honest with the new guy. She warned him that her ex-boyfriend would be there. Emma and her ex were in the same friend group; they got along. She'd offered to make another plan for that weekend, but the new guy assured her he'd be fine.

But when he arrived at the party, her stomach dropped. Something felt off. She led him to an area of her friend's house where they could be alone. She hoped that they could connect, she could share her nervousness with him, and they could talk through it. Instead, he tried to kiss her. "I'm not in the mood," she told him. "I'm just so anxious right now. I just can't." He responded with angry silence. Then, Emma's ex-boyfriend and the boy who was hosting the party came into the room. They tried, Emma said, to make the new guy feel welcome.

He wouldn't look at them. He stared at the ceiling. Emma paid attention to her feelings, and when her friends left, she voiced them. "'Can I be honest with you?'" she told him. "'Your presence is making me more anxious.' And he was like, 'Do you want me to leave?' And I thought about it for a second. And I was like, 'Actually, yeah, I do want you to leave.'"

Emma went with him to his car, hoping to clear the air. Initially, she felt bad for asking him to leave after he'd driven all the way to the party. But the more he yelled, the more convinced she was that she'd made the right decision. "I would never hit you or yell at you," he told her. Emma was alarmed. "You don't say that unless you've done something like that before," she thought. It took her an hour to get him to leave.

She'd seen other red flags. This guy texted her incessantly, even when she was in class. When she didn't respond immediately, he sent more desperate messages. "Do you still like me?" he would ask. Or he'd tell her he hated when people didn't text back right away. "This situation could have become very abusive very fast," she tells me.

She had a clarity about the situation. This guy's harassing words felt familiar because she had practiced holding her own while an instructor harassed and threatened her. Outside the party at his car, she used the skills she'd practiced—stating and restating a simple message: *I need you to leave*. "Had I not taken the self-defense class, I don't think I would have been able to say the things I did," Emma tells me. "I'm less fearful but more aware."

The next day, she broke up with him. Some of her friends supported her decision, but others tried to cast her as a bitch or a tease. One person in her friend group told her that she "did him dirty" and "now you have a track record." But the other parts of the self-defense class helped her navigate the pressure she got. She had learned about social and political inequities, wage gaps based on gender and race, and sexual harassment at work. She learned not to discount her own reality, and that lesson fortified her. "The fact that I was uncomfortable," she explained to a friend who told her she was wrong to break up with him, "I shouldn't even need to justify it."

Emma left for college a few months later without the burden of a jealous boyfriend. "I want to go out. I want to have fun. I don't want to be afraid," she tells me.

A qualitative study of 445 college women by psychologists Sara Crann and Charlene Senn is consistent with Emma's experience. Nearly half of the participants used a skill they'd learned from a feminist self-defense program, and 78 percent of those who had used a skill found it helpful. In response to detailed questions about how they applied self-defense training to their lives, women responded that they prioritized their own safety and comfort rather than feeling compelled to please and placate men. They paid attention when they felt uncomfortable, challenged gender expectations, and supported other women.[4]

Women in this study used a wide range of skills, from physical striking to forceful assertive communication to leaving uncomfortable social situations. One woman was watching a movie with a male friend, but when he began making sexual advances, she left. Another woman told researchers about a sexual situation in which her partner ignored her limits: "I used 'No' and 'Get off me,' and 'I'm not having sex,' and 'Stop' in a loud firm voice. I felt powerful and confident to stand up for myself and he backed off." One woman said that a man wanted to change the location of their date from a public place to his home, and she refused because she didn't want to be alone with him. An important theme was that women located the problem with men who pushed past their boundaries and did not blame themselves. As these young women began their adult dating lives, they did so with an analysis of gender inequity and a set of practical resistance skills that helped them navigate social and intimate situations.

Sociologist Jocelyn Hollander's earlier study of college women found similar effects. In response to open-ended questions, women reported taking up more space in public, being more assertive with intimate partners and friends, having more positive body image, and being less worried about being perceived as rude. Hollander also found statistically significant decreases in their fear of taking public transportation, going to bars, or doing laundry alone after dark. Women also described communicating assertively in a range of potentially harmful situations including unwanted sexual advances from intoxicated men. Others spoke up about their sexual limits and desires with their boyfriends.[5]

A study led by criminologist Laura Siller, which examined just over one hundred Indigenous teen girls on a tribal reservation in the Midwest, found that a self-defense program focused on resisting sexual assault resulted in increased confidence, strength, and assertiveness. The study included in-depth interviews with teachers, guardians, and other community stakeholders, many of whom noted that girls in the program appeared more confident and were more likely to tell an adult if they were having a problem. Adults also noticed that the girls were using the skills to refuse unwanted attention and to resist being pressured to drink, use drugs, or bully others.[6]

Bridget got anxious every time a man looked at her. Maybe he was into her or maybe he was just spaced out and staring in her direction. A survivor of child sexual abuse, Bridget lives with complex post-traumatic stress disorder. When she got any kind of attention from men, she felt helpless and stuck. Every interaction felt like a threat; every threat felt like an emergency. She was scared all the time—in the grocery store, on the subway, always wondering "What would I do if someone came at me again?" Bridget had gone to group therapy and individual therapy. She'd tried meditation and yoga. As a result, she felt a lot better, but better wasn't the same as safer. "I didn't feel safe in my body," she tells me.

At the treatment center where Bridget went for therapy, she learned about a self-defense class for abuse survivors. One of the teachers was a social worker. The class included practice in realistic scenarios and time to reflect on what it meant to take back power. The social worker stayed next to each participant, coaching and supporting them, while they practiced. Bridget learned to identify different types of threats—dismissing your limits, getting too close to you, yelling at you, or blocking exits. Once she understood specific threatening behaviors, she realized she didn't have to see every man as a threat. But it wasn't just the education. Getting to practice using her voice and body made her believe she could do it. Repeated practice has helped her internalize what she learned.

Years later, Bridget was breastfeeding her baby after a church service. She was sitting in the back pew, talking to a woman from the congregation while everyone else was in a room down the hall. The woman's husband, who had been abusive in the past, came over to them and leaned against the pew, hovering over them. He began yelling and pointing at Bridget, threatening her. Bridget knew this man was capable of severe violence. He'd once thrown his wife down the stairs. Without thinking, Bridget accessed the self-defense skills she'd learned. "I don't feel safe. Please back up," she told the man. "What do you mean you think I'm not safe?" the man responded. Bridget didn't get sucked into an argument. Instead she kept repeating herself, yelling at him to leave her alone. "I got louder and louder," she explains. "Finally people started coming in. And they got him under control." Bridget was surprised that it took so long for other people to intervene, but she was also prepared in case nobody came to help her. "I had a baby and my boob out," she says. "And I was like, that's okay because I have my legs and I will kick you in the groin if we're going there."

Bridget is one of many survivors who feel less fearful after learning self-defense. For Julia Liu, having self-defense skills means she doesn't have to constrict her life: "I find that reviewing the skills when I am walking alone somewhere that I may find threatening or potentially dangerous gives me courage and allows me to do things on my own that I might not otherwise do." Knowing how to keep herself safe enables Julia to live in a way that is consistent with her beliefs. "I feel I deserve to be in that space and deserve to move freely in it without risk of harm," she says. "There are a number of nonverbal and verbal strategies that give me strength and confidence." Self-defense also gave Julia the tools to speak up "without being aggressive or belligerent, which was my default mode if I wasn't being passive and submissive."

Julia is vigilant about victim blame. "Systemic and structural violence becomes internalized," she explains. "By starting there and then challenging it directly, the self-defense program starts by fortifying our minds, liberating us from the notion that we deserve any violence we experience, that we should just take it and that we do not have the right to defend ourselves and are incapable of defending ourselves." She sees this analysis play out in her daily use of the skills: "I move through the world in ways that root me in strength." One skill Julia practiced was advocating for herself in a conversation with a coworker she feared. The realistic practice helped her trust herself. "Practicing the skills in that role-play allowed me to overcome that fear in that instance but also to give me confidence (and trust in myself) that I could handle any future fears of coworkers with a reputation for inappropriate behavior."

"If I hadn't become a mother," Julia tells me, "I'm not sure if I would have had the courage to take the course." Julia had insisted her daughter learn self-defense when she started middle school and decided that it was only fair to take the class herself. Seeing the change in her daughter strengthened Julia's own resolve. "She looked and moved freely," Julia says, "like someone who was comfortable in her own body and confident to go out into the wide world, which is what she did and continues to do."

Watching Christine Blasey Ford testify about Brett Kavanaugh's sexual assault motivated Brigit McCallum to learn self-defense. The assault Blasey Ford described was similar to the one that Brigit had survived as a teenager. She felt unmoored watching just over half the US Senate declare that a man who reminded her of a boy who assaulted her long ago was fit to be on the Supreme Court. She wanted to feel the ground under her again. But when she started searching for self-defense, all she could find was classes offered by the police. "My dad was a cop and my dad was brutal," she explains. So the police were the last place she wanted to go.

She called a rape crisis hotline to find other options, and got connected with Prevention.Action.Change, a feminist program based in Portland, Maine. They had just started a class called Healing Through Empowerment, and it was exactly what Brigit needed. "I had the expectation that I would probably be the oldest person there," she says. Brigit was almost eighty at the time. But after decades of trying to move past her history, she tells me, "I felt like I had left my body behind and

I wanted to do something that was very much about physical strength. I felt like my body got robbed."

"I am a person with a trauma history," Brigit explains. "So what I present to the world and what's going on inside are not always the same." Brigit often presented as confident. People who knew her described her as a strong person, but she spent most of her life being afraid of her power, like if she ever stopped reining herself in, she would destroy herself and everyone around her. So Brigit hid her power for most of her life, feeling like she had to "take care of everybody else by being smaller." As a kid, she beat up bullies. She never hesitated before smacking the boys who were terrorizing smaller kids. She felt like she was giving them justice but she never felt worthy of having justice for herself.

Self-defense gave Brigit the space to hit and kick. Then, she could sit in a circle with other survivors and talk about all the complicated feelings that come up when you experience your strength. Brigit now feels freer to access her power and trust that she can be strong without becoming destructive. Over the years, she's been told many times not to blame herself for the abuse she survived. She appreciates the affirmation, but without the skills to protect herself, she finds it insufficient. "It's one thing to go to therapy and try to heal from what happened in my past and to see myself as a more deserving person," she says. "But if I don't have the tools to stand up for myself then that doesn't give me hope." Letting go of self-blame was critical for Brigit, but it was only possible when she learned to trust her power. Now, she feels like her responses to stressful situations are more conscious and deliberate. "It's more strategic rather than involuntary or reactionary," she says.

Research on the impact of feminist self-defense on abuse survivors is consistent with the experiences of Bridget, Julia, and Brigit. A study led by psychologist Maiya Hotchkiss found that group therapy combined with Prepare, a New York City–based feminist self-defense program, significantly decreased symptoms of post-traumatic stress disorder. Hotchkiss also found significant increases in survivors' confidence navigating interpersonal relationships. "Participants reported a greater valuing of their boundaries, and comfort using verbal and physical skills to set and defend these boundaries," the authors note, "[and] feeling safe enough to resume dating post-assault, and experiencing benefits within their intimate and non-intimate relationships."[7] A study of a Prepare program for transgender women and transfeminine people, led by psychologist Danielle Berke, had similar outcomes, including decreases in post-traumatic stress symptoms and increases in assertiveness in intimate relationships.[8]

For some people, the benefits are both psychological and practical. "Living in a shelter was the worst time in my life," Ashley tells me. She was in her early twenties and homeless with her infant son. She was also in college, trying to learn every skill she could, so when the shelter offered a self-defense class, she signed up. "I grew up in an abusive household," she says. "I felt that a self-defense class would help me protect myself if I ever came into contact with someone who was trying to hurt me." Fifteen years later, Ashley was stable, housed, and pursuing a social work degree. After ten years in a job that paid decently but wasn't her passion, she began working for a social service agency. A teenage client tried to put Ashley in a headlock. Her self-defense skills came back immediately. She protected her airway, pulled his hands off her neck, and escaped. Thanks to Ashley's quick thinking, nobody was hurt.

Ashley's experience of using self-defense skills more than a decade after she'd learned them is consistent with research by sociologist Martha Thompson. In a study of ninety-seven women who had participated in an IMPACT program, almost 90 percent faced at least one situation in which they'd used the skills. Some study participants described being more aware of abusive and coercive behaviors. Others noticed increases in their ability to advocate for themselves and others. Study participants reported being able to speak up in situations where they felt fear, because they trusted they could protect themselves. Women also described feeling physically stronger, more confident, and less immobilized by fear.

A defining characteristic of IMPACT is practicing physical and verbal resistance skills in realistic simulations of attempted violence. Study participants reported that the practice had helped them. One woman described her reaction when she was being threatened: "I remember thinking how clear everything seemed—the little spike of adrenaline and suddenly the file drawer containing all my options opened and I knew exactly what to do/say, exactly what my targets were."⁹

———————

In 2017, a political discussion between Camilla Howard and her brother escalated and he began threatening her. "Having taken self-defense drastically changed the way I was responding," she explains. She walked away from her brother rather than feeling like she had to win. "All of this anger and rage that is being directed at me, it's not actually mine to carry," she says now. After that confrontation, she brought a quiet confidence to a range of situations. "I can tolerate more stressful situations without feeling as much stress," she explains. Learning to protect her body helped Camilla "approach conflict with curiosity" trusting she could hold her own without getting pushed over or escalated.

In 2021, as theaters began to reopen after Covid, Camilla worked as a house manager at a performance venue that required masks and proof of vaccination. The rules were printed on every theater ticket. They were posted in the lobby, too, but that didn't stop some audience members from yelling at Camilla when she told them to put on a mask. She laughs as she tells me about one person who was in the middle of yelling at her, accusing her and everyone else of not telling people they needed to show proof of vaccination. "And they're holding up a printable ticket," Camilla remarks, "that has the Covid policy written on it." With her physical response to stress under control, Camilla was able to calmly show the audience member the policy. She didn't get intimidated or get sucked into an argument. "I've done a lot of not backing down, but not stepping forward," she says.

Chani Larocque took an Uber to a tattoo studio in downtown Boston. When the driver dropped her off in the wrong place, she didn't panic. She was calm and comfortable walking the six blocks to the right address. She said hello to the people she passed on the street, no longer feeling compelled to keep her head down. She got an ouroboros, a mythical dragon that eats its own tail, tattooed on her upper back. She chose the upper back because it's a painful place to get a tattoo and she wanted to test her strength. She chose the ouroboros because it's a symbol of destruction and rebirth. It was a way to honor how she tried to destroy herself in the past—drinking, eating disorders, and cutting her own skin—and how she now feels reborn, into a person who can walk around a city by herself, who speaks up, who isn't plagued by night terrors. Her previous tattoo was a butterfly, another symbol of transformation. She got that one on her upper thigh. It covers scars from where she used to cut herself.

After getting the tattoo, Chani bought a black dress from a thrift store. The next night she wore it to a party at a hotel jazz club, where she enjoyed the music and the warm energy in the room.

The people who love Chani most reacted with delight—and disbelief—when they saw pictures of her, not wearing her glasses, not hiding her body under clothes a couple sizes too big. "To see me fix up and fix my hair and take off my glasses and to invest in myself," she tells me. "To not be afraid of attention. Because that was one of my triggers—unwanted attention. So to be comfortable with my body to be comfortable with myself to mingle with people."

Before Chani learned self-defense, there was a three-year period when her anxiety was so bad she almost never left the house. Driving to the grocery store felt like a nightmare; she imagined a thousand things that could go wrong. She imagined a thousand more if she was with her kids. She knew she would blame herself if anything happened to them. She missed their parent-teacher conferences. They missed out on extracurricular activities because she was too afraid to drive them.

Then, in 2021, Chani Larocque took a class on the Turtle Mountain Chippewa reservation where she lives. It was offered by my collaborators at Turtle Mountain IMPACT, the first Indigenous-led IMPACT program. Turtle Mountain IMPACT is led by people with deep community roots, women and men who work together to make sure Indigenous people have the skills to resist violence. As a woman who had carried the weight of personal and historical trauma for most of her life, Chani experienced healing and community she couldn't have imagined. Self-defense also helped with her anxiety. "I could drive to the grocery store now," she says. "I could talk to people now. I'm actually starting to show up and be present in my life."

The Turtle Mountain reservation is a twelve by six mile stretch in northern North Dakota, surrounded on all sides by farm towns and oil workers. Racism is bitter and persistent there, Angie Decoteau tells me. Being called a drunk or a welfare rat when they leave the reservation is painfully common. Angie grew up fighting. Self-defense helped her see when she didn't have to. "I used to be a fighter," she tells me. "I fought all the time. But taking this class let me know that I don't have to be that person to look for a fight. I don't have to be that person to just jump into a fight and try and hurt somebody because it could affect me and my future. And my kids' future. So they taught me how to de-escalate."

The physical skills were taught step-by-step and repeated until everyone caught on. "I didn't feel inferior," she says. "I didn't feel like I was gonna get beat up." She came in worried that she might be judged, that someone might tell her that the violence she survived was her fault. But she found just the opposite. "They basically helped me get over a lot of what I was worried about," she says. "And the courage, the confidence I got at the end of that class was amazing."

A few weeks later, Angie was at work at the tribe-owned casino. There was a carnival in town. She saw a man she didn't recognize trying to steal money from a child. "I got my strong stance. And I said, 'Leave him alone.' I said, 'He don't know you.' And I used my voice a lot. I spoke up as loud as I could. And he ended up taking off."

Angie kept going back. She became what she calls a "professional student," not only coming to all the classes but showing up on weekends and after her kids went to bed to help the teachers—one of whom is her husband—practice. "I've learned how to use my voice," she tells me. "I've learned how to have that confidence and letting people know that I'm not afraid to defend myself if I have to."

The IMPACT program came to Turtle Mountain because of Shanda Poitra, who also grew up on the reservation. In 2005, she was a student at the University of North Dakota in Grand Forks, 180 miles from home. She signed up for an IMPACT class because she needed a gym credit. She had read the class description. She tells me she "sort of took in" what it said about women's empowerment and finding your voice. But the opportunity to fulfill a requirement in just three days was the main motivator. Shanda was struggling to keep up with her classes. She had three kids in diapers and a partner who offered little support. Ten years older than most of her classmates, who could study in the library until ten at night and go to parties on weekends, she had to be home for dinner and bath time. She was also cleaning houses to earn extra money.

Shanda Poitra was one of only two Indigenous women in the class. Most of the other students, she tells me, were nineteen-year-old white women who grew up in farm towns near the university. In a lot of ways the curriculum was built for them, focused on sexual assaults at fraternity parties on campus. Shanda once showed me pictures of some of those parties, the ones with "Indian" themes and students who painted their faces red and wore fake feather headdresses.

Still, Shanda is not exaggerating when she says that gym credit saved her life. She realized for the first time how much trauma she was carrying. "I knew about genocide," she explains. "I knew about the whole historical legacy of Native Americans. But I didn't know what I was carrying, what I was bringing to the table personally, until I was asked those tough questions and I was seeing these scenarios happen." The instructors showed examples of abuse in intimate relationships, and for the first time, she realized that her partner was abusive. As the weekend progressed, she had a realization: "Women back home could really use this."

Shanda had grown up witnessing abuse in her home and community. It was common to the point of being normalized. "Couples fight," she says. "We always heard stories of like what Grandpa used to do to Grandma. And I mean, the stories were fucking awful and treacherous and alarming, but you know, in their old age, Grandma and Grandpa are still together. So it's like, 'We made it through, you know?'" IMPACT changed Shanda's understanding of these situations: "It's like, 'No, she survived you.'"

There was a skill she learned in the self-defense class called a three-part statement, which consists of the answers to three questions: *What's happening? How does it make you feel? What do you want to happen instead?* Shanda remembers a night shortly after the class when she was in a heated argument with her partner. She was standing by the sink, and he was standing over her. "I'm terrified right now," she remembers telling him. "I feel like I can't say anything. And what I want you to do right now is I want you just to walk away from me and leave me alone tonight." Shanda is careful not to take responsibility for her ex's actions or to say that any one strategy works for every person living with an abusive partner. But watching her ex respond to verbal self-defense was a revelation. "I remember him looking around and realizing he did have me cornered. And he was in my face. And what I was saying was very true," Shanda tells me. "He ended up walking away. And I felt like, Oh, my God, oh, my God, you know, like, it worked. And I just, like, couldn't believe it. And like, how strong my words were just calling out what exactly is happening and how it's making you feel is so fucking incredibly powerful. And I've done it ever since."

Shanda Poitra left her partner not long after taking the IMPACT class. She began playing Roller Derby, where she met friends who supported her. She left the university to enroll in a two-year college, a sacrifice she made so she could get a job sooner and support her kids on her own. Shanda worked as a surgical technologist in hospitals in Grand Forks.

Ten years later, Shanda moved back home to the reservation. Right away, she was surrounded by violence. Hate speech from white people in neighboring towns and threats from intoxicated people on the reservation. A man pulled a knife on her mother while she was getting her mail. But the hardest violence for Shanda to witness was abuse from intimate partners. One of her close friends was beaten so severely that she had to be airlifted to a hospital hours away.

Shanda felt an urgency to get IMPACT to Indigenous women, so she convinced two friends to drive the 180 miles to the University of North Dakota to take the class. Two years later, I met her at a conference, and we began collaborating to create an IMPACT program for Indigenous women and communities.

She knew that she couldn't just take a curriculum that was designed for predominantly white communities and bring it to the reservation. "I knew that we had to get real with the things that we were going through," Shanda explains. That meant scenarios to address hate speech and intimate violence. The movement to address the crisis of missing and murdered Indigenous women (MMIW) was gaining momentum. "We had to really dig deep into what is causing these issues," Shanda says. "How are our women disappearing and being murdered?" She came to understand the crisis by learning more about the women from her tribe who'd gone missing or been murdered. They were trying to escape poverty and escape the reservation. "And they're finding themselves alone out there in situations where they don't have support, and they don't have people looking out for them." Some were struggling with drugs or alcohol when they went missing. "With being Native American," Shanda explains, "there's gonna be little to no justice if you disappear." She made sure to address abduction, and in every class, she makes the same point: *It's not that we're vulnerable as Indigenous women, it's that we're targeted.*

Another issue Shanda wanted to address was the way Indigenous women were treated by doctors. Working as a surgical technologist in the federally run Indian Health Service (IHS) hospital on the reservation, she saw a lot of exploitation. Turtle Mountain is in a remote rural area. Temperatures can drop below zero in October and stay there for months, so it's hard to get quality doctors who want to live there. When Shanda moved home, the first thing she noticed was the quality of surgery was not as high as it was in other operating rooms she'd worked in. One surgeon spent four hours removing a gall bladder, a procedure Shanda had seen done in forty-five minutes. But she soon realized a worse problem—at least two doctors were performing pelvic exams that were medically unnecessary.

"Even if the report went to headquarters," Shanda tells me. "It wouldn't go any further." She knew she could not trust official channels to stop the doctors. "The solution was to teach women that this happens," she says. So Shanda created a scenario in which an instructor plays the role of a doctor trying to coerce a woman to let him do a pelvic exam when she came in for a sore throat. Shanda models communicating a boundary and refusing the exam. She shows women how they can get farther away from a doctor, even in a small exam room, and how they can get loud to attract attention if the doctor tries to stop them from leaving the room. Shanda has taught classes in which almost every woman in the room has had a similar experience.

In addition to addressing the violence Indigenous women and communities face, Turtle Mountain IMPACT integrates cultural and spiritual traditions. "It's designed for our way of life," Angie Decoteau says of the program. "Things that happen on the reservation, and then it actually pulls a lot of people in, because they're like, 'Hey, I know, this happened to this person,' or 'It happened to me,' and exactly, you know, it's kind of like, they're living their life over again, in those scenarios that we do. And it helps them heal." This is important to Shanda because she holds on to the experience of a self-defense class that both saved her life and wasn't built for her community. Traditional singing and rituals like smudging—burning sage and letting the smoke cover your entire body—are part of the program. "I know what it's like to walk into that class for the first time," Shanda says. "I know what it's like to feel like you're in a group of people you don't belong to and can't relate, and it's scary and you're going to face a lot of hard truths and you're going to face a lot of things that you've been through whether you know it or not. I know that's what would have made that experience easier or better for me walking into the room and smudging. Wow, you know that would have made me so comfortable right off the bat." Some classes start with passing around the smudge. Instructors introduce themselves using their traditional Ojibwe names and encourage students to do the same.

The space Shanda created helped Chani Larocque heal. "Every class, I was letting a different part of my anxiety go. I was actually telling my story," Chani says. "I've been in therapy since I was like fourteen, fifteen years old. And in those years, I was lying my ass off, you know. I didn't want them to know the extent of what was happening. We live in a small town; everybody knows each other. So I figured a lot of people aren't very professional. So they might talk and be like, 'Oh, that family is messed up' or whatever. So I kind of protected my privacy from them. But in, in self-defense, like I could let all that fear go."

Chani Larocque never asserted her boundaries before she learned self-defense. She describes herself as having been a pushover, a people pleaser. It's never easy, but Chani is much better at speaking up for herself, even with her children's father, a man who has tried to strangle her on multiple occasions. She used to freeze in fear when she saw him, but now she doesn't. "He came up to my house, and he was just all worked up. And he came and he started hollering at me. Instead of giving him ammunition and arguing with him back and escalating it, I was just like, 'Okay, we'll talk about it later. You need to leave for now. I'm uncomfortable. You're scaring me.'" He didn't leave right away, but Chani persisted. Her daughter then came out of the house and told her father to leave. "She's like, 'Dad, this is not okay, you don't treat women like this. I don't want you yelling at my mom.'" He eventually left. "It took a couple of days," says Chani, "but we were able to de-escalate."

Chani also sets boundaries with her father. "I had an instance where my dad was hollering at my mom. My mom, she's been sick with multiple sclerosis from a very young age, and my dad gets impatient with her. And so he was kind of picking on her. And I, I'm able to stand up for my mom," Chani tells me. "It just shut him right up."

When Shanda Poitra presented the sexual assault scenarios, she said things Chani had never heard before. When teaching skills to resist a sexual assault, Shanda framed it like many feminist self-defense teachers do: *This is something you could do, not something you should do, or should have done.* Resisting victim blame is as crucial as resisting violence. Chani had been abused from such a young age, she initially thought it was normal. But once she realized that it was not, that "these were things that should not be happening to little girls," she began blaming herself for not doing something to stop it. "I started to think, like, I should have fought back. I should have done something. And I blamed myself for a lot of years. And that's one of the hardest things to shake." So to have people tell her that she wasn't wrong made the environment feel safe.

After a year as a professional student, Angie Decoteau joined Shanda Poitra as a self-defense teacher. She is grounded and unflappable. In a room full of kids, she knows who to separate and how to get them to pay attention. Her tough maternal energy motivates them. "Listen. You're going to need this," she tells them. And they do. Angie always notices who looks away when Shanda says, "Even if it's your partner, if they force you to have sex after you've said no, it's sexual assault or rape."

"We have a lot of people that have taken the classes and actually have taken over my role as the professional student," Angie tells me. "And they love it." "Not only," she explains, "does it help them memorize the moves and let them, you know, train. But it also lets them take out anger." A year later, Chani Larocque also started teaching. She is energetic and compassionate. She reads the room and offers the exact encouragement people need.

Turtle Mountain IMPACT has become involved in the cultural revitalization movement on the reservation. This includes traditional arts and talking circles for women, but just as importantly, they've begun offering healing circles to men. "Having this here on the reservation is building our people's confidence up, not only for the women, but the men's talking circles. The guys are actually able to go there and learn, sit and talk about their feelings without being called a cry baby," Angie explains. "Our traditional men are helping other men learn that it's okay to cry. It's okay. It's okay to have feelings. It's okay to talk things out." Her husband, James, leads a traditional drum circle that teaches healthy masculinity through drumming. Mike Davis, another member of the Turtle Mountain IMPACT team, leads a men's circle. It's a place for men to talk openly about their struggles and joys, to let go of toxic behaviors and become better people. These circles are rooted in culture and tradition. "We either use an eagle feather or wing fan or a bundle of sage to hold when we speak," Mike explains. "When we hold these things we put our traumas, problems, or whatever it may be into what it is we're holding. When we're done speaking, we take a little piece off and smudge with it. By doing that we're cleansing ourselves of what is bothering us. Everything has a spirit. Words, traumas, everything. That medicine and the act of smudging with it helps to release those spirits."

After two years of being invited to teach self-defense at a coming of age ceremony for girls and two-spirit youth on the Standing Rock reservation in South Dakota, the Turtle Mountain IMPACT team became inspired to create one for their own tribe. Most elders on the reservation live with trauma from boarding schools and laws prohibiting Indigenous traditions. As a result, there have been no coming of age ceremonies open to the entire community in at least three decades.

The ceremony took place in the summer of 2023. It included a traditional water ceremony, a women's sweat lodge, traditional crafts, and a tipi ceremony. Central to the ceremony were teachings on healthy relationships, safe and healthy sexuality, and self-defense, further integrating cultural preservation and resistance. Angie Decoteau sees a connection between giving people a space to claim their power and being part of a movement in the community to reclaim culture and traditions.

The Turtle Mountain reservation is home to a Catholic church, a small but imposing building where white priests prohibited traditional drumming for decades. Drum groups were required to stay outside the church, even when they were attending a tribe member's funeral. Angie told me she once showed up to a relative's funeral in a traditional ribbon skirt. The priest gave her a look and told her about catechism classes. Most of the elders on this land are survivors of Christian boarding schools. Forced to leave their families, they lived at US government-funded schools that were explicit in their mission to "kill the Indian and save the man." Countless investigations have revealed widespread torture, sexual and physical abuse, starvation, and mass graves. While official sources say the last boarding school in the US closed in 1983, Shanda knows people in their thirties and forties that went to some pretty abusive schools. Boarding school trauma endures. Angie tells me it ripples through generations. She has seen the effects on her young students, some of whom walk into class with their heads down and struggle to find words for how the violence their parents and grandparents endured has impacted them. Chani's father was abused in a residential school, and she sees that as a reason why it was so hard for him to be a good parent.

Though the church has no official standing, its influence was once widely felt on the reservation. And it used to be, says Angie, that the church had the power to stop two-spirit pride events. "Up until recently, the church is what had handled everything. You know, like for our LGBTQ, we tried having a walk one year. And the church stepped in and said, no, it wasn't happening. So everybody in our community said, no, it wasn't happening." The resistance and movement to reclaim Indigenous pride and heritage comes from many sources. But Angie sees the self-defense program as a contributor, helping people find their voices and reclaim their power. She has seen a lot of people in her community develop the confidence to push back. The two-spirit community held a Pride celebration and a drag show. One performer started her act by placing a red handprint across her mouth, a symbol that honors missing and murdered Indigenous people.

Angie notices a groundswell of people practicing Ojibwe traditions. "We're getting our native pride back," Chani concurs. "We're getting our identity back. This little inner fire being sparked, it's just, it's amazing. It gives you hope, you know, that, that things will change, you know, that we can defend ourselves, that we will stop going missing, we could look out for ourselves, we could look out for each other." Shanda notes that church membership is shrinking. Some people she knows walked out on a sermon in which the priest declared homosexuality a sin. She knows a parent of a two-spirit person who never went back to church after hearing that message.

"We could recreate an entire generation of people who don't have to be broken," Chani Larocque says. "I never thought I would ever have a good life. I never thought I would ever be able to defend myself if bad things were to happen. All I knew is these good, amazing, beautiful feelings that I never thought I deserved."

Empowerment self-defense is a change strategy that is as intimate as gender-based violence. It is big and fierce enough to fortify us against the threats and harassment that try to keep us small.

| CHAPTER 7 |

THE EVIDENCE AND
ITS DISCONTENTS

In June 2015, the *New York Times* published an article about a "rare success" in the struggle to prevent sexual assault on college campuses.[1] The Obama administration had brought unrelenting attention to the issue. There were changes in federal regulations and a media campaign in which the president himself urged men to be part of the solution. The Justice Department launched high profile investigations of universities that mishandled students' reports. The newly enacted Campus Sexual Violence Elimination (SaVE) Act required colleges and universities to provide prevention education to students and staff. Hundreds of campus administrators complied with this law by requiring students to click through webinars about sexual violence or sit in auditoriums watching skits about how to get consent. Everyone from CDC scientists[2] to students themselves[3] agreed that these efforts were ineffective. So, when the *New England Journal of Medicine* published a research report about a program that worked, there should have been a sea change.

The program, Enhanced Assess, Acknowledge, Act (EAAA), commonly known as Flip the Script, was developed by Charlene Senn for university women in Canada. Flip the Script combines physical self-defense with education that helps women recognize both blatant and subtle sexual coercion. It also helps women define and pursue their own sexual desires. Senn's study of almost one thousand first-year students at three Canadian universities found that women who participated in Flip the Script were 63 percent less likely than a control group to experience sexual assault and 46 percent less likely to experience rape.[4] Senn's study is larger and more sophisticated than most, but its findings are consistent with decades of similar research.

Sociologist Jocelyn Hollander found that women who participated in a self-defense course at a community center in Oregon were 50 percent less likely to experience sexual assault than a control group.[5] Her research on college women found even greater differences between women who took a thirty-hour feminist self-defense course and a comparison group. She found that 9 percent of self-defense students experienced unwanted sexual contact compared to 20 percent of the comparison group, that 4 percent of self-defense students experienced sexual coercion compared to 13 percent of the comparison group, that 3 percent experienced attempted rape compared to 8 percent of the comparison group, and that none experienced completed rape compared to 3 percent of the comparison group.[6] Research led by Clea Sarnquist of Stanford University found that girls in Nairobi, Kenya, who took self-defense were 63 percent less likely to experience sexual assault. Her research also found that half the girls who participated in the program had used a self-defense skill to stop an attempted assault within a year, and that schools that implemented self-defense programs for girls saw the number of students who dropped out due to pregnancy decrease by almost half.[7]

Instead of creating a sea change, Senn's research mobilized some unlikely detractors: feminists and public health experts who share her commitment to ending gender-based violence. Feminist author Jessica Valenti published an op-ed in *The Guardian* about Senn's work titled "We Need to Stop Rapists, Not Change Who Gets Raped."[8] While Valenti acknowledged that the "impressive reduction" in sexual assaults that resulted from Senn's program is "reason to celebrate," she still argued that educating women is the wrong approach. "What if rape reduction programs are actually just *redirecting* assault?" she asked, citing no evidence that this is actually happening. I confirmed with Centers for Disease Control and

Prevention scientists that they are not aware of any research that supports this claim. Still, Valenti sounded the alarm about Flip the Script: "There's a real danger in believing the solution to sexual assault is on the shoulders of women who might be attacked," she argued. "Sending the message that stopping rape is women's work is a slippery slope." Liberal media outlets piled on. *Vice* ran an article that described Flip the Script as a "controversial program" that "teaches women to spot 'pre-rape' warning signs."[9] A *Vox* article proclaimed, "Teaching women to avoid rape works, but it's controversial."[10] Even a mostly supportive article in *The Cut* devoted about a third of its word count to criticisms based on claims that programs like Flip the Script put the burden for stopping rape on women.[11]

An op-ed by CDC scientist Kathleen Basile appeared in the same issue of the *New England Journal of Medicine* as Senn's study.[12] In it, she acknowledged that Flip the Script is rigorously studied, and consistent with best practices for sexual assault prevention education. Yet she still cast doubt on its value. "Its primary weakness," she writes, "is that it places the onus for prevention on potential victims, possibly obscuring the responsibility of perpetrators and others. What happens when women who complete the intervention cannot successfully resist rape?" The question was rhetorical in her op-ed, but some research has already answered it. A 2008 study by psychologists Lindsay Orchowski, Christine Gidycz, and Holly Raffle showed that women who experienced sexual assault after having taken a feminist self-defense class had lower levels of self-blame than other survivors.[13] Two years later, Senn published a study showing that in addition to reducing rates of sexual violence, Flip the Script also reduced victim-blaming attitudes.[14]

Basile went on to critique Flip the Script for not conforming to a specific definition of public health. "With a public health approach," she argued, "the most efficient way to have a population-level effect on violence is through a focus on primary prevention with potential perpetrators as part of a comprehensive, multilevel approach." However, several of the examples she gave of sexual violence prevention programs she prefers don't have strong evidence that they work. She referenced a program for boys' sports teams that has some positive outcomes but overall mixed results. She mentioned a study that found that neighborhoods with a high concentration of liquor stores had more rapes reported to the police than other geographic areas. However, the majority of sexual violence is not reported to the police, and Basile gave no examples of sexual violence prevention programs that have operated successfully in these neighborhoods.

A feminist and a survivor herself, Senn was shocked by these reactions. She'd spent the first decade of her academic career studying the prevalence of gender-based violence, but after years of asking women about their experiences of victimization, she explains, "I was fed up with just measuring what was happening to us because we already knew what was happening to us." It was the early 2000s, and sexual violence prevention research was a nascent field with few programs demonstrating any lasting effects. She was drawn to feminist self-defense, both because of early research showing that it was effective and because of her own experience learning self-defense and its lasting impact on her.

Dismissing Senn's work could be warranted if evidence for the effectiveness of other strategies to prevent rape was conclusively stronger, but it's not. In 2019, Laurie Graham conducted a systematic review of published studies of violence prevention programs for boys and men.[15] Of the more than four thousand academic articles her team reviewed, they found only ten studies of seven educational programs that measured changes in abusive and coercive behaviors. The majority of published studies measured changes in knowledge or attitudes, which don't necessarily lead to behavior change. Coaching Boys Into Men is a program in which coaches of boys' sports teams start practices with ten to fifteen minute lessons about topics like gender norms and abusive behaviors. Research showed no significant changes in dating violence perpetration three months after the program. When participants were surveyed a year after the program, they reported less dating violence perpetration in the preceding three months. Another study of Coaching Boys Into Men found no significant changes in dating violence perpetration at any time point.

The Men's Program is a one-hour discussion group for male undergraduates that includes definitions of consent, a presentation about the impact of rape on survivors, and a video that depicts a male police officer who was raped by two men. Researchers found no significant changes in sexual assault perpetration for study participants as a whole. They did find that men who participated in the discussions who joined fraternities were less likely to sexually coerce than men in the comparison group who joined fraternities. Yet an earlier review of campus sexual violence prevention programs by psychologists Rory Newlands and William O'Donohue gives more context to this finding.[16] Prior to the start of college, the men in this study who later joined fraternities were no more likely to sexually coerce than those who did not. But seven months later, this study found that men who joined fraternities in the sample as a whole (both those who got the program and the control group) were over three times more likely to sexually coerce than those who did not. Fraternity men who participated in the Men's Program reported significantly fewer acts of sexual coercion at the seven-month follow-up (6 percent compared to 10 percent) but the difference was not as great as the overall disparity between those involved in Greek life and those who were not.

A college program called RealConsent, consisting of six thirty-minute online sessions, found that men who got the program reported less sexual coercion than the control group six months after watching the videos. Of men who reported that they'd sexually assaulted in the past, those who got the program were 73 percent less likely to report having sexually abused. However, Newlands and O'Donohue note that the study population decreased from 743 participants to 215. With more than two-thirds of the sample not participating in follow-up surveys, it's hard to interpret the results. Additionally, Newlands and O'Donohue note that before the study, the control group had higher rates of sexual assault perpetration, coercion, and hostility toward women.

A study of the Men's Project, another campus-based discussion group, found that four months after the program, those who participated in the groups had significantly lower rates of sexual aggression than the control group. But those gains were not maintained. Seven months after the program, there were no differences between the discussion group and the control group. By contrast, a 2017 study of Senn's program showed that women who took Flip the Script were still experiencing lower rates of sexual violence than the control group two years later.

Research on the Sexual Assault Prevention Program for College Men, a single-session program, found no significant differences between the treatment and control group at three and seven month follow-ups.[17] Another program that included a video about how to get consent produced change in the wrong direction. Those who watched the video were slightly more likely to sexually coerce than those in the control group, though the difference was not statistically significant. However, for men who reported that they'd sexually coerced in the past, those who saw the video were significantly more likely to sexually coerce.

The only study in Graham's review that didn't rely on boys and men reporting their own behavior changes was a discussion group in Côte d'Ivoire, which measured physical and sexual violence perpetration by asking the men's female partners about their experiences of abuse. That study found that the discussions produced no significant changes.

A meta-analysis of sexual assault prevention programs for men led by Lauren Wright was published around the same time.[18] The authors reviewed sixteen published studies along with thirteen dissertations and masters theses that contained original research. Taken together, these studies showed small improvements in men's attitudes about sexual assault and intentions not to perpetrate, but when sexual assault perpetration behaviors were measured, they found no significant changes. "As sexual assault perpetration is the most important outcome under investigation in the present study," the authors note, "this finding is both important and disappointing."

Other approaches to preventing sexual violence focus on framing sexual and gender-based violence as a community problem. Treating men as part of the solution rather than as potential rapists is seen by many as a way to motivate and engage them. The reality is that, despite the high prevalence of sexual violence, the majority of men do not assault. Changing social norms is the goal of many prevention strategies.

In her first semester of college, Sharyn Potter was given a whistle and told to be careful. The women students, she remembers, were separated from the men and given a clear message: *Don't go out and get raped*. Potter, executive director of research at the University of New Hampshire's Prevention Innovations Research Center, is one of the leaders of an important shift in how colleges and universities address gender-based violence. Rather than focusing on individual victims and perpetrators, this strategy works to get communities to take responsibility for everyone's safety. Known as bystander intervention, this approach is designed to help people develop the skills and willingness to speak up if they suspect someone is at risk.

Bystander intervention strategies include everything from directly confronting someone trying to hook up with a person who is too drunk to consent to causing a distraction to diffuse street harassment. Bystander intervention is arguably the most widely accepted prevention strategy in the United States, with more federally funded research than any other approach to stopping gender-based violence. Over the past two decades, it's been championed by everyone from the Obama White House to the US military to organizational psychologists who see it as a promising strategy to prevent workplace sexual harassment. The University of New Hampshire's Bringing in the Bystander curriculum is one of the best-studied approaches.

There are hundreds of studies demonstrating the effects of bystander intervention programs, but whether these programs reduce incidents of assault remains unclear. In a systematic review of bystander programs for sexual assault prevention, Gabriela Mujal and her colleagues found lots of evidence that bystander programs make changes, but almost none of those changes were in how often people perpetrate or experience gender-based violence.[19] Her research identified forty-four studies of bystander intervention programs published between 2007 and 2017. Some showed changes in people's attitudes. Others showed decreases in people's acceptance of myths about rape or date rape. Twenty-five studies found significant changes in participants' confidence in their ability to be effective bystanders, and fourteen found that students who received bystander intervention education were more likely to say they would do something if they witnessed a risky situation.

Only one of the studies Mujal reviewed measured changes in sexually coercive behaviors—Nadia Elias-Lambert and Beverly Black's study of 142 fraternity men, half of whom were randomly assigned to a ninety-minute version of Bringing in the Bystander. Only fifty-five participants completed follow-up surveys five weeks later, and at that point, there was a modest difference in sexually coercive behaviors between the intervention and control groups. They also surveyed men about their intentions to engage in sexually aggressive behaviors like using force to obtain sex or pressuring potential partners to drink alcohol. In the bystander group, they found a significant decrease in these intentions immediately after the training, but five weeks later, the bystander group reverted to their previous levels of sexually aggressive intentions, which were not significantly different from the control group.[20]

A 2023 review led by Kelsey Banton had similar findings: bystander programs are widely accepted but evidence of their effectiveness isn't consistent or conclusive.[21] Some evidence also shows that racial bias may impact students' willingness to intervene. A study by psychologist Jennifer Katz found that white college women, when given a scenario in which a man was dragging an intoxicated woman to his room, were less likely to say they intended to intervene when the intoxicated student in the scenario was Black.[22]

That said, some bystander intervention programs do change some behaviors. The Green Dot program, developed at the University of Kentucky, teaches students to intervene when they notice that someone is at risk for sexual assault, laughing at a rape joke, or calling someone a fag. "Green dots" refer to small actions people can take to counteract unhealthy or abusive situations, defined as "red dots." The rationale behind the program is that everyone taking small actions to make their communities safer adds up to large-scale change, making gender-based violence socially unacceptable. Green Dot recruits influential students like fraternity and sorority members and student government leaders to attend a training that teaches them the skills to influence their peers. In a 2015 study, epidemiologist Ann Coker and her colleagues compared the rates of sexual assault, intimate partner violence, sexual harassment, and stalking on the University of Kentucky campus with the rates on two demographically similar campuses in Ohio and South Carolina that don't have bystander programs. The study design was well-suited to a program that aims to prevent abuse by changing the culture of a whole campus.[23]

Coker's team found significantly lower rates of sexual harassment and stalking on the University of Kentucky's campus, but no significant differences in intimate partner violence. They found no significant differences in rates of sexual assault, with the exception of intoxicated sexual assault, which was lower at the University of Kentucky. And when rates of intoxicated sexual assault were stratified by gender, according to Newlands and O'Donohue, it was only men who were less likely to be sexually assaulted when drunk.[24] It makes sense that programs aimed at changing social norms would be more effective at reducing the types of gender-based violence that are most public.

Changing social norms and expectations is important, but doing so may not have an immediate effect on people's experiences of sexual violence. Estimates vary about what percentage of sexual assaults are witnessed by third parties who could be trained to intervene, but every credible source places the number well below half. Lindsay Orchowski addressed this question by surveying college students about heterosexual sexual encounters that men initiated and women didn't want.[25] Her aim was to determine how often these encounters were stopped and what stopped them. Her team surveyed 635 men and 650 women in their first year of college, asking them about unwanted experiences of sexual touching, intercourse, giving a woman alcohol to facilitate sexual activity, and taking a woman to an isolated location. Women and men differed in their estimates of how many sexual advances were unwanted, how often unwanted sexual activity stopped, and what actions stopped it. But both groups reported that, in most cases, the reason the encounters stopped was women's resistance, which Orchowski defined as saying "Stop!" or "No," having a conversation about sexual limits, or using a physical self-defense skill. According to the women, 85 percent of unwanted advances were stopped by women's resistance and only 4.5 percent were stopped by bystanders. (The rest were stopped by what the researchers defined as "nonverbal cues.") The men reported that 73 percent of the encounters were interrupted by women's resistance and only 1.6 percent by bystanders. In a smaller study of heavy drinking college men, Orchowski found that, in these men's experiences, only 5 of the 237 unwanted advances (2.1 percent) were stopped by bystanders.[26]

I asked Sharyn Potter and Jane Stapleton, executive director of practice at the Prevention Innovations Research Center, how they understand the relationship between the outcomes they measure and the actual rates of sexual assault. "I don't know that we, as researchers, have figured out what the formula is to really decrease perpetration," Stapleton says. "It just takes a long time and we don't have the evidence." Potter's team got federal grants to examine whether bystander training reduced sexual assaults, but they didn't publish their results because they weren't able to show that the program made a difference. There weren't enough people in the study to see any change, Potter explained.

One of the reasons why Bringing in the Bystander is not having an effect on the overall prevalence of sexual violence at the university, Potter and Stapleton tell me, is lack of institutional support. Students who participate in Bringing in the Bystander do so voluntarily, as there is no requirement from the university. New Hampshire has legislation that requires colleges and universities to provide sexual assault prevention education to all matriculating students. But administrators have chosen to comply with this law by having students complete a brief webinar, even though more than a decade of research shows that passive single-session programs don't work. For a program like Bringing in the Bystander to significantly reduce sexual assault on campus, Stapleton and Potter note, there would need to be a complete reorganization of campus life, academically, administratively, and socially. And despite the devastating and widespread effects of sexual violence, there is not enough political will to make those changes.

The kind of organizational transformation Potter and Stapleton described was shown to reduce sexual and dating violence in a much younger group of students. In 2009 and 2010, thirty New York City middle schools participated in a program called Shifting Boundaries, developed and researched by Nan Stein of the Wellesley Centers for Women.[27] Stein and her team implemented the comprehensive program that included educational sessions for students and the use of posters on teen dating violence. But it also involved teachers and administrators in two important ways. One was called hot spot mapping. The team gave out maps of the school and asked students to identify places where they experienced or witnessed harassment, bullying, or abuse. Administrators then ensured adults were stationed at these "hot spots" between classes. Another institutional change was the implementation of Respecting Boundaries Agreements. Any student who felt that their boundaries had been violated could create an enforceable agreement about how the student who harmed them was expected to treat them in the future. Stein's research found schools that implemented both the educational sessions for students and the institutional changes had the biggest decreases in sexual and dating violence. Schools that implemented the institutional changes but did not educate students saw more modest changes, while those that only educated students saw no significant decreases in violence. Stein doesn't know if the schools involved in the study are still implementing Shifting Boundaries. It's nearly impossible, she explains, to keep up with all the schools she studies. The Centers for Disease Control and Prevention is aware of two states implementing Shifting Boundaries in a combined total of ten counties and an additional four states that are using their own forms of hot spot mapping in schools.

There is some evidence that bystander intervention programs are having more significant effects on younger people. Ann Coker led a study of Green Dot in Kentucky public high schools.[28] She randomly selected thirteen schools to receive the program and thirteen others to serve as the control group. The program was implemented over a four-year period. Schools that got Green Dot had an average of 120 fewer sexually violent incidents in year three, and an average of eighty-eight fewer incidents in year four. This represents a reduction of 17 percent in year three and 21 percent in year four. According to more recent studies of Green Dot, it is especially effective for students who witness family violence in their homes. A study of a Bringing in the Bystander program for Indigenous middle school students in South Dakota found lower rates of sexual violence among those who participated in an intensive education program led by their peers, but not among those who only attended a brief kickoff event.[29]

––––––––––

When I interview Kathleen Basile, she maintains that she's always seen the value of programs like Flip the Script. "I think that my op-ed was misconstrued a little bit," she tells me. She points out that empowerment-based programs for women were included in the CDC's 2016 guide for educators and policymakers that gives an overview of effective and promising strategies to prevent sexual violence.[30] But at the same time, Basile says, the CDC is a public health agency, so it has to focus its resources on prevention strategies that have a broader impact on the population. "A focus on perpetrators makes more sense with the limited funds that we have," she tells me. "Because if we can stop perpetration, we can also stop victimization. But if we stop victimization, we're not necessarily stopping perpetration. We're just stopping some victims from experiencing that perpetrator."

In addition to preventing individuals from perpetrating, the CDC, Basile notes, is investing in research on structural changes like laws and public policies. For example, do changes in municipal alcohol ordinances affect the prevalence of gender-based violence? "It takes longer to see community level changes," she explains. "You don't always have the best data sources." But she contends that learning more about which policies are the most effective has the potential to affect the greatest number of people.

Public health is, in many ways, a better framework for understanding gender-based violence than crime. Its focus on collective and systemic solutions is in line with the goals of early feminists, who fought to ensure that rape and abuse were seen as social injustices, not family secrets. Public health helps us see how our individual well-being is shaped by our environment. On my first day of graduate school in public health, a professor gave us a lecture about the spittoon, a bowl used in the nineteenth century to spit out chewing tobacco. He showed us old newspaper clippings with headlines that blamed the spittoon for the spread of disease.

It was public health, he told us, that used evidence to identify the real cause of the problem, which was sewage systems that were unsafe because local governments were not maintaining them. Using solid evidence leads to effective solutions, he told us. It also helps us hold governments accountable when they try to abdicate responsibility and blame people for their own poor health.

One example of the value of public health advocacy is the fight to ban smoking in restaurants and bars. Noting the dire health effects of secondhand smoke, advocates argued that allowing people to smoke indoors violated occupational health and safety standards for workers. Patrons could choose a different restaurant, but servers and bartenders couldn't just leave—and shouldn't be risking their lives to serve us food and alcohol. Offering smoking cessation counseling to one restaurant patron at a time would have been inefficient and probably ineffective since smoking is addictive and the presence of other smokers would make it hard to abstain. Instead, public health advocates changed people's behavior by changing the environment. People who didn't want to leave their friends to have a cigarette alone in the freezing cold smoked less. A statewide smoking ban in Massachusetts went into effect in 2004. A year later, epidemiologist Melanie Dove demonstrated that the law was responsible for a significant decrease in heart disease deaths.[31] Similarly, in a history of the advocacy group Mothers Against Drunk Driving (MADD), James Fell and Robert Voas note that the number of alcohol-related traffic deaths in the US dropped from thirty thousand in 1980 to just under seventeen thousand in 2004.[32] This was the result of stricter penalties for driving drunk, media campaigns that promoted designated drivers, and sobriety checkpoints that kept intoxicated people off the roads.

I'm sure that a decade before smoking bans went into effect, they seemed inconceivable. Now, I can't imagine being in a smoke-filled bar. But with smoking and drunk driving, there are clear and measurable connections between environmental changes and improved well-being. You can test somebody's blood to know if they've smoked and check readily available government records to measure heart disease and lung cancer deaths. You can convince someone to leave a bar with a designated driver and they can't go home and secretly drive drunk in their bedroom. But someone telling a researcher they think rape myths are wrong says almost nothing about how they'll treat the eighteen-year-old who came back to their apartment after dancing in a club and can't afford a cab back to campus. She doesn't look thrilled to be having sex, but she isn't screaming or crying either.

The disconnect between public statements and private actions is seen in high-profile gender-based violence cases. In a 2016 *Vanity Fair* article about the trial of Owen Labrie, who was convicted of sexual offenses for assaulting a fellow student at St. Paul's, an elite boarding school, author Todd Purdum illustrates this reality.[33] The assault was part of a tradition at St. Paul's called the "senior salute," in which high school seniors compete to see who can have the most sexual encounters with younger students. Purdum notes that Labrie, nineteen at the time of the assaults, had participated in a mandatory training about statutory rape and signed a statement that he understood his obligation to follow the law. Labrie was a dorm leader, a role for which this training and pledge was required. But Labrie went even further. Purdum dug up an editorial Labrie had written for the school newspaper condemning the senior salute. What Labrie did in the relative privacy of a dark mechanical room in the school's math and science building was a sharp departure from what he'd said publicly. If his assaults hadn't gone to trial—as most sexual assaults don't—his public statements might have led people to believe that the education the school gave him had changed his behavior. In 2018, then New York attorney general Eric Schneiderman, a champion of the #MeToo movement and a leader in the prosecution of serial sexual abuser Harvey Weinstein, was forced to resign as a result of allegations that he physically and sexually assaulted several of his women partners.[34]

I've been at this for thirty years. I've spent hours clustered around flip chart paper with smart and dedicated people, trying to envision what types of social and environmental changes could stop sexual assault. We've uncapped the markers the facilitators gave us and written bold aspirations on the paper, things like "an end to patriarchy and all forms of oppression." But finding doable steps that will make measurable changes too often evades us.

The difficulty of applying public health principles to gender-based violence is apparent from reviewing the results of eight years of CDC-funded research. Between 2014 and 2022, the agency funded forty-nine studies of efforts that were supposed to prevent sexual assault, child sexual abuse, intimate partner violence, and teen dating violence.[35] This included eight grants for studies of educational programs for boys and men. One of those programs, Manhood 2.0, was shown to have had no significant effect on perpetration of sexual or dating violence.[36] A later study of Manhood 2.0 found increases in abusive behaviors among men who had not sexually coerced or assaulted before they participated in the program. This increase was not seen in the comparison group.[37] The other seven have produced no published studies about the effectiveness of their programs. I asked Basile's office if I'd missed anything, if any CDC-funded research had demonstrated that programs for boys and men reduced perpetration. They sent me two studies of mixed-gender programs that have been shown to reduce perpetration, but nothing specific to men and boys.

Of another eight CDC-funded studies of bystander programs, two produced changes in sexual assault, two showed no changes, and the remaining four did not produce any published studies. Of the nine studies on the impact of legislation on abuse, the results were also mixed. The Earned Income Tax Credit was associated with decreases in abuse reports to state authorities but not with changes in domestic violence homicide. States with low-income housing tax credits and more affordable units had lower rates of domestic violence homicide. State increases in SNAP benefits were associated with fewer reports to child protective authorities. And states that participated in Medicaid expansion as a result of the Affordable Care Act had lower rates of reported child neglect but not abuse. Identifying connections between public policy and the prevalence of abuse is an important way to address gender-based violence using the tools of public health. Maybe there is an equivalent to laws that ban smoking in restaurants or reduce the legal blood alcohol content that is considered drunk driving, but it will take more work to identify.

I support the CDC's efforts to study the impacts of laws and policies. It will be complicated to isolate the impact of any particular law or policy, but if it can be done, the effect will be broader than that of any educational program that reaches a few dozen people at a time. It's possible that states that implemented Medicaid expansion also invest more funding in domestic violence services, so it will take work to distinguish the impact of the expansion from the effects of having more and better social services. The connection is much less clear than Melanie Dove's analysis of how the Massachusetts smoking ban decreased heart disease deaths.

In our interview, Kathleen Basile said that the CDC does not have any policies against funding studies of feminist self-defense, but in practice, they have not done so. I respect the constraints she is facing. Research on gender-based violence is under-resourced. A study led by psychologist Randall Waechter found that US government funding for research on sexual violence is between 15 and 81 percent lower than research funding for heart disease, cancer, diabetes, and HIV/AIDS, all of which are less prevalent than sexual assault.[38] But compared to other prevention strategies, funding for research on feminist self-defense fares consistently worse. Psychologist Sarah Ullman was one of the first researchers to demonstrate that forceful resistance stops sexual assault. She has published some of the most important academic articles about feminist self-defense but told me that she had to change her research focus because she couldn't get grants. Jocelyn Hollander has gotten only small grants from her university to support her work. She gave up applying to the Department of Justice after several rejections. Lindsay Orchowski, a prolific researcher in numerous areas of gender-based violence has likewise never gotten a major grant for her work on feminist self-defense. Senn is Canadian, and unlike her US-based colleagues, her research is funded by the federal public health agency. The availability of government support is one reason why Flip the Script has the most robust evidence.

One of the most impressive examples of public health research on sexual violence is the SHIFT (Sexual Health Initiative to Foster Transformation) study at Columbia University, which began in 2015.[39] Led by sociologist Jennifer Hirsh and psychologist Claude A. Mellins, SHIFT dove deep into the sexual and social lives of students with the goal of understanding how and why sexual violence is so intractable. The book

Sexual Citizens, coauthored by Hirsh and sociologist Shamus Khan, who was a coinvestigator on the study, is based on that research.[40] Over a two-year period, SHIFT researchers interviewed 150 students and held focus groups reaching close to 200 more. A representative sample of 1,671 undergraduates completed a survey, and 427 kept daily diaries in which they reported experiences of mood, stress, substance use, sleep, sexual behavior, sexual assault, and self-esteem for two months. The SHIFT team also sent ethnographic researchers to observe dorms, academic buildings, fraternities, sororities, events, and parties, with more intimate gatherings observed by younger researchers who could blend in.

The SHIFT team maintained their commitment to understanding sexual violence as a public health issue with a view toward solutions that don't rely on changing one person at a time. Their research demonstrated a relationship between sexual violence and structural inequalities like racism and classism—students of color and those on significant financial aid were the most likely to experience sexual violence. Relatively privileged students avoided some assaults by getting themselves out of risky situations with money for Ubers or hotel rooms. The students with money who experienced sexual violence were able to mitigate some of the trauma with privilege. One survivor told researchers she felt lucky to have easy access to emergency contraception and enough money to travel to her parents' house to get away from the student who assaulted her. Another interviewed student had the opposite experience. A nonbinary Latinx first-generation college student from a low-income family went to a bar off campus to hear Dominican music that felt like home. There, they met a guy who offered to buy them a drink. They initially refused, but changed their mind because drinks in New York City clubs are expensive. The drink was drugged, and they felt too woozy to take the subway. Unable to afford a cab, and unaware they'd been drugged, they went to the guy's apartment, where he raped them.

SHIFT found that students of color were more likely to be sexually assaulted by a familiar person who used verbal coercion while both people were sober than white students, who were more likely to experience assaults at or after parties while both people were drunk. Hirsh and Khan note that bystander intervention programs are more tailored to the types of assaults most common for white students.

SHIFT also shed light on the disconnect between university policies and students' experiences. Only 2 percent of the survivors they surveyed reported their assault to the university through official channels. All students said they were aware of Columbia's policy requiring students to get affirmative consent for any sexual activity, but 69 percent said that the way they got consent was to just make a move and keep going if the person didn't say no.

The SHIFT team identified changes to the campus environment that could prevent sexual assaults, some of which Columbia implemented. For example, the university now keeps an on-campus dining room that doesn't serve alcohol open late at night so students have a place to talk and flirt without drinking or winding up in someone's room. Hirsh has advocated other environmental changes, like offering single rooms to first-year students so they can have sex in a familiar place.

But even with this emphasis on structural change, Hirsh and Khan's work illuminates the reality that systemic change to prevent sexual assault is really a coordinated, critical mass of individual changes. The students they interviewed—the ones who assaulted, the ones who survived assaults, and the ones who didn't want to give their weird hookup a label—had something in common. They lacked the skills to balance one person's sexual desires with another person's humanity. For some, this meant subordinating themselves to their partners, having never learned that they could have agency in sexual relationships. Others had the opposite problem, a sense of entitlement. These people were sometimes so focused on their desires they cared too little about their partners' limits. Trends followed prevalent gender norms—the vast majority of those who reported having been sexually assaulted, 83 percent, were women. Still, two-thirds of the men who experienced sexual violence were assaulted by women.

One of the key structural changes Hirsh and Khan advocate is for students to have access to comprehensive sex education long before college, education that teaches them to claim their sexual desires and pleasures, to communicate yes and no clearly, and most importantly, to get what they want out of sex in a way that respects the full humanity of their partners. "Sex is a critical life skill," Hirsh and Khan argue.[41] Nobody would let thousands of teenagers behind the wheel without driver's education. Sex education, they contend, should be just as common. Hirsh and Khan further argue that while anger at university administrators for mishandling sexual assault reports is warranted, at least as much outrage should be directed at politicians and school administrators who fail young people by allowing them to come of age without effective sex education. They note that while political parties are polarized about sex education, there is some evidence that American parents are not. They cite a Planned Parenthood study in which 93 percent of parents across multiple political affiliations want sex education for their children.

Chief among their findings was that women who got comprehensive sex education in which they learned the skills to refuse unwanted sex were half as likely to experience sexual assault. Abstinence-only education did not produce this result. "If there were a vaccine that could prevent half of all campus rapes and it was only provided to young people in half the school districts in the country and those whose parents could afford a progressive private education, there'd be a national outcry. And yet that is essentially the situation in the United States," the researchers conclude.[42] This "vaccine"—sex education with refusal skills—is essentially feminist self-defense.

While there are policy decisions and political fights that make quality sex education available or not, the actual change is happening on a deeply intimate level. The ability to navigate fear of rejection, gender socialization, internalized racism or transphobia, and erotic urges and pleasure is not done in any public arena.

There are good reasons to be hesitant about trying to stop sexual violence by teaching women to defend themselves, but a more careful look at the research shows that the effective programs are those most aligned with public health and social justice. A review by Senn, Hollander, and Gidycz identified common characteristics of self-defense programs that reduce sexual assault.[43] They are explicit in challenging victim blame and placing responsibility for sexual assault on those who perpetrate.

They encourage women to trust themselves and to look critically at the ways societal sexism affects their intimate relationships. This includes challenging sexist expectations that they avoid conflict by subordinating their wants and needs to men's. Effective self-defense programs focus on sexual assault by familiar people and teach physical resistance skills designed for the realities of gender-based violence. Most of them also include sex education, because when women know what they want out of sexual relationships, it's easier to spot when they're being coerced into doing something they don't want.

No compliance-based self-defense program has been shown by published peer-reviewed research to reduce any type of violence. The police-led RAD self-defense program is the only one that has been the subject of published studies, most of which are small and limited in scope. A 2014 study of thirty-four women who took a RAD class at a Midwestern university found that they enjoyed being part of a group, and the younger women felt inspired by watching older women practice physical skills. One participant told researchers that she wished the police officers who taught the class had made more space for honest conversation about fears and past experiences of violence, but this observation was not reflected in other interviews. This study reports on the participants' mostly positive experiences but provides no analysis of the program's outcomes.[44]

A 2018 study of RAD programs across the country found that one week after taking the class, women reported higher confidence in their ability to defend themselves. But this study found that RAD produced no significant changes in women's confidence in their ability to address challenges in interpersonal relationships and social interactions. Another limitation of this study is that 233 women completed the survey before their RAD class but only 71 took the post-class survey. With more than two-thirds of the women dropping out of the study, the outcomes are even more limited.[45]

A 1999 study compared women who took a RAD class, a martial arts class, or no self-defense class at all, with about thirty in each group. Immediately following the program, those who took the RAD class or the martial arts class reported higher levels of confidence in their ability to defend themselves and manage interpersonal relationships. However, neither RAD nor martial arts made women feel less vulnerable or vigilant. They were no less likely to avoid certain places and activities to stay safe and they did not see themselves as less likely to experience sexual assault. Women in this study who were survivors of sexual violence reported lower levels of confidence in their ability to navigate challenges in interpersonal relationships after taking RAD or martial arts than they had before the classes.[46] By contrast, a 1990 study of a feminist self-defense program found positive changes in all these domains, changes that were maintained for six months.[47]

The difference between feminist and compliance-based self-defense programs is not widely understood, but differences in the evidence are stark. The self-defense programs with the strongest evidence are the ones that teach women that we are not the problem, the ones that help us learn how easily gender inequities creep into our intimate relationships and what we can do to recognize and resist coercion.

It's understandable to want to stop sexual violence by teaching men and boys not to rape, but that doesn't mean it's always possible. I remember how hard we tried in the mid-2000s. We held meetings and conferences focused on engaging men. We invited male allies to be keynote speakers, and we listened intently as they brought themselves to tears telling us about their work. During lunch at one conference the men were asked to stand for a round of applause. We who had staffed the shelters and crisis lines for decades clapped for what felt like five minutes.

It's important, too, to interpret the research with care. When I say that educational programs that teach boys and men not to abuse are mostly ineffective, what I mean is that most of the programs that are quick and cheap enough to attract funders and participants are not comprehensive enough to create lasting change. Learning to respect someone else's limits when you're overwhelmed by your own desires is hard. It's even harder when you're trying to reconcile those intimate choices with everything you've been told about what it means to be a man. Waiting until boys are in high school or college and then having them watch videos or have discussions for less time than we spend waiting in line at the DMV is not enough. The Framingham Heart Study has been following thousands of people for more than seventy-five years, looking at their stress levels and smoking and family relationships and diet.[48] From that investment, they've learned what factors contribute to cardiovascular disease. If the people who made decisions about government funding cared enough about stopping sexual violence, we could do something similar.

We could study a cohort of parents who insist their kids get explicit permission for touching anyone from the time they're toddlers. Parents who explain that wanting to hug or kiss someone isn't enough. Parents who help their kids learn how to hold the disappointment that comes when another person's wishes are not the same as theirs and who teach their kids to find joy in mutuality and no pleasure in anything else. We could compare these parents with others and find ways to determine which kids grow up to respect other people's sexual boundaries and which kids grow up to abuse. It would be harder and more complicated than anything we can measure with blood tests. But it only sounds impossible because we don't have the will to invest in it.

It makes sense, too, to mobilize decent people to interrupt sexual harm. Bystander intervention is one of the most powerful shifts in how we understand gender-based violence. Calling on friends and teammates and fraternity brothers and coworkers to speak up makes abuse a community problem, not a private tragedy.

Changing social norms and expectations is essential. Our lives would be worse if more rape jokes went unchallenged, if more parents, teachers, and school administrators felt entitled to shrug their shoulders and say "Boys will be boys." But the difference between what people say in public and what they do in private is a defining characteristic of gender-based violence. Changing social expectations and public spaces is essential, but it's equally important to make sure people have the skills to create change in intimate spaces.

PART 3

WHAT MOVES US FORWARD

| CHAPTER 8 |

RESISTING RACISM

Wriply Bennet lets out a sarcastic laugh when I ask her who she trusts. Sometimes other Black transgender women, she says, but usually just herself. She loves lots of people, she tells me, but love is not the same as trust. Wriply grew up in poor and working-class neighborhoods in Columbus, Ohio. She was bullied at school. Adults in her neighborhood threw soda and beer cans at her from their car windows. She also survived sexual abuse by family members and friends.

Wriply grew up fighting. She loved Power Rangers cartoons and felt like an action hero when she fought with other kids. But as an adult, her ability to fight—and to know when not to—is a matter of survival. As a child and teenager, Wriply was visibly queer. "It wasn't anything that I was outwardly trying to do," she tells me. "It was just me." The older she got, the better she understood that being different meant being targeted. "I started to take my safety very seriously," she says. "Learning how to defend myself was paramount to growing up Black, but also growing up queer."

Wriply never leaves her house without weapons; knives, brass knuckles, batons. Sometimes she hides them in her coat pockets, but at least as often, she brandishes them. "Men just follow me places," she explains. One man drove his car onto a sidewalk to get close to her, but drove away when she showed him her baton. "So taking the bus and taking the train and just walking down the street. That doesn't happen anymore.

That will never ever happen again. At least not without my baton, my knives, my taser, and my pepper spray, my personal alarm," she tells me. Self-defense is urgent and complicated. She is more likely than most to be assaulted on the street. There are times she orders in groceries to avoid leaving home.

But she faces just as many threats from the institutions that protect more privileged women. She knows that if she physically hurts someone, even someone who is trying to hurt her, she is the one who will be arrested. She corresponds with a Black trans woman who is incarcerated in a men's prison because her partner forced her to participate in his crimes. Knowing this reality, she explains, "I have to learn different ways of defending myself, especially when it comes to institutions that are built around vilifying folks who protect themselves."

Wriply is a cofounder of THORN, a grassroots group that gives self-defense tools to Black transgender women. "I got tired of seeing Black trans women being beat in the streets," she explains. "And no one raises a hand to try and help them. I got tired of seeing those videos and hearing those stories." THORN's self-care kits come with brass knuckles, alarms, tasers, batons, and other weapons. They also include Wriply's drawings of comic book characters in brilliant greens and oranges—Black queer superheroes fighting the systems that try to obliterate them. "People like me are disposable," she says. "You're considered an elder by the time you're thirty."

As a Black trans woman, Wriply has a clear understanding of what safety would look like. "Safety means me being excited to go outside," she tells me. "To walk down the street or taking public transportation would be nice so I don't have to waste my money Ubering everywhere." More than that, she says, "Safety means not having to explain myself to people in order to feel safe, not making excuses for who I am in order to feel safe."

THORN's work is funded by Venmo contributions and coordinated through encrypted messages. Wriply has learned that she can't trust the social service agencies that are supposed to be a safety net. One LGBTQ agency tried to collaborate with her because serving the Black transgender community was a way to get grants. But, Wriply tells me, "these larger organizations were strangling the work we were trying to do." One social service agency canceled a safety summit she'd tried to organize because they wouldn't endorse a group that gave people weapons. "We understand how severe the violence is towards Black trans people," Wriply says, so whether to arm people never came up for discussion. THORN stays grassroots and unincorporated, Wriply tells me, because the trade-offs required by state funding would make the work ineffective.

The most marginalized women of color and LGBTQ people of color live with the constant threat of severe violence and the equally serious threat of facing criminal charges for acting in self-defense. The same week Kyle Rittenhouse was acquitted for killing two people and injuring a third when he shot them at a Black Lives Matter protest, Indigenous woman Maddesyn George was sentenced to six years in prison for killing a white man who had raped her at gunpoint. Unlike Rittenhouse, George knew the man who attacked her. And unlike Rittenhouse, she was prohibited by federal prosecutors from arguing self-defense.

In August 2010, Marissa Alexander was less than two weeks postpartum when her ex strangled and threatened to kill her. She went to the garage to get her legally registered gun. She fired one round into a ceiling, injuring no one. The baby and her two other children were safe, but she was charged with three counts of aggravated assault with a deadly weapon, a crime with a mandatory minimum sentence of twenty years.[1]

Marissa Alexander lives in Florida, a state with strong "stand your ground" laws that give armed citizens the right to shoot without having to make an effort to retreat. Those laws gained national attention in 2012 when they were invoked to defend George Zimmerman, who shot and killed Black teenager Trayvon Martin. Based on the belief that she had the same rights to stand her ground, Marissa Alexander rejected a plea deal that would have put her in prison for three years and went to trial. Alexander was convicted in May 2012. The jury deliberated for twelve minutes. She got a mandatory minimum sentence of twenty years.[2]

Shortly after the conviction, activist and philosophy professor Alisa Bierria joined the campaign to free her. She remembers a website put together by Alexander's family[3] that caught the attention of women of color who were leaders in anti-violence activism. Grassroots organizations formed in cities around the country. The most visible was the Chicago Alliance to Free Marissa Alexander, led by now-prominent abolitionist author Mariame Kaba. "Defense campaigns and any kind of community organizing always seems to me to be like some kind of magic," Alisa tells me.

The stakes of their work were frightening. With Florida's harsh sentencing laws, Marissa Alexander could have gone to prison for decades. The defense committee walked a delicate line, careful to be guided by what was best for Alexander, even when they were committed to a broad political vision that included ending incarceration. "As feminist advocates, one of the highest principles is to support survivors' self-determination," says Alisa.

Another role of a defense campaign, Alisa tells me, is to show how incarceration replicates the dynamics of intimate abuse. "The context of the violence that they've already experienced includes isolation," she says. "Isolation is one of the most powerful tools in abusive relationships." So the defense campaign made efforts to keep Marissa Alexander connected. Some people visited her in prison, others wrote letters. Mariame Kaba created a book and art exhibit called *No Selves to Defend*, which featured artwork and stories about Marissa Alexander and other women of color throughout history who had been criminalized for protecting their bodies.[4] The Free Marissa Now campaign raised money for her legal fees by selling T-shirts, buttons, and posters. In artist-rendered images in bold yellows and browns, Marissa Alexander wears hoop earrings and a floral top. You see joy and resolve in her facial expression.

Alisa Bierria remembers a strong collaboration between Marissa Alexander's lawyers and the activists who fought to free her. "The legal process is organized to be untouchable and unknowable because it likes to pretend that it's neutral," she tells me. So the defense committee used protest and social media to bring attention to her case. With the amount of stigma Alexander faced, her lawyers understood that keeping her out of prison would take more than courtroom strategies. The stigma was most clearly illustrated by the fact that prosecutor Angela Corey charged her with such a serious crime even after Corey had acknowledged the threat her ex had posed. No one disputed that he had tried to strangle Alexander before she fired the gun. "They knew that he attacked her. They understood what situation she was in," Alisa tells me. "They just bypassed it and went directly to the gunshot." A key strategy for the Free Marissa Now campaign was to draw media attention to how differently Florida's "stand your ground" laws were applied to a white man who killed a Black teenager he didn't know and to a Black woman who used a gun to startle but not injure a man she'd once loved. The campaign succeeded at getting news outlets like the *New York Times* and *The Guardian* to cover the case.

In 2013, Marissa Alexander's legal team succeeded in getting her conviction overturned on appeal due to improper jury instructions. In response, Angela Corey announced that she would prosecute Marissa Alexander again, this time aiming for three consecutive twenty-year sentences. Alexander opted for a plea deal—three years in prison followed by two years under house arrest. She'd already served most of the prison time. She went back for sixty-five days. "I was revved up, we were getting ready for a trial," Alisa tells me, so when Alexander chose the deal, Alisa says, "It was a little bit deflating," but also a relief given the prospect of prison for sixty years. It was Alexander who chose to go to trial in 2012, based on her belief that she'd done nothing wrong. She had a brand-new baby and the plea would have put her in prison for three years. And it was Alexander who chose not to risk a sixty-year sentence. "In her choice making," Alisa says, "she is doing self-defense. She was doing self-defense when she chose to go to trial. And she was doing self-defense when she took the plea deal."

Defense campaigns to free survivors who were imprisoned for defending themselves date back at least to the 1970s. Historian Emily Thuma chronicled four pivotal defense campaigns from that time: campaigns to free Joan Little, Dessie Woods, Inez Garcia, and Yvonne Wanrow.[5] All four were poor and working-class women of color. All four had killed men who tried to rape them.

These four cases gained momentum during a complicated time in the history of feminist activism to end rape and abuse. Throughout the 1970s, radical feminists in cities around the US had founded rape crisis centers. Most were explicitly political. They organized speak-outs to draw attention to the magnitude of rape. Some groups publicized the names of men who had sexually assaulted. Others protested police departments that dismissed survivors. They operated hotlines, staffed entirely by volunteers, that survivors could call if they needed support. Most hotlines were inundated with calls from women struggling with everything from the immediate aftermath of rape to the decades-old trauma of child sexual abuse. The urgent needs of survivors sometimes eclipsed the political organizing that was central to most rape crisis centers' missions. Relying on the unpaid labor of activists to staff crisis lines was becoming unsustainable.

Sociologist Nancy Matthews followed six rape crisis centers in southern California from the mid 1970s to the early '80s as they made the transition from grassroots activist groups to government-funded social service providers.[6] She concluded that an infusion of feminist values into social work and an availability of advocates to help survivors navigate court, police, and health care systems resulted in more humane treatment for individuals and more understanding of sexual violence by professionals. Matthews also acknowledges that while the Reagan administration was cutting social services, it was getting tough on crime. Framing rape survivors as crime victims meant money for services. But it also meant closer collaboration with the police. Radical feminists of the 1970s saw the police as the opposition, but liberal, disproportionately white feminists believed that if rape crisis centers wanted to change public opinion, they needed to become more mainstream. "Being labeled as deviant vigilantes also marginalized the movement rather than promoting society-wide change," Matthews notes.[7] But at the same time, government funding changed the character of rape crisis work from political activism to social service provision. Government funding, she found, was a "conservatizing influence," a shift she bluntly described as going "from stopping violence to managing rape."[8]

Black feminist sociologist Beth Richie characterizes this evolution as having "won the mainstream but lost the movement."[9] In analyzing the ways Black women are targeted for violence and then failed by police and social service systems that are supposed to help crime victims, Richie argues that the incredible peril Black women survivors face is partly a result of ineffective feminist leadership. "It is possible to imagine that if the feminist organizing that led to these changes in research, in the law, in services, and in public awareness had included a broader, more radical anti-racist agenda, Black women in disadvantaged communities might have been protected."[10]

Researcher and activist Mimi Kim conducted an analysis of feminist domestic violence activism between 1973 and 1983 that shows the limitations of early efforts to hold the police accountable for dismissing survivors.[11] In 1976, lawyers Eva Jefferson Patterson and Pauline Gee, both women of color, won a lawsuit against the Oakland Police Department by successfully arguing that failing to respond to domestic violence calls was a violation of women's constitutional right to equal protection. In order to ensure that the legal victory created meaningful change, Gee began working inside the system. She designed the domestic violence protocol for the Oakland police and was appointed to the commission that oversaw police training for the state of California. Activists in San Francisco and Duluth, Minnesota, used similar strategies. "Assurance of success depended upon maintaining a strong arm of feminism in an ongoing struggle with a recalcitrant criminal justice system," Kim explains. Advocates working inside police and court systems maintained close collaborations with more radical activists who could mobilize protests and lawsuits.

But as victim advocacy, police training, and community response programs proliferated across the country, the oversight structures and political alliances that made systems-change work effective were diluted. As a result, advocates in other cities and towns operated in these systems without institutional power, their roles often dictated by police officers and judges. Kim calls this phenomenon "carceral creep," the gradual and sometimes imperceptible eroding of activists' power and influence until they became subordinate to police officers and prosecutors.

That was my experience working as a family court advocate in Upstate New York in the 1990s. There was no external pressure to bolster my work inside the system. Domestic violence advocates made requests, not demands. We were so grateful to be allowed inside the courtrooms that we accepted every rule the judges imposed on us. We were not allowed to say anything in the courtroom, which meant having to stay silent while judges berated or dismissed survivors. All the judges and court officers were men. Men made the rules, or they enforced them with their thick, imposing bodies. Women were secretaries and social workers, tasked with carrying out men's orders or providing emotional support. I wanted my presence to hold the system accountable, but in practice, I became just another woman who cleaned up after the law.

During this complicated time, Emily Thuma's research shows that campaigns for survivors who had been criminalized for self-defense posed a direct challenge to advocates who saw the police and prosecutors as allies in their efforts to hold abusers accountable.[12] These campaigns were bigger than the individual women they fought to free. By focusing public attention on women of color who were in prison for protecting themselves from rape, activists exposed a violence inherent in the criminal legal system.

In 1974, Joan Little, a Black woman, was serving time for a robbery in a North Carolina prison. A white guard, Clarence Alligood, tried to rape her. He came into her cell, wielding an ice pick. She took the ice pick and killed him in self-defense. Evidence that Little acted in self-defense, Thuma notes, comes from Alligood's autopsy report, which stated that he was found dead in her cell with his shoes in the corridor. He was naked from the waist down, with fluid presumed to be his semen on his penis and inner thigh. Still, Little was charged with his murder. Her lawyers, a multiracial team of civil rights attorneys, quickly realized it would take more than a court proceeding to secure her freedom. They would need an activist groundswell to draw attention to her case.

Little's lawyers saw how the prosecution was using her life history to discredit her. Joan Little had run away from an unsafe home as a teen, did not have a high school diploma, and had been arrested multiple times for shoplifting though all the charges were dropped due to lack of evidence. So the prosecution tried to brand her as scheming Jezebel, playing on stereotypes of oversexualized Black women. In response, her lawyers established the Joan Little Defense Fund. Headquartered in Durham, the fund brought together a broad coalition of feminist, civil rights, and Black Power activists with professors, students, and everyday people. Defense committees were formed in cities across the country including New York and Pittsburgh, raising funds for Little's bail bond and legal fees. Prominent civil rights activist Rosa Parks founded a Joan Little Defense Committee in Detroit. Through publicity, protests, and speaking engagements, the fund bought attention to Little's case but also to broader issues like the right of women to defend themselves against rape and inhumane conditions in women's prisons, which included sexual coercion and abuse by guards. The campaign included prominent partners like the Black Panther Party and the National Organization for Women. The Southern Poverty Law Center worked with Little's defense team to sue the state of North Carolina for abusive treatment of women in prisons.

Bolstered by grassroots activism, Little's legal team won a change of venue to Wake County, which is much more racially diverse than Beaufort, where Little was incarcerated. The legal team called other incarcerated women as witnesses. These women testified to the sexual harassment and assaults perpetrated against them by Clarence Alligood. Nearly one hundred journalists covered the case. A jury of mostly women, split evenly between Black and white jurors, acquitted her. Little was deemed the first woman in US history to be acquitted for using deadly force to stop rape.

Joan Little's case galvanized activism against systemic racism and sexism in the criminal legal system. It also led to the founding of a defense campaign for Inez Garcia, a Latina woman found guilty of murder in California for killing a man who had raped her and threatened to kill her if she told anyone. Feminist activists organized car pools from the Bay Area to the coastal town near Salinas, where Garcia was being tried. They packed the courtroom with Garcia supporters and journalists. After Inez Garcia was sentenced to five years to life, activists continued protests outside the prison, and prominent feminists Gloria Steinem and Simone de Beauvoir made statements supporting her. Inez Garcia appeared on the cover of *Ms.* magazine in May 1975. Activists both nationally and in

California continued to protest, fundraise, and apply political pressure, even petitioning then governor Jerry Brown to commute her sentence. In 1976, Garcia won her appeal for a new trial and was acquitted on the grounds of self-defense the following year.

In 1975, Dessie Woods, a working-class Black woman in Georgia, traveled to the prison in Reidsville with her friend Cheryl Todd. They planned to advocate for Todd's brother, who was incarcerated there and needed medical care, but they were denied access. When Todd fainted from heat exhaustion, both women were charged with public drunkenness and incarcerated for three days without a Breathalyzer test to establish intoxication. After this ordeal they hitchhiked home. A white man impersonating a detective picked the women up. He tried to rape Woods at gunpoint, but she took his gun and shot him. She was convicted in 1976, in a trial that was mostly closed to the public, a reaction, Thuma argues, to the mass protests and packed courtrooms for Joan Little and Inez Garcia. But activists continued to raise awareness and apply political pressure until she was released six years later, in 1981.

Yvonne Wanrow, an Indigenous woman, fatally shot a white man who had broken into her friend's home. This man had threatened Wanrow's son with a knife and sexually assaulted the friend's daughter. Wanrow and her friend had called the police but got no help from them. Wanrow was on crutches at the time of the break-in and physically smaller than the man, who was intoxicated. She used a gun to stop him when he began lurching toward the children. She was initially convicted and incarcerated in 1973. But then, a defense committee got involved and the Washington Supreme Court affirmed her right to claim self-defense and released her from prison in 1977. The court then denied the prosecution's request for a new hearing, so they charged her with different crimes. Not wanting to endure another trial, Wanrow agreed to five years' probation.

Defense campaigns have seen a resurgence since Marissa Alexander's case. In 2016, Alisa Bierria was part of a group of organizers that founded Survived & Punished, a national coalition working to free survivors of sexual and intimate partner violence who are criminalized for defending themselves. Beyond individual defense campaigns, Survived & Punished works to "abolish gender violence, policing, prisons, and deportations." In March 2022, Survived & Punished, in collaboration with the UCLA Center for the Study of Women, released a research report titled *Defending Self-Defense: A Call to Action by Survived & Punished.*[13] The research team, which included Alexander and Bierria, was overseen by an advisory council of survivors who had spent time in prison for defending themselves.

The report includes a long section describing the research process. Advisory council members were paid for their time and expertise. They interviewed each other, rather than being interviewed by researchers who didn't share their lived experience. They also reviewed the findings at multiple stages of the process and had the power to decide what conclusions were drawn from their stories.

The main finding of the *Defending Self-Defense* report is that the most stigmatized survivors were put in an impossible position: they couldn't get help from the police or social service agencies. Because they couldn't trust the institutions that were supposed to help them, the violence escalated to the point where their lives were in danger. And because their lives were in danger, they had no choice but to hurt or kill the person abusing them. In the report's introduction, Marissa Alexander described this impossible situation: "If the violence is unabated, we risk losing our lives. If we defend ourselves, we risk losing our freedom."

Some survivors couldn't call the police because they were involved in criminalized activities like sex work or drug use. Other times racist and transphobic violence that they or their communities had experienced in the past kept them from trusting the police. Social service agencies, including rape crisis and domestic violence programs, were also out of reach because they were seen as being too connected to the police or child protective services. Advisory committee members didn't see a way to get support without becoming entangled in those systems. After being criminalized, committee members noted the conspicuous absence of support from survivor advocacy groups, even those that espoused feminist values: "Participants raised concerns about how government funding and investments in having 'good' relations with prosecutors can play a role in organizations' decisions to not publicly support survivors."

On top of the realities of unresponsive or hostile systems, the danger of being killed by an intimate partner is greater for the most marginalized survivors. The report cites data that Black and Indigenous women experience the highest rates of intimate partner homicides. Black women are almost three times more likely than white women to be killed by a current or former partner.

The *Defending Self-Defense* report exposes vast inequities in the application of self-defense laws. In every US state, people have the right to engage in behaviors otherwise illegal (like hitting or shooting someone) to protect themselves from imminent bodily harm. You can't just punch someone on the street, but if their hands are around your neck and you punch them to stop them from strangling you, you shouldn't be convicted of a crime. Laws vary from state to state, but in general, people need to prove that a "reasonable person" would be afraid of serious bodily harm or death. Most states require this "reasonable" person to believe that the violence is imminent and the force used in self-defense was necessary to stop it—if someone points a gun at you, you can shoot them, but if they only make a verbal threat, it's harder to prove that shooting them is justified. Some states have a "duty to retreat," which requires a person to show that they attempted to leave the situation or otherwise avoid using force. Some, like Massachusetts, have a duty to retreat in public places but not in a person's own home. However, most US states have enacted "stand your ground" laws, which assert that a person has no duty to retreat from any place that they have a legal right to be.

Self-defense laws, the report argues, are biased toward white men protecting themselves from strangers. Shortly after Marissa Alexander's conviction, the Urban Institute published an analysis of FBI data by political scientist John Roman. He found that homicides in which a white person killed a Black person were the most likely to be ruled as "justified," 281 percent more likely than homicides in which a white person shot and killed another white person.[14] Beyond racial disparities, it can be harder to convince a jury that an act of violence is "imminent" in the context of an intimate or familiar relationship. Survivors can be in serious danger even if a gun is not pointed at them at the exact moment they resist. Also, women who defend themselves against men in the context of intimate abuse are overcoming disparities of size and strength. Some survivors overcome these disparities by using guns or other weapons. This leaves them vulnerable to being charged with additional crimes or receiving longer sentences, because in most states, using a weapon makes a crime more serious.

Colby Lenz is the deputy director of policy and community research for the UCLA Center for the Study of Women and a cofounder of Survived & Punished. Before joining the Defending Self-Defense research team, she worked on defense campaigns with the California Coalition for Women Prisoners. One of the most important challenges, Colby explains, is navigating the relationship with a survivor's lawyer, who is primarily focused on the court case. Colby has experienced a wide range of reactions from lawyers. Roshawn Knight, a member of the advisory council who spent nineteen months in prison for killing her abusive partner in self-defense, was represented by public defender Janae Torrez. Torrez understood the complexity of the case, Colby tells me. She understood how much research and investigation it would take and how hard it would be to prove self-defense. She understood that the public defender's office didn't have the funding or staffing to do everything that would be needed to build a successful case, and she saw that the defense committee could raise money, find the right expert witnesses, and support Roshawn Knight and her family in all the ways that fell outside the scope of legal representation. So Janae Torrez added Colby and other members of Survived & Punished to the legal team, giving them the status to do legal visits with Knight in prison.

Other times the collaboration is not as close. "There's often a push and pull," Colby tells me. "A kind of tension around whether or not the attorney is comfortable with a more public facing campaign or even behind the scenes advocacy." Some campaigns build public support and outrage by getting media attention for a criminalized survivor. And some lawyers have understandable concerns that sharing too many details about the incidents with the media could work against the survivor in court. She's worked with lawyers who were wholly unprepared for the hatred and stigma their clients face. They see the severity of the abuse and expect judges and juries to understand why their client had no choice but to shoot or stab. Colby describes one legal team who didn't understand the need for a defense campaign until they saw how badly the judge treated their client. "Once you're in the category of quote, unquote, 'murderer' there's no way out," she says. "You can't be seen in a more complex way even if you have the most egregious evidence of domestic violence. So, eventually, in that case, and I've seen it in other cases, they got so overwhelmed with the inability to move the case forward that they were more open to advocacy and organizing strategies."

Some low-income survivors rely on big law firms for pro bono attorneys, and their expertise is sometimes a wild mismatch for the complexity of arguing self-defense. One firm, Colby remembers, had a tax lawyer working on a murder charge. In cases like that one, defense campaign members walk a tightrope, respecting the lawyer's role while making sure the survivor benefits from their knowledge of the criminal system. Other times, defense campaigns have no relationships with lawyers. Colby has sometimes supported survivors in advocating for themselves and making sure their lawyer represents their interests.

Colby described a pivotal time in 2017 and 2018, when then governor Jerry Brown sharply increased the number of pardons and sentence commutations he granted. Also, Colby notes, it wasn't just for safer sentences like non-violent drug crimes. The California Coalition for Women Prisoners and other organizations had created strong communication "across the walls." And because of those relationships, Colby and other activists noticed a pattern. Brown was commuting sentences of women convicted of crimes that resulted from domestic violence. And for the first time, women sentenced to life without parole were being interviewed for clemency. So, Colby tells me, Survived & Punished got involved. They developed relationships with the people in Brown's office who were conducting clemency interviews. In one instance, a survivor's attorney was convinced that their client wasn't eligible because her case was ongoing. But because of the relationships Survived & Punished had built with incarcerated survivors, they understood that wasn't the case.

So they scrambled to submit her petition, doing their best to maintain a good relationship with the lawyer.

In 2016, then-fourteen-year-old Bresha Meadows shot and killed her father, who had physically and sexually abused her and her mother. He'd caused serious injuries for years and threatened to kill them. Bresha Meadows was part of the Defending Self-Defense advisory council. In the report, she explains why self-defense was her only choice, describing a time she tried to get help from the police after she'd run away from home. "I called the cops to let them know I had run away and I didn't feel comfortable going back. They told me to come to the police station because I was still a runaway and whoever I was with would get a kidnapping charge. So I did go to the police station and they sent me home with no questions whatsoever."

Bresha Meadows was charged with aggravated murder and prosecutors attempted to try her as an adult. In response, a groundswell of activism was mobilized by a group Colby Lenz and Mariame Kaba described in a *Teen Vogue* op-ed as a "small organizing collective that brought Bresha's case to national and international attention."[15]

Hundreds of people wrote letters to the prosecutor and made phone calls demanding her release. Others sent Bresha postcards and books while she was incarcerated. They raised money to pay for legal fees, including expert witnesses. Organizers packed the courtroom. There were protests outside too, and hundreds of journalists calling for comment, overwhelming the staff of that small courthouse in Warren, Ohio. "That day of her big court hearing," Colby tells me, "there were people calling from all over including international outlets calling the court trying to get access. I think it felt more significant because that kind of activity was not happening in that region." Colby is confident that the defense committee had an impact on the outcome of the case. "They're under scrutiny," she says. Together, the defense campaign and legal team put enough pressure on the prosecution that they gave Bresha Meadows a plea deal. Instead of being tried as an adult and facing life in prison, she was sentenced to one year in juvenile jail followed by six months in a psychiatric facility.

Another impact of the defense campaign was to keep the prison system from allowing Bresha Meadows to disappear. "We made Bresha's case visible," Colby Lenz and Mariame Kaba wrote in the *Teen Vogue* op-ed, "to demand her freedom and to pressure prosecutors to stop pressing charges against survivors, if for no better reason than to avoid the organized threat of public exposure and shame. In Ohio, we heard from people who would know that prosecutors were nervous and concerned about the level of public attention and public pressure being brought to bear around Bresha's case." Criminalization and incarceration, Colby tells me, is a "disappearance process," a way of removing survivors from their homes and communities, isolating them from the rest of us so they are eventually forgotten. Defense campaigns resist this. They keep criminalized survivors visible, and they shine just as much light on the institutions that treat them as predators.

The most marginalized women and queer survivors are fighting for the integrity of their bodies. Fighting to be included in what it means to be a "reasonable" person, a person whose judgment matters, a person whose fear of being raped or killed doesn't get buried under a million racist narratives that cast them as angry or out of control or inherently violent. Defense campaigns shine an uncomfortable light on what it means to be a person pushed to the breaking point and then blamed for breaking. In doing this, they expose the jeopardies of depending on the criminal legal system to stop gender-based violence.

CHAPTER 9

STRENGTHENING ACTIVISM

Denise Velasco and her parents were in the United States legally, but she still understood Proposition 187 as an attack. She was only fourteen in 1994, the year a majority of California voters supported a referendum making it illegal for undocumented immigrants to get health care or go to school. Worse than that, teachers and health care workers were expected to call the INS if they suspected any of their students or patients of being undocumented. Proposition 187 didn't survive legal challenges and never went into effect, but the impact of voter-approved hatred stayed with Denise for a lifetime.

Denise Velasco became a labor organizer, working with janitorial workers in California, most of whom are Latina immigrants. She is now the director of strategic initiatives at the Maintenance Cooperation Trust Fund (MCTF), a statewide watchdog group that works to end illegal and unfair practices in California's nonunionized janitorial industry.

MCTF was founded in 1999, a rare but effective alliance between labor activists and more ethical cleaning companies that were getting outbid for janitorial contracts because it costs more to do business when you're not stealing from your workers. MCTF's goal, Denise tells me, is to make it "so unscrupulous employers get weeded out of the janitorial industry." For years the organization's main focus was wage theft. MCTF was instrumental in passing legislation that created a statewide registry of companies that illegally withhold pay from janitorial workers. Then, as organizers gained workers' trust, they began hearing stories about sexual harassment and assault. Janitorial workers, some of whom are undocumented, work night shifts cleaning office buildings. "We know that they're oftentimes in buildings by themselves," explains Sandra Henriquez, the CEO of ValorUS, an organization that works to end sexual violence by advancing equity in California and nationally. "People who want to cause them harm often know that they're there and intentionally target them," she tells me in an interview.

In 2015, janitorial worker Georgina Hernandez began speaking publicly about her experience of sexual violence.[1] She worked in a hotel, cleaning the lobby at night. Her supervisor, she told reporters, harassed her constantly. He sexually assaulted her in the parking garage where there were no security cameras. That year, the PBS *Frontline* documentary "Rape on the Night Shift" first aired, bringing national attention to the magnitude of sexual abuse janitorial workers experience on the job.[2] Often working alone at night in deserted office parks, these workers were seen as vulnerable. They didn't know their rights, were undocumented, weren't fluent in English, or lived in poverty and were too afraid to risk their jobs by making a report. The documentary also exposed how difficult it was to hold employers accountable. Many janitorial companies hire a complicated web of subcontractors, making it hard to determine which company is the worker's actual employer. This structure diffuses the responsibility for maintaining safe working conditions. Even the most committed investigators had to sift through pages of documents just to determine which entity was responsible for protecting a worker's rights.

Lilia Garcia-Brower was executive director of MCTF at the time. She led the organization from 2000 to 2020 when she became the labor commissioner for the state of California. Her experience taught her that any response to sexual violence had to be led by the workers, because more privileged people would not have been able to build trust. "When you're dealing with a vulnerable population," she tells me in an interview, "they are more astute at sniffing out BS. Because they have so few chips available." She had already seen that college-educated organizers were not successful, because they couldn't connect with the workers. "The organizing work had to be done by janitors," she explains. "You have two to three minutes. You're talking to a janitor at night, while they're working, trying to not get on the boss's radar. You're often talking to them out by a trash can, or in a bathroom. You're trying to do it in the shadow of the night, and you don't want the employer to see you." That might expose the worker to retaliation. "Our investigators who came from the industry had that ability to say, 'I know what's going on with you, because I lived it,'" she tells me. "And so I made a deliberate choice to protect all of our investigator jobs for former janitors."

Lilia knew she would need support in order to do right by janitors who had survived abuse on the job or even in their homes. So she reached out to Sandra Henriquez. Sandra connected MCTF with the East Los Angeles Women's Center to get help for workers who were struggling with current or past abuse. Several members of the MCTF staff, including Lilia herself, completed training for their promotora program. The promotora model trains women who are trusted in their communities to understand sexual and domestic violence. Promotoras are leaders in their communities who help other women get access to practical support and healing.

The other resource Sandra Henriquez offered was self-defense. Before joining Valor, she had spent years teaching self-defense to sexual assault survivors and advocates across California. When she thought about how isolated the workers were, how unlikely it would be for anyone to be around to help them, she realized they needed something they could do for themselves. She had seen the impact self-defense had on the survivors she'd taught. "The assertiveness that they get to practice and the actual physical techniques," Sandra tells me, "informs their ability to speak up on their behalf, to exercise their rights to live free from violence." So Sandra volunteered her time to train janitorial workers to teach self-defense. A daughter of immigrant parents, Sandra Henriquez moved to the US when she was a child. She'd seen family members work in jobs where they were treated like they were invisible. So it meant a lot to her to help janitorial workers access their power. The program, now called Ya Basta!, has reached over five hundred janitorial workers across California.

Denise Velasco wasn't sold on self-defense right away. She didn't want to put more burdens on women, especially the workers whose stories she knew intimately. Women who had survived war and poverty, who had lost their children to disease or violence. "Just one of those things is a big deal in somebody's life," Denise tells me. "So, at the end of the day," she thought, "men just need to stop abusing." But after seeing Ya Basta! in action, she says, "I came to a point where I understood that self-defense wasn't just about defending yourself; it was about changing the way you looked at the world in terms of your own power."

In an article published in *Ms.* magazine in 2018, Lilia Garcia-Brower explained how the Ya Basta! program works.[3] "For four hours, we carefully take women through a journey of healing and empowerment," she said. "This special investment of time and resources is critical because we find that most of the women who participate have never had the time or the space to think about their emotional well-being, their physical body and the pain they carry." Then, she explained, "For the last hour, the women practice how to punch, kick and jab to protect themselves from potential attackers. They channel their pain, anger, and rage into a positive outcome—understanding the principles of self-defense. So much anger comes from feeling powerless. The self-defense training gives them power. The power to change your life, your workplace and the way you understand the world."

In an interview with me, Lilia Garcia-Brower talks about the barriers women overcome just to make it to class. "For poor working people, you're working three, four jobs, and you just can't stay afloat," she tells me. They don't have the protections unionized workers have. Sometimes several family members work for the same company: "So if I take on the boss, it's not just me, it's my brother. It's my cousin. It's my aunt," Lilia explains. "So you have no room to think. You have no room to consider another way. And so the power of this program is that we create safe space for the women to breathe." MCTF provides child care and healthy food to make Ya Basta! accessible. At the height of Covid, they taught parts of the class virtually.

Marlene Herrera is a former janitorial worker who now oversees organizing in Orange County for MCTF. She was one of the promotoras trained by Sandra Henriquez to teach self-defense. Before coming to MCTF, she worked for a company that cleaned airports. She'd been a union steward. When the workers lost union representation, she fought to bring it back with tactics that included a hunger strike and civil disobedience. In response, the company fired her. She met the field director for MCTF, and they helped her file a retaliation complaint. After that, she went to work for MCTF. Marlene works closely with janitorial workers, and she's seen firsthand how learning self-defense improves their confidence. Some said they feel safer at bus stops on long commutes to work during off hours. Others have spoken up and resisted sexual advances from their bosses. Ya Basta! has also made more women aware of what constitutes sexual harassment—sexual jokes, a supervisor who keeps asking for dates, or unwanted attention from office workers in the buildings where they clean.

Denise Velasco describes the unique role self-defense plays in organizing women who have lived through unrelenting trauma. "The huge difference," she says, "is reclaiming your personal power. And that's something no police report or no lawsuit will give you." Once women are able to do that, she has noticed, there's a domino effect: "One is finding your voice. The second is understanding that your body belongs to you." The Ya Basta! program begins with women using their voices. Yelling the words "Yo soy alguien" ("I am someone") as loud as they can.

"Those are small shifts," Denise explains, "where you start realizing that you are a powerful person, you can stop things from happening." She notices a strong connection between self-defense and organizing. "When we talk about self-defense, we're saying, 'You have immense value.' Sexual assault is an affront to that. Harassment at work, wage theft, health and safety violations. All of these are trying to tell you you're not human and you don't matter and you don't have any value." So self-defense plays an important role in shifting that narrative. "You're decolonizing people from these ideas that made them believe that their body wasn't worth anything, that their labor wasn't worth anything."

This work, Lilia Garcia-Brower says, is about "creating opportunities for women to know that they are more valuable than how they are being treated at home or at work. We recovered $80 million in back wages. But they were going back out in a revolving door into the same industry having the same experiences." From that, Lilia came to understand that Ya Basta! and the trauma healing from the East Los Angeles Women's Center promotora program were essential to keeping janitorial workers motivated to fight for their rights. "We needed to invest in emotional and mental healing," she tells me. "That was our secret ingredient that we had been missing. We created space. And so these women were feeling powerful."

Everyone I interviewed about MCTF spoke about the strong connection between protecting your body and protecting your rights. Shortly after initiating the self-defense program, Denise Velasco and other leaders realized that they wanted to integrate Ya Basta! with the classes they teach janitorial workers about labor law. Doing this helps make important connections between workers knowing their rights and finding the power of their voices and bodies.

In 2019, after two years of intensive self-defense training and work with the East Los Angeles Women's Center, MCTF and their allies achieved an important legislative victory. A new state law requires all cleaning companies to implement in-person sexual harassment training for all workers and managers. More importantly, the training must be led by janitorial workers who know the industry. This law also requires companies to register trainings with the state, and if they fail to do so, that information will be available to the public.

From these individual shifts come the collective power needed to fight against injustice in the janitorial industry. "We are creating an army of women—a support network committed to reaching as many female janitors as possible," Lilia Garcia-Brower wrote in *Ms.* magazine. "As each women connects with her power, she will be prepared to denounce her abusers in a self-empowering way. We want as many workers to transform their profound pain into a courageous, bold, proud light that celebrates the powerful person they actually are. And as we go from training to training, we're making that internal shift one worker at a time."

CHAPTER 10

EMBRACING RESISTANCE

O n a rainy August morning in the basement of a community center, Gloucester Stage Company holds its first rehearsal for a new play by a local playwright. Folding tables are arranged in a rectangle. Fluorescent lights reflect off bright white floor tiles. Actors, the director, stage and production managers, lighting, scenic, and costume designers sit on metal chairs. Loud laughter echoes off the walls of this large basement space.

Chris Griffith, the theater's managing director, welcomes the cast and production team. They are all freelancers, employed only for the six or eight weeks it will take to put on this play. He wants to make sure they understand what to do if they experience harassment or harm. Detailed policies have been emailed to everyone in the room. They are available, too, on the theater's website.[1] But this issue is important enough that Gloucester Stage starts the first rehearsal of every production with a presentation. There's a colorful flier with graphics, a flow chart of the conflict resolution process.

Chris starts by talking about conflict—a joke that doesn't land, a racial microaggression, any action by one person that could make another person wonder if the rehearsal space is safe. The first step outlined in the policy is a direct conversation. "If you feel comfortable doing so," it states. "This helps foster an honest, open community and is often the fastest path to a resolution." The policy gives a structure for addressing these moments. The person who was harmed says "Ouch" and explains the words or actions that caused harm. In response, the person who did something harmful is supposed to say "Oops" and then listen and apologize. The words sound silly to some, but using them creates a shared language that is recognizable to everyone involved in the company. This practice comes from Not in Our House, a group of Chicago theater makers who developed abuse prevention standards for performing arts organizations.

Chris tells the cast and production team about a time he made an insensitive comment to a person he supervises. In line with the policy, she initiated a direct conversation with him, and he apologized for the comment. Using himself as an example, he illustrates that the organization supports people who speak up when they experience harm just as it expects people who cause harm to take responsibility.

The policy acknowledges that sometimes a direct conversation isn't possible. In those cases, Gloucester Stage provides names and phone numbers of people who can receive reports. Some are part of the production, like the director and stage manager. Others are not. They include Chris, the theater's artistic director, a member of the board of directors, and a former board member. This clear and comprehensive reporting structure corrects the deficits of past approaches, some of which were identified in a 2018 survey and focus groups led by IMPACT Boston.[2] As part of the Line Drawn initiative, which works to prevent harassment and abuse in the New England performing arts sector, we identified key barriers that have kept theater professionals silent.

Most jobs in theater are short-term and competitive. Actors audition constantly, up against dozens of people with a similar physical appearance for a single part. Designers and technicians depend on their reputations. If one producer recommends them to others, they'll keep working. If they get a reputation for being hard to work with, they might not. The scarcity and precarity of employment, our survey found, made freelance theater professionals reluctant to do anything that could brand them as "difficult." They told us it was safer for their careers to just endure the harassment because after a month or two, the show would close. Another problem the survey identified was that freelancers were unclear about how to make a report. Because their relationship with the organization was brief, they often didn't interact with the company's leadership or know how to contact them discreetly. Even if a theater organization had a sexual harassment policy, they weren't told how to contact the person responsible for addressing it.

This practice of presenting the theater's abuse prevention policies at the first rehearsal came from Not in Our House, a coalition of Chicago theater artists who developed standards after a sexual abuse crisis in 2017.[3] The *Chicago Reader* had just published an investigation that uncovered decades of sexual abuse at Profiles Theatre by artistic director Darrell W. Cox. Not in Our House's *Chicago Theatre Standards* outlines a series of practices designed to create safe and equitable workplaces. It includes everything from harassment policies to intimacy onstage to physical safety for people who get on ladders to hang lights.

Next, Chris Griffith presents the theater's policy about intimate moments onstage. "Honor your boundaries," the document reads. "Honor your cast members' boundaries." The policy explicitly encourages performers to start each day of work by assessing whether they are comfortable with any sexual or intimate scenes that are part of their role. If they are not, Chris states the organization's commitment to changing the choreography so that every intimate moment is truly consensual. "There is no boundary that will get in the way of us telling this story," the policy reads.

Most importantly, Chris states Gloucester Stage's commitment to hiring an intimacy director any time a play includes sex, physical intimacy, or sexual violence. Intimacy directors are specialized choreographers who stage scenes that are especially vulnerable to perform, usually because they require close touch between performers. Intimacy directors also create structures and protocols that help performers communicate their boundaries. They serve as advocates for actors, ensuring that the power imbalance between performer and director doesn't result in performers being compelled to be vulnerable in ways that don't feel safe. "You don't have to put your emotional self, your physical self in harm's way to get to an authentic, raw, beautiful performance," Chris Griffith explains to me.

Having sexual and intimate scenes choreographed in a way that gives actors the choice and opportunity to refuse to do what the director wants is a dramatic shift in the industry. "Actors are trained to say yes," explains Chelsea Pace, founder of Theatrical Intimacy Education and an intimacy director in regional and Broadway theater. In her book *Staging Sex: Best Practices, Tools, and Techniques for Theatrical Intimacy*, she explains that expecting actors to develop "chemistry" on their own or improvise intimate scenes erodes the boundary between the person and the character they are playing.[4] Without clear and consistent choreography, it is almost impossible to ensure that what happens onstage is consensual. No director, Pace explains, would let performers improvise a fight scene. The risk of injury is clear when one performer hits or kicks another. The risk of injury for sex and other onstage intimacy is just as present, even if it wasn't acknowledged until the proliferation of intimacy direction.

The Line Drawn survey and focus groups found problems with sexual and intimate scenes. Sometimes they weren't choreographed. Other times, intimacy was choreographed, but actors told us that their scene partners would change the choreography in the middle of a performance. One woman told us her scene partner put his tongue in her mouth onstage in the middle of a show, a violation she felt unable to address in the moment because it would have meant breaking character and stopping the show. It was a small theater, with no understudy to replace him, so she had to finish several weeks of performances with him.

Gloucester Stage presents its policy to the cast and production team on the first day of rehearsal, but every actor who will perform an intimate moment already knows about it. Actors are informed when they audition for a role, Chris told me in an interview, if there will be nudity, sex, intimacy, or sexual assault. They give actors pages from the script so they can get a concrete sense of what the intimate scenes look like.

There's an ease and authenticity in the way Chis talks to the cast and production team. I look around the room. No hunched shoulders, or averted eyes. No pained or somber expressions. Chris looks comfortable, fully embodying the values and practices he describes. There's a weight to the lightness, though. A significance to all these invitations to speak up, to have boundaries, to resist. A significance because everything Chris Griffith is saying is the stark opposite of the way Gloucester Stage operated for most of its history.

Paula Plum was an actor at Gloucester Stage in the early 1990s. Israel Horovitz, the theater's founder, was a respected playwright. He wrote seventy plays, one of which was performed on Broadway starring Al Pacino. The fact that Horovitz raped and sexually assaulted women was an open secret. Horovitz was blatant too. Paula tells me about a time he forced his tongue into a young woman's mouth in the middle of a rehearsal. Paula isn't sure how many of the men who ran the theater company in the 1990s knew how bad the abuse was, but every woman had a clear understanding of the type of woman Horovitz targeted: "boyish, slim, vulnerable, young." She and the other women in the company made it their job to warn every woman who matched this physical type. They lingered in dressing rooms and backstage, a silent army doing everything they could to keep other women safe. "As soon as we knew he was in the building," Paula explains, "we just made sure no one was alone." They prevented a lot of assaults, but it was impossible stop all of them. One woman, she tells me, was about to go onstage, when Horovitz grabbed her and groped her. Paula compares the experience to living with an alcoholic family member. "You manage around it."

I ask Paula Plum if she ever thought about reporting the abuse. She says she could not have imagined that the men in leadership at the time would have done anything to hold Horovitz accountable. "It was a culture of not reporting," she explains. "We wouldn't even think of reporting." Everyone who worked at Gloucester Stage was beholden to him. "He was the top. He founded the theater. The way he presented was just, you know, king of the world." But despite a complete absence of institutional support, women found ways to support each other. "We weren't disempowered," she explains. "We had an understanding whereby we could protect each other."

At the theater, a mood of tension came over everyone when he entered, Paula says. If he didn't like a set design, he would order that the scenery be torn up and it was. "He had the sort of effect of an autocrat," she explains.

"He could smash everything down." Sally Richardson had a similar experience when she was hired as a costume designer in 2014. She was just out of school, and it was her first professional job. Before she started work, she got the same warnings Paula Plum had given twenty years earlier. "At the time I was just like, 'Oh, that's good to know, thanks,'" she says. But looking back she finds it bizarre that she didn't ask more questions. "Why did I not question more about that?" she asks. "Or wonder why is anyone working with this person if that's the advice you give to women?" The play Sally worked on was written and directed by Horovitz. In the final scene, a woman murders a house painter who had tried to blackmail her for sex. Horovitz insisted the actor be dressed in lingerie, though neither Sally nor the actor thought it made sense. Horovitz didn't listen, and insisted on the lingerie. Sally found a garment the actress could live with.

When the show began tech rehearsals, Horovitz stopped speaking to Sally. After constant emails with feedback about the costumes, he didn't say a single word. "That's odd," she remembers thinking. At a break in the rehearsal, she approached him hoping to talk about the costumes. "I took a step forward to talk to him and started to open my mouth to speak. And he just caressed my cheek, smiled at me, and walked away. And that was the end of it," she explains. "And that night at the production meeting, I said, 'Oh, I didn't get a chance to check in with you. I have a couple notes.' And he just told me not to do them, that he liked everything the way it was, and he didn't want me to do any more work."

The next summer, Sally was hired to design costumes for another Israel Horovitz play. Horovitz wasn't supposed to direct, but a week before rehearsals started, the director's travel visa got rejected, so he stepped in. "The whole show was designed," Sally explains. "The whole team had done their jobs." But Horovitz insisted on throwing out the sets and costumes and lights, making the designers start over and redo their work with no additional pay. "It says something about the culture that nobody felt they could push back and nobody felt like they could advocate for their work," she says.

Sally also remembers bizarre and unnecessary intrusions. Horovitz, she tells me, would go into the women's dressing room to give notes to the cast, sometimes when actors were still changing. Marsha Smith, a stage manager, remembers having to keep track of Horovitz to make sure he wasn't still backstage. "He was lingering in the greenroom after half hour. And I went in and said, 'Really, you cannot be here,'" she tells me. He would say he just came backstage for some cough drops. She would tell him she just saw him put two cough drops in his pocket: "You have your cough drops. Now get out." He would respond by calling her a bully. Marsha could take Horovitz's anger at her. And she understood how important it was that she did. "Everybody knew Israel was not okay," she tells me, "that he was always making passes at women and would deny people roles if they weren't reciprocated."

"I had actresses ask me to make sure they were never alone with him. I said, 'Of course, you are exactly his type. You are five foot seven, and you are blond, you are adorable. You are playing the ingenue in his play, and you are exactly, as I understand it, his type. So yes, of course, I'm going to make sure,'" she tells me. "And every time he would show up at rehearsal, I would have to fold something right next to where they were talking. Every time they were talking. Go figure. And he never seemed to notice."

Still, his plays brought in more money than the theater's other productions. He was beloved by many in Gloucester, a mixed-class fishing town an hour north of Boston with no other professional theaters. Liz Neumeier remembers the first Gloucester Stage play she saw. It was ninety degrees with no air conditioning. She sat in the back row of the theater, dripping with sweat, but was so moved and delighted by what she saw onstage that she didn't care. A lawyer and lifelong theater lover, she bought a subscription and eventually joined the board of directors. Horovitz, not just his work, was loved and respected. "I had a great fondness for Israel," Paula Plum tells me, "and had a hard time believing he would do that." She never let her love or disbelief get in the way of her vigilance about other women's safety, but it was a struggle to reconcile his abusive behavior with how kind he was to her.

In 1993, theater critic Bill Marx published an article in the *Boston Phoenix* about six women actors who reported having been groped or harassed by Horovitz.[5] None felt safe enough to let the paper print their names, but all agreed to come forward if Marx or the paper was sued. They described incidents of kissing, groping, and harassment, and talked about the same buddy system Paula and Sally explained. Bill Marx also interviewed then board president Barry Weiner. He characterized the women as "tightly wound if you know what I mean." When asked if he thought the women had been sexually harassed, Weiner responded by saying, "People throw around that charge like manhole covers." Weiner further asserted the women who spoke to Marx were just upset by the theater's decision to fire the business director, at the time the only woman in leadership. Weiner characterized the former business director as "very emotional about everything." The next week the *Phoenix* published a follow-up article. One more actor and three women who had worked as nannies for Horovitz's children added their stories of sexual assault. Barry Weiner responded to the additional reports by saying that the board did not have enough information to investigate Horovitz: "We need to be mindful of people's reputations. It's very frustrating."

Paula Plum remembers hearing about the article. She remembers, too, being unsurprised that nothing at Gloucester Stage changed. "A lot of us, and I'll put myself in that category, are from another generation that sort of accepted male behavior in a way that's unhealthy," she tells me.

Then, in 2017, the *New York Times* published a story about Horovitz's abuses based on reports from nine women.[6] The incidents were similar to those described in the *Phoenix* article fourteen years earlier—young women theater artists who believed Israel Horovitz was their mentor until he groped or assaulted them. Trust shattered, careers cut short. Careers other than Horovitz's that is. The story was picked up by NPR, the BBC, and other media outlets.

About a month before the article was published, Liz Neumeier, then the Gloucester Stage board president, was at a conference out of town when she got a text message from one of the volunteer ushers. A theater artist in New York who had considered Horovitz to be a mentor and parent figure had written a long social media post about how he'd sexually assaulted her. The post was going viral. In response, Bill Marx rescued the *Phoenix* articles from obscurity and posted them on his website. Liz Neumeier walked out of the conference and called an emergency meeting of the board's executive committee. A board member met with Israel Horovitz. Then, the whole board met on a Saturday morning at a library, not wanting to gather in the theater. With only forty-eight hours' notice, every member of the board was present. Israel Horovitz was not. The board had requested to talk to him, but he cited health issues and didn't show.

Then, on November 17, at the board's insistence, Horovitz stepped down as artistic director emeritus. Though he'd been retired from day-to-day operations, the board decided to cut all ties with him and stop producing his plays. The board agreed to speak to the *New York Times* reporter and to answer her questions with full transparency. "To the extent we know anything," Liz Neumeier told me, "we share it." Her quotes in the *Times* article reflect the integrity the board was aspiring to. "I apologize to the brave women who came forward in 1992 and 1993 but were not listened to," she told the *New York Times*. "We are individually and collectively appalled by the allegations, both old and new."

This is where Gloucester Stage departs from the typical organizational response to an abuse crisis. No canned apologies written by PR companies. No lawyers drafting non-disparagement agreements. No imposed silences prohibiting people from talking about the ways the organization failed survivors. Instead, they dug deep into why so many people in leadership did nothing when they knew how many women Horovitz had harmed. At the time, the Line Drawn initiative had just begun. Leaders from Gloucester Stage attended every meeting, full of humility, eager to learn.

In an interview, Chris Griffith tells me about the impact of the board's decisive action. "A staff member would never have been able to effect the amount of change we needed," he explains. But he also recognizes the magnitude of the risk they took: "All of them know that the livelihood of the theater is on this one man's name."

Chris had just moved to Gloucester from central Indiana. As the brand-new director of marketing and development, he thought he'd be helping Gloucester Stage improve its fundraising. He'd been charmed by Gloucester, with its ocean views and vibrant visual arts scene, and looking for a new professional challenge. That first fall, at a performance of *To*

Kill a Mockingbird, a volunteer usher pulled him aside. "You know about Israel, right?" she asked. Chris knew what he'd Googled: the accolades, the accomplishments. As a marketing and development professional, he also knew that when Gloucester Stage produced a Horovitz play, ticket sales were significantly higher than they were for any other production. The difference was as much as $1,500 per night, which is a lot for a small theater. He'd worked at the theater for less than two months when the *Times* story broke.

Liz Neumeier remembers a day she was at a restaurant in downtown Gloucester with another board member. Her neighbor called to say there was a TV news truck in front of her house. The board tried to work with a PR consultant. Liz is diplomatic and measured when she describes the experience: he was "coming from such a different place from where the board was coming from." He wanted to protect the organization, to say as little as possible. The board wanted accountability and repair, so they got rid of him. Liz wonders how many leaders are led away from their better inclinations by the advice of PR consultants.

The Contact Us page of the theater's website was flooded. Liz Neumeier read as many messages as she could. She told me about one that stuck with her. It was from a woman who had been sexually harassed by Horovitz decades earlier when she worked in the box office. She'd heard the story on the radio while she was driving and had to pull over. She had loved theater, but after working at Gloucester Stage, she decided not to pursue it. "People want to talk about the talent of these men who engage in this behavior," Liz tells me. "But how much talent are they costing the arts? By the people they drive away?"

The bold and terrifying step of removing Israel Horovitz was only the beginning. His outsized artistic voice had drowned out most others. "Could we continue without Israel?" was a question a lot of people in Gloucester asked. "The immediate reaction from so many folks was so polarizing," Chris Griffith tells me. "You have folks that are calling going, 'How could you let this happen for so long?'" But just as many were angry at the board for throwing Horovitz under the bus. A lot of people in town loved Israel Horovitz, Chris explains. Or even if they hated him, they loved the thrill of hating someone famous.

The staff pulled together. They read every news story. Then managing directors Jeff Zinn and Robert Walsh reached out to the Not in Our House group in Chicago, wanting to learn everything they could about how they made theater organizations safer. They quickly implemented *Chicago Theatre Standards* and began the heartbreaking work of rebuilding the theater. Being an outsider gave Chris Griffith distance and perspective. But for those who were around in 1993 when ten anonymous women went to the *Phoenix* because they had no faith in the organization, the questions were harder. How had they been complicit? What had they known and chosen not to acknowledge? Why hadn't they taken the situation more seriously?

They knew they couldn't just get rid of Horovitz and write an email saying they were sorry. They had to take a deep and painful look at the culture he created and figure out what it would take to thoroughly transform it. "That whole year," Chris says. "was just learning how to speak about the company without talking about him, and reassessing what it is that we provide to our community."

"It sounds a little cliché," Chris says, "but it felt like a new day. But not like, 'Everything's great.' It was almost like after a hurricane came through, we have some work to do to build this house again. There are large parts of this house that are missing. But all of a sudden, here are some more people in our neighborhood that are going to come help us."

In the months following Horovitz's removal, board members greeted the audience at every performance. "I was really quite surprised," Liz Neumeier says, "at the number of people who came up and said to me, 'I have not been at this theater for decades because of that man. And now that he's gone, I bought a subscription.'" They lost some audience members. But Liz took those losses in stride. Gloucester Stage's mission gave her clarity: to be a safe harbor for new playwrights. Continuing to produce plays by its established and internationally recognized founder was the opposite of the theater's purpose.

A big part of the transformation was taking a serious look at what it means to be a person in a position of authority. "There'd be all these times when people wouldn't say anything to me," Chris Griffith explains. "There would be this culture of fear." So as a person in leadership, especially a man trying to understand the magnitude of sexual violence, he had to work hard to make sure people understood that it was safe to challenge him.

Chris described a moment that illustrated for him how much the organizational culture had changed. He had tried to encourage a young staff member in an entry level position to take initiative, by saying, "You're a big girl, figure it out." She later reached out to him to tell him she had a concern she needed to address. When they met, she told him she found the comment demeaning. "It was condescending," she told him. "It was a little sexist." But he was thankful and relieved she felt she could say something to him. "I'm so glad that she brought it up. It helped me reset into a place where I'm not falling over the line," he tells me. He shares this story with actors on the first day of rehearsal. It's a concrete example of "ouch" and "oops," but it's also an invitation to speak up when someone crosses a line, even if that person has "director" in their title. "When conflicts arise, the most authentic way I can show myself that I'm available to these moments is that I will put the brakes on for conversations like this, and then we'll create some type of action plan," he says.

The most defining change is that everyone in leadership at Gloucester Stage welcomes and embraces resistance. They've created a culture that encourages people to advocate for themselves even when it means challenging people in leadership. Invitations to resist are a part of administrative processes and rehearsals. Paula Plum told me about a "gates and fences" exercise developed by intimacy director Chelsea Pace. At the beginning of each rehearsal, every actor states what touch is acceptable that day (the gates) and what touch is not (the fences). "There's a huge awareness that we have been through this history," Paula tells me. "And we are determined and committed to making the theater a safe place." Stage manager Marsha Smith told me about a rehearsal where actors played a game called "No" in which they practiced refusing requests.

Since actors have been trained to be agreeable and compliant, this game helped them advocate for themselves, and it demonstrated that Gloucester Stage is an organization that makes space for that. She describes people in leadership finding "joy in the ability to let an actor say no to them, because they spent years not being able to do that."

Chris Griffith believes that when artists feel less precarious, they create better theater. He doesn't want anyone who works for Gloucester Stage to feel the need to be consumed by theater or do it in a way that compromises their well-being. "I want you to come to do what you're passionate about. I want you to not worry that you're not going to be compensated, you're not going to be supported," he explains. Another important change is making sure actors don't worry that "if you don't go out to cocktails with the artistic director, you're never going to be in a show again."

Freelancers who worked for Gloucester Stage before Horovitz was removed have noticed the changes. "I feel like the culture is different," Sally Richardson says. She says Chris's presentation at the first rehearsal is especially helpful. As a designer who works for multiple theaters at once, she finds it's hard to keep track of each company's policies. So to have them communicated clearly on the first day of work makes a difference. She's noticed changes in the theater's hiring practices too: "A lot more women are working there now at least on the shows that I'm working on. And no one has ever said, 'Don't be alone in a room with this person.'" For Sally, Chris's first-day presentation reflects the reality of how the theater works. "People feel more equipped to protect themselves and the other people in the room, and it doesn't feel as much like you need to be wary of anything," she says. "It feels like a much safer space."

The ultimate example of how much the theater has changed was an experience that Sally had in the middle of a tech rehearsal. Someone made an insensitive comment and, Sally tells me, "One of the actors said, 'Can we hold, because I have an ouch.' And they talked it out. It only took a couple minutes, and then everyone was able to move on from it instead of everyone going home thinking about it." The more she thought about that moment, the more she understood how deep the change was. "There's so much space to be able to handle it now. Instead of sitting on it and feeling like you have to suppress it." Tech is the hardest and busiest time when putting up a play. It's the week before a show opens when all the sound, lighting, costumes, and stagecraft are integrated with the actors. Historically, it's a time when theater professionals are expected to work late and set aside their needs and put their lives outside the production on hold. It's a time when everything feels urgent. So to have space for an actor to speak up and resolve a conflict says something important about how much the organization lives its values. "You're in such a time crunch, like nothing else matters," Sally says of tech rehearsals, "except it does."

Sally has noticed other changes that show the theater's commitment to inviting and respecting boundaries. "There's more flexibility instead of having to bend over backwards through a hoop of fire." Before Horovitz left, she remembers having to sit in rush hour traffic to get to Gloucester for a forty-five-minute meeting. But now theater leadership respects freelancers' time. Meetings are hybrid, decisions about scheduling are collaborative. She notices more trust too. She's not inundated by constant emails from a director backseat driving her designs. She feels her knowledge and skills are respected in a way they weren't when she worked for Horovitz.

"Took them long enough," was stage manager Marsha Smith's first reaction when she heard that Horovitz had been removed from Gloucester Stage. But at the same time, she appreciates that the board's decision to remove him was years in the making. When she started working for the theater in 2003, she told me, everyone was in Israel Horovitz's corner. The board and staff were handpicked by him, friends and allies who quashed efforts to hold him accountable. But over the years, Marsha noticed gradual changes. The board turned over, and newer members were more independent. They hired managing directors who were more professional. "By the time we really started addressing the legacy of Israel's hand on the lower back and kissing everyone on the face, I had seen this other big step," she says.

I asked Marsha what it was like to be in the room while Chris Griffith presented the policies. She said she believes the ease I observed comes from being open about the theater's history. The use of silly words like "ouch" and "oops" to address conflicts, for her, makes it possible to resolve hurtful comments in the moment, so nothing festers.

Living their values is a work in progress, but the progress is real. "We're taking the producing power of the Gloucester Stage Company away from this one man who had been abusing it and ruining careers with it for all these years. And now we're spreading it out to new playwrights to women," Chris explains, "trying to lift those voices up, promote those shows and give them the same love that Israel gave himself." Gloucester Stage is still white-led, but it is employing more people of color and producing more shows by and about people of color.

Liz Neumeier encapsulates what she learned from leading the board through this crisis in one thought: *Do the right thing and get good insurance.* "If Israel had sued us," she tells me, "I would be perfectly comfortable with putting that before a jury or a judge."

What the leadership at Gloucester Stage did could be understood as *institutional courage*, a term created by psychologist Jennifer Freyd.[7] Freyd, who founded a research center to study organizational responses to abuse and other crises, defines institutional courage as "an institution's commitment to seek the truth and engage in moral action despite risk, unpleasantness, and short-term cost." According to some preliminary research conducted by Freyd and her colleagues, employees who experienced acts of institutional courage after having been sexually harassed at work had higher levels of job satisfaction. A more unexpected result is that workers who experienced institutional courage reported less physical pain compared to those who experienced what Freyd calls *institutional betrayal.*[8]

That said, neither Freyd's institute nor my colleagues who are leaders of national sexual assault prevention organizations could give me a list of organizations that acted like Gloucester Stage. Because so much abuse is made possible by organizational inaction, it is crucial to understand the few promising examples of genuine change.

Community organizer Nico Aguilar Shank told me about another instance of this kind of courage. They remember standing outside a hotel in central Oregon on a freezing cold evening. Immersed in a long conversation with immigration rights leader Ramon Ramirez, Nico noticed the chairs in the lobby. They thought about how much warmer it would have been if they'd gone inside. But later Nico realized Ramirez was being careful. After the sexual harassment they'd experienced from another movement leader, Francisco Lopez, Nico suspected that Ramirez didn't want to do anything that could have looked like he was inviting them to his room.

Ramon Ramirez had already earned Nico's trust. He's a cisgender heterosexual man and was, at the time, the executive director of a respected immigrant rights organization. Nico noticed how respectfully he talked about issues relevant to queer people. He listened to younger women organizers. All of this gave Nico the confidence that if they talked about their experiences of harassment, Ramirez would believe them.

In 2017, Nico Aguilar Shank (who then used the name Amanda), posted an article on *Medium* that was later published in the transformative justice anthology *Beyond Survival*.[9] It was the height of the #MeToo movement. But unlike most stories published at the time, this one was not about organizational failure. The immigrant rights organization where Nico worked was asked to cosponsor a United Against Hate rally in Portland, Oregon. Nico was reluctant because one of the other sponsoring organizations, Voz Hispana, was led by Francisco Lopez, the man who had sexually harassed them and three other organizers. Nico and the other harassment survivors wrote detailed letters to the coalition about the harm they had experienced. Their experiences were similar, and taken together, they showed a pattern of calculated and systematic harm. In response, coalition members voted unanimously to remove Voz Hispana as a cosponsor. "The response from rally organizers was swift and appreciated," Nico says in the article. The coalition sent a letter to Voz Hispana. The organization would not be welcome as long as it was led by a man who refused to be accountable for sexually harassing young women organizers.

Nico was concerned about stoking racism and xenophobia. Not a year earlier, Donald Trump had called Mexicans rapists, and though Lopez was not of Mexican descent, the broad brush of white supremacy could have been used to undermine their organizing. But Nico spoke up because they felt responsible for making organizing spaces safer. "The primary motivator for me was making sure this never happens again," Nico tells me in an interview. "And that is a big fucking burden to carry as a person who's surviving this type of abuse or harm. It can feel overwhelming, and it can feel urgent, and it can feel very isolating to know that this has happened, and is likely to continue happening." But Nico and the other harassment survivors were clear that they didn't want the burden of fixing the problem to fall on them. "I'm ringing the alarm bell," Nico explained to me in an interview. "And I need people to come out and fight the fire."

"We mostly got support," Nico says of the organizing community's response, "which was kind of like the baseline to be honest." But Nico's organizing community gave more than sympathy and compassion. Other activists took the issue on themselves. They were conscious of making sure the burden of changing the culture didn't fall on the four survivors. "They came to me and said, 'Here's our plan. This is what we want to do. We've already discussed it; is this okay with you? Is there anything else that would be supportive?'" Nico tells me. "They didn't make me go to meetings about it; they didn't make me come up with ideas about how to address it; they had their own ideas." Nico experienced this as "true solidarity." "They were not taking it on for me," Nico says. "They were taking it on for the whole community." This, to Nico, made the work feel more permanent.

The work went deeper than one rally. Those who had worked with Lopez in the past began thinking about how their groups had shielded him from accountability. "There's a lot of ways that a person may not be accountable and there's a lot of ways that the culture of an organization may be enabling that type of leadership," Nico says. "So you start to unravel this one thing, which was sexual harassment by one man against several people. And you start to see that there were other challenges of leadership style that people were experiencing from this same person." One thing they realized was they needed to make it safe to express disagreement or dissent. When people feel free to speak up and challenge leaders about a range of issues, then it's less likely that someone in power will be able to avoid accountability for sexually harassing.

Distancing ourselves from organizational leaders who enabled abuse is an understandable impulse, but some of the most effective prevention comes from doing just the opposite.

———————

The coaches are alert and focused. It's 2018 and US Olympic officials are being grilled about sexual abuse on Capitol Hill. Images of Larry Nassar in a prison jumpsuit are on every TV screen. That and local news stories about much less famous abusive coaches have motivated them to come to this training, hoping I'll teach them how to prevent sexual abuse in the sports organizations they lead. Almost everyone in this room works for an adaptive sports organization. They coach disabled athletes, a group that is much more likely to experience sexual abuse and less likely to be included in any of the major news stories.

I give them news stories that range from Olympic volleyball to middle school swimming, and I give them a direction they don't expect: Identify with someone in the story who dropped the ball on preventing abuse. There's a stunned silence in the room as I ask them to imagine themselves as the administrator who ignored an abuse report because it was made by another teammate, not the athlete herself. Or the coach who stood by while a popular doctor gave examinations in private because she didn't think the rules the doctor broke were any big deal.

"I could see myself doing what the athletic director did," one participant says. The article is about a high school sports coach who sexually abused teenage girls. This coach had been banned from the school a decade earlier for some unspecified inappropriate conduct, only to be hired back when his friend became the athletic director. *I could see myself wanting to help a friend. And we all want to have faith that people can change.* We compile a list of all the reasons they could see themselves dropping the ball: ordinary lapses of courage, single-minded professional ambition, and inclinations against assuming the worst. We then generate a second list, of commitments they make to themselves and each other, promises to listen and believe and ask hard questions even when it scares them. The next question is the most important: *What can you do to guard against these tendencies?*

If it works, the result is a plan to keep each other honest and challenge each other to see that abuse is possible. When we can see ourselves and the leaders we revere as capable of abusing power, then it becomes possible to develop accountability practices to guard against those abuses. If it works, we create communities that welcome the kind of constructive resistance that keeps everyone safer.

In July 2021, the United Church of Christ (UCC) made this kind of bold decision. The Southern Baptist Convention was in the news. A damning recording of their president, Ronnie Floyd, urging leaders to downplay sexual abuse had been leaked to the media, and their annual meeting was interrupted by protests from survivors.

In response, minister Elizabeth Dilley encouraged members and leaders of the UCC not to distance themselves from the Southern Baptists. "Let me be clear: this is not a 'Thank God we are not like those other groups' post," she wrote in an article published on the website of the UCC's central governing body. "I know that we have further to go to make our denomination one where all people are safe from sexual violence and where anyone can share their stories of abuse with confidence that they will be heard and respected." Her blog post described the UCC's strategy for preventing sexual abuse, which is comprehensive and holistic. It includes everything from resources to help individual churches develop abuse prevention policies to guidelines for teaching sex education to parameters for including those who have sexually abused in the community without leaving them alone with children.

Sharing power and inviting church members to challenge their leaders and each other is a defining characteristic of how UCC churches approach abuse prevention. "The UCC fundamentally believes in the sacred and holy wisdom among the gathered community," Elizabeth Dilley tells me. "We make good decisions when we do it together, as opposed to just receiving it from someone."

The UCC offers a guide for congregations to develop abuse prevention policies. It outlines a year-long process overseen by a work group of parishioners and church leaders. The work group and the congregation are encouraged to debate and dissent. Preventing sexual abuse is complicated.

It requires us to introduce suspicion into communities where we come to relax and be accepted. It requires us to balance fellowship and trust with discernment. The difference between genuine trustworthiness and skillful manipulation is near impossible to get right every time, and many people who sexually abuse are especially good at that kind of manipulation. This is why the UCC's approach to building these policies is focused on getting as close to consensus as possible. It's easy to put something stern and responsible in writing but not have the stomach to do it in reality. If your policy says that no adult can be alone with a child, then most of the church community needs to wholeheartedly support it. Otherwise it would be too possible to do nothing when a beloved Sunday school teacher takes a kid upstairs, because you can't imagine he would ever do anything.

At the same time, shared power does not mean abdicating accountability. Local UCC churches, Elizabeth Dilley tells me, have a lot of autonomy. They choose their own leaders and write their own bylaws. Each congregation is free to choose their minister, but they are not eligible for insurance unless they hire one who is in good standing with the denomination. If minister does anything to cause people to question whether they belong in leadership, an oversight body conducts what is called a fitness review. "Non-hierarchical denominations," she tells me, "do, in fact have the ability to hold ministers accountable." In the fitness review, the minister could be assigned to what is called a "program of growth," which consists of self-reflection and behavior change strategies. The typical program lasts a year and a half and involves everything from spiritual reflection to psychotherapy. "The purpose of the program of growth," Elizabeth Dilley tells me, "is to attempt to restore that person to full fitness for ministry." But if the conduct is too egregious or the minister is not sincerely engaged in change, then the denomination has the authority to revoke a minister's good standing.

There's a specific type of resilience that guards against abuse in organizations, and it comes from welcoming resistance. It means creating space for people to communicate their boundaries, and more importantly, giving people repeated experiences of seeing boundaries respected. It means that it's safe, even welcome, to challenge people in leadership. It means believing that people do their best work when they have space to advocate for themselves. It means sharing power so no single person can overrule the good judgment of others.

Leadership that welcomes resistance is hard. Nico Aguilar Shank explains the delicate balance it requires: "As an organizational leader, you're balancing, how do I keep this organization functional? Like, I don't want to implode it by releasing too much of this information or allowing dissent or discontent to just take over. And that's a real risk. And at the same time, you don't want to stifle that. And it takes a lot of very nuanced understanding, and very little baby steps, to be able to move towards a healthy organization." This work is conspicuously absent at the largest and most powerful institutions. Still, the deep change that leaders of smaller organizations are creating is vital.

In November 2020, almost exactly three years after he was removed from Gloucester Stage, Israel Horovitz died. His anticlimactic death, despite obituaries in major media outlets, was drowned out by a news cycle dominated by the presidential election and the pandemic. Gloucester Stage published a eulogy on their website that celebrated his artistic accomplishments without pretending away his abuse: "Gloucester Stage acknowledges that accusations of sexual harassment led to Horovitz's separation from the organization. The Company has since focused the core mission of developing new works to invest in women playwrights, raise up BIPOC storytellers, and create a residency program that is a safe harbor for new playwrights," it read. "Gloucester Stage is equally committed to a respectful and professional creative environment where new work can develop, company members are engaged to bring it forward, and an increased dialogue with our artists and audience is promoted. Israel Horovitz's dedication to socially relevant and intellectually stimulating theater was the cornerstone of Gloucester Stage Company's first forty years. That concept will live on, through new voices, for the next forty more."[10]

SO, WHAT SHOULD I DO?
WHAT SHOULD I TELL
MY DAUGHTER?

There's a reason compliance-based safety advice has an endless shelf life on the internet. It makes us feel like we're in control. It takes the complex and unpredictable realities of violence and promises to spare us. All we have to do in return is stay away from white vans or stop wearing ponytails or never go shopping alone.

It's important to challenge simplistic directives like these, but it can be just as unsatisfying to replace them with too much nuance. Having nothing more than "It's complicated" or "Trust yourself" or "If anything happens, it's not your fault" may not be enough. The need to feel a sense of control is compelling. A research review led by neuropsychologist Lauren Leotti shows that believing we have choice in stressful situations has both psychological and biological benefits, from increased immune functioning to a stronger sense of self.[1]

Other people's violence is not your fault. But that doesn't have to mean there is nothing you can do about it. There are practical strategies that can keep you safer that don't perpetuate stereotypes or stigma. You don't have to restrict your life or diminish yourself to use them. I had a conversation years ago with a group of parents whose daughters were taking a self-defense class. Some took comfort knowing their girls were learning to protect themselves, but others were frustrated. *Why do we live in a world where interrupting a sexual assault is as much a life skill as doing laundry?*

It's a fair question. That's why safety through resistance is so important. It doesn't just prepare people for the worst; it also prepares them for the best. Sometimes we feel fear because our safety is at risk. Other times, we're afraid because we're taking bold steps to make our lives bigger—traveling to a new country, taking a challenging job, speaking up for an important cause. Being bold and focused when we're afraid helps us interrupt violence. It also helps us live our values and pursue our dreams.

You can make safety choices that challenge the shame, secrecy, and inequity that help gender-based violence thrive. You can make safety choices that further social change.

Here are some options:

Communicate your boundaries and pay attention to how people react. One of the most powerful tools we have to assess whether a person is trustworthy is to say what we want and don't want. If that person ignores or dismisses you, it could mean they are capable of serious harm. Not everyone who disregards our limits is capable of violence, but many people who abuse start by eroding smaller boundaries.

Describe the behavior that alarms you. Be specific. You're getting too close to me. I said 'No' and you didn't stop. You're blocking my exit. Statements like these can clarify what line is being crossed. Much abuse and violence requires secrecy. A person who tries to hurt us may want us to be too embarrassed or afraid to call attention to what they're doing. Naming the specific behavior makes it harder for this person to hide or deny their actions.

Get loud. It works. The National Crime Victimization Survey and other data show that forceful resistance is more likely to stop an attempted sexual assault than non-forceful resistance.[2] Using a strong voice can also call attention to a situation.

Keep it simple. We don't owe someone who is harassing or threatening an explanation. Use simple phrases that state what you want: "Leave me alone!" or "Don't come any closer!" or "Stop!" It's OK to repeat yourself. If there's a bystander around who might be inclined to help us, yelling simple, descriptive phrases helps that person understand what's going on. If we are being recorded—by a person with a smartphone or an unseen surveillance camera—using phrases that make it clear that we don't feel safe can help us later if we need to establish that we acted in self-defense. Also, if you keep it simple and repeat yourself, you're not wasting energy on a complicated argument, energy that could be better used for making sure the person doesn't get too close to you.

Can you leave? If someone is threatening you or trying to start a fight, leaving may be the safest option. This is true whether the person trying to hurt you is someone you know or not. Leaving is safest when you have somewhere safer to go and a way to get there. If you're at a party and you have friends you trust downstairs, or you're close to a public place where you feel safer, go there. If possible, stay out of their reach while you exit, two or three arms' lengths apart if you can. While you're leaving, split your attention between looking where you're going and at the person who is threatening you. If you turn your back to the person, you can't see if they're coming after you. If you don't watch where you're going, you could fall or run into something.

Get distance and use obstacles. If leaving is not possible, get as far away from the person as you can, without putting yourself in a corner. This can mean stepping back to show that you feel threatened and don't want a fight. It can mean putting objects between you and them. Can you move around the room so there's a chair or couch or table between you? That way it will be harder for the person to grab or touch you.

Ask yourself, "Do I want this attention?" and feel free to end an interaction if the answer is no. This could be someone you don't know well asking increasingly intrusive questions about your life or a boss or coworker commenting on your appearance. We are not obligated to entertain people just because they want our attention.

Recognize and resist "parting shots." Nadia Telsey and Lauren Taylor, authors of *Get Empowered: A Practical Guide to Thrive, Heal, and Embrace Your Confidence in a Sexist World*, have identified what they call *parting shots*.[3] "When someone's manipulating us, they're likely to react to our assertiveness or other efforts to be safe by saying something designed to make us feel guilty, uncertain, bad, unworthy, unattractive, threatened, or some other difficult emotion. These statements may be a last-ditch attempt to get us to go along with them," they explain, "a way to keep us from talking about what they did, or a way for them to save face as they give up and leave us alone." Telsey and Taylor acknowledge that recognizing parting shots can help us keep from prolonging an unwanted interaction. "When faced with a parting shot," they suggest, "resist the urge to deny, argue, or respond. Instead you can choose not to respond or you can agree and reframe it." They also identify ways to prevent parting shots from affecting us psychologically. "Knowing that an aggressor is likely to use a parting shot can protect us from damage to our self-esteem and avoid kicking up self-doubt." The safest aggressor is the one who is walking away from you. So if someone is making a parting shot while they are on their way out, it can be helpful to let it go, especially if doing so can let them go.

Use a strong part of your body against a weak part of theirs. Physical striking is the least safe way to defend yourself, but sometimes it's the best option for a particular situation. Forceful resistance works. National Crime Victimization Survey (NCVS) research shows that yelling and fighting back are effective at stopping sexual assaults. At the same time, there is no evidence that any particular kick or strike is more effective than any other. In 2005, criminologists Jongyeon Tark and Gary Kleck published an analysis of the NCVS data looking for trends in the types of strikes that were most effective. They found none.[4] If physical resistance is your best—or only—choice, strike a part of the body that is vulnerable on everyone, like the eyes, head, or groin. If the person trying to hurt you is bigger or has more muscle, striking a vulnerable part of the body can equalize these advantages. The goal is not to be Ultimate Fighting Champions; it's to cause enough pain to end the threat.

If you are a parent, teach your kid that they can choose who they touch. And back them up when other adults try to touch them in ways they don't like. Teaching kids that they get to decide who they hug or kiss helps them learn their boundaries. Showing them you respect their boundaries, and you will support them when other adults might not, can help them learn to expect not to be touched in ways they don't like. This makes it easier for your kid to recognize boundary violations that are subtle and covert and to resist unwanted sexual advances across the lifespan.

If you are part of a highly targeted community, leaders in your community know best. For Black transgender women, disabled people, Indigenous women, or other highly targeted people, the prevailing evidence may not be relevant. People who aren't being effectively reached by researchers—or those who have cause to distrust government-run surveys—are not well represented by large-scale national surveys. Anti-violence activists and leaders in your community probably know the most about how to reduce harm.

If you are part of a community that is disproportionately criminalized for using self-defense, use resources like Survived & Punished and the Defending Self-Defense project to better understand how to protect yourself legally.

In some (but not all) cases, it can be effective to use a recording device that is in your control, like your personal phone, to make it harder for someone to argue that you were the aggressor. Resisting verbal harassment and threats with language that comes from self-defense law will make it harder to build a case against you. More than that, people who are leading legal defense efforts for survivors who have been criminalized will know the best strategies for establishing that you acted in self-defense.

Know when to de-escalate. If someone is angry but is not treating you like prey, the strategies are different. Listen to the nuance when people yell. Are they threatening you with violence or are they feeling wronged? Are they yelling at you because they're in the middle of their own crisis? If someone is agitated, the situation could still become violent, so do what you can to avoid being too close to them. But also if they are posing a threat to you because they are scared or frustrated, shutting them down may not be effective or ethical.

If they're escalated because they're trying to start a fight, use a calm and assertive tone and say, "I don't want to fight." Focus on keeping your distance, so they can't reach you. Be aware of the exit and give yourself a clear path to it. Also try to avoid blocking their path to the exit. If they're escalated because they are struggling with a crisis, offer empathy and do what you can to help. Listen to what they have to say. Some people become calmer if they feel like they're being heard.

If someone gives you safety advice, ask questions. If they don't have an answer, it could be baseless. If you're told not to go to the mall alone, ask if there is a documented increase in violence at the mall and if so, what types. Be critical of "common sense" if it's really just attempts to make your life smaller.

Gender-based violence is a systemic injustice that is enacted in intimate moments. A family friend is tickling your four-year-old and doesn't stop when she says she doesn't like it. A friend is passed out in an upstairs bedroom and the person who was giving them drinks all night wants to check on them and keeps pushing even when you assure him that they're fine. Intimate acts of resistance are not a substitute for political change, but they are integral to social change. Work to stop gender-based violence is incomplete without thousands of people making brave choices in small moments. People who aren't afraid of being labeled "uptight" or told they're overreacting. People who are afraid but are willing to take the risk. These intimate moments create a specific type of agency. They fortify us to create safer communities, and they enable us to interrupt harm. Small moments of resistance alone cannot bring about systemic change, but systemic change is impossible without them.

ACKNOWLEDGMENTS

I consider myself to be one of the luckiest people in the world to have Leila Campoli as an agent. Leila, you are discerning, encouraging, thoughtful, and engaged. Thank you for sticking with me for the years—and I mean years—it took to write this book. And thank you editor Haley Lynch for making my dream of publishing my book with Beacon Press a reality. Haley, you too are discerning, encouraging, thoughtful, and engaged. Every one of your comments made this book better, and your genuine enthusiasm kept me going. Thanks to the rest of the Beacon team: Marcy Barnes, Louis Roe, Alyssa Hassan, Frankie Karnedy, Caitlin Meyer, and Beth Richards.

A special thank-you to Emily Dolbear and Susan Lumenello for a copyediting process that far exceeded any reasonable expectations. Working with a team that understands the value of precision significantly improved this book. Emily, you are meticulous and diligent. The errors in my manuscript took seconds to make and hours to correct, so I am grateful for the care you took to make sure every quote was accurate, every person's name was spelled correctly, and every grammatical mistake was fixed. Susan, thank you for your discerning questions and genuine effort to understand all the nuances of my writing and my work. Thank you for exchanging a week's worth of emails over whether a sentence in the introduction should include the word "or" or "and." (I am not making this up or exaggerating.)

Thank you to the executive directors of the other IMPACT Violence Prevention organizations in the US and around the world: Donna Chaiet, Karen Chasen, Richard Chipping, Linda Leu, Carol Middleton, Rocio

Molina, Shanda Poitra, Alena Schaim, Jill Shames, Katie Skibbie, and Martha Thompson. Anyone who tries to sustain an IMPACT organization knows that there are times when the path will be twisted and risky and slow, but getting to share this work with you all makes the effort worth it. Thank you to my friends and collaborators in the empowerment self-defense movement: Lauren Bailey, Tasha Ina Church, Rachel Collins, Darlene DeFour, Coty DeLacretaz, Magdalena Dirico, Carmel Drewes, Kyren Epperson, Justine Halliwill, Julie Harmon, Jocelyn Hollander, Amy Jones, Brenda Jones, Ellen Krause-Grossman, Anne Kuzminsky, Arlene Limas, Brigit McCallum, Mark Nessel, Lindsay Orchowski, Michelle Pereira, Clara Porter, Kim Rivers, Candace Rushton, Clea Sarnquist, Susan "George" Schorn, Charlene Senn, Silvia Smart, Lauren R. Taylor, Yuko Uchikawa, and Lynne Marie Wanamaker. I have been changed for good by your brilliance, support, and integrity.

Thank you to the IMPACT Boston staff: Josh Alba, Autumn Buhl, Ben Comeau, Katiana Gordon, Sean Greene, Aaron Grossman, Will Lau, Michelle Morales, Lindsay Orchowski, Shay Orent, Alicia Ortiz, Rene Rives, Elaine Sanfilippo, Ruby Smolin, Kaya van der Meer, B Whitney, and Jeanine Woods. The whole world changed and everything stayed the same when I started writing this book. I could not have made it through the past few years if each of you hadn't stepped up and kept IMPACT going in ways that made it possible for me to give this book the time it needed. Thank you to all past members of the IMPACT Boston team. The work we do is complex, and no one person has all the ideas, so thank you to everyone who has influenced my thinking about safety, violence, and resistance. Not a day goes by that I don't feel grateful for the IMPACT Boston board of directors. What more do I need than your wisdom, clarity, and trust. Thank you to board president Elizabeth Bostic and board members Claudia Castillo, Rania Henriquez, Keith Jones, Jorge Ledesma, Nancy Lee, Yuki Nishizawa, Janice Philpot, and Bonnie Tai.

Thanks to our Turtle Mountain IMPACT family for bringing this work to Indigenous communities and showing us how IMPACT can be a force for cultural reclamation and strengthen the connections between body sovereignty and tribal sovereignty. In addition to fierce leader

Shanda Poitra, thanks to Mike Davis, Angie Decoteau, James Decoteau, Dorothy Henry, Loren Henry, and Chani Larocque. Centuries of silence will end because of your work.

Thank you to my Tuesday-night writing group: Shaya French, Elliot Marrow, Jules Patigian, Jenna Schlags, Rowan Wielblad, and the others who have dropped in over the years. Thank you for listening to draft after draft of this book with the rare combination of cheerleading and critical thinking I needed. Thank you also to the Wayward Writers for a drop-in writing group that got me writing on Saturday mornings and kept me going throughout the week.

I would not be a writer without skilled and thoughtful teachers. Thank you most of all to Alex Marzano-Lesnevich. I spent ten years writing the wrong book with no idea why it wasn't working. But after one conversation with Alex, after they read my very stuck five hundredth draft, I came to understand the kind of writer I am. Thank you to Grub Street, the writing center in Boston where I first took classes with Alex. Thanks to all the Grub Street writers whose classes helped me, notably Jenn DeLeon, Katrin Schumann, and Chris Boginski. Thanks to all the writing centers that went virtual in 2020, giving me the chance to write with skilled teachers from across the country. Most notably, thanks to Catapult, where Boyce Upholt taught a masterful class on how to weave reporting and narration together and Sari Botton taught an essay class that gave me the space and structure I needed to write the first paragraphs of *The Cost of Fear*. Thank you Susan Shapiro for virtual classes that taught me how to write pitches. Thank you to Claire Dederer and Hedgebrook for including me in the Radical Craft Retreat. And thank you Tony Amato, whose writing workshops turned me into a serious writer. Your prompts were provocative in the best way. How could I ever forget the day you handed each of us a deck of cards and told us to make a house? When mine fell, I started writing about the years I spent working nights in a domestic violence shelter. I trace every bit of clarity I have about my writing to that moment.

Thanks to everyone I interviewed. Thanks for being generous with your time, your insights, and your stories. Thank you to Lilia Garcia-Brower and Sandra Henriquez for fitting me into your schedules, which are busier than anything I could imagine.

And, I mean, when you've got friends like mine . . . Thank you David Pollack for being kind, gentle, intelligent, and perceptive. I'm always grateful for your fascinating questions. I don't know the words to tell you how it feels to watch someone with a PhD in math think through the realities of teaching feminist self-defense, but wow, do our conversations sharpen my mind. Thank you Martha Thompson for your warmth, wisdom, and academic library access. Thanks for the hours you spent helping me to talk through chapter 7. Thank you Molly Singer for helping me put the chapters in the right order. I will always be grateful for your smart and critical mind, and your talent with flipchart paper. Thank you to Lauren Bailey for sincere and meticulous editing help on early drafts. Emily and Susan, your job was much easier because Lauren taught me a few things about the right way to use a semicolon. Thank you to Patrick Calhoun, Ilene Fischer, Greg Lanza, Neil Savage, Amita Swadhin, and so many others.

Thank you to my family. Thanks to my mom, Carole Stone, for always knowing when I was on the right track, even when I didn't. Thanks to my sisters and their kids, and thank you to the rest of my giant, vibrant family, who can always be counted on to show up for celebrations, funerals, and everything in between. I don't know many other people who have actual relationships with more than ten of their first cousins once removed, but I'm glad I do. Thank you also to my dad, Jim.

There is a special relationship between writers and cafés where people can sit for hours with a laptop. It's not an exaggeration to say that half this book was written at Mariposa Bakery and Café in Cambridge, Massachusetts. It's up to the barista to create an environment where writers thrive. Thank you for all the encouragement, warmth, and extra orange slices. On the day I submitted my manuscript, they gave me a latte with foam in the shape of my name. Thank you to Aloe Domizio, Hiawatha King, Annie McGillen, Cindy Mei, Michele Mei, Ruth Park, Dina Preffer, Suhayl, Meaghan Sullivan, Eugene Xi, owner Suzanne Mermelstein, and everyone else who worked at Mariposa between 2022 and 2024.

Most of all, thank you to my partner, Mal Malme. Mal, you are the most human person I know—generous, funny, and always soaking up life down to your toes. I can only go to the hard and painful places that a person goes to when they write a book because I have you waiting on the other end. There's nothing we two can't face, and I never forget how lucky I am to go through life with you. Thank you also for having the ability to keep house plants alive. I do not share this talent.

NOTES

INTRODUCTION: SCARED AND POWERFUL

1. Jennifer S. Wong and Samantha Balemba, "The Effect of Victim Resistance on Rape Completion: A Meta-Analysis," *Trauma, Violence, & Abuse 19, no. 3* (2018): 352–65, https://doi.org/10.1177/1524838016663934.

2. Martha Thompson, "Falling Short: The White House Task Force to Protect Students from Sexual Assault," *IMPACT Chicago Blog*, July 21, 2014, http://impact chicago.blogspot.com/2014/07/stopping-sexual-assault-on-college.html.

3. UNICEF, "Gender-Based Violence in Emergencies," https://www.unicef.org /protection/gender-based-violence-in-emergencies.

4. Fiona Vera-Gray, *The Right Amount of Panic: How Women Trade Freedom for Safety* (Bristol, UK: Policy Press, 2018).

5. Jocelyn A. Hollander, "Women's Self-Defense and Sexual Assault Resistance: The State of the Field," *Sociology Compass* (June 19, 2018), https://doi.org/10.1111 /soc4.12597.

6. Amy Arnsten, "The Effects of Stress on Prefrontal Cortical Function," https:// www.youtube.com/watch?v=pFrdkDcPbjo.

7. US Bureau of Justice Statistics, "National Crime Victimization Survey Dashboard (N-DASH)," last updated April 23, 2024, ncvs.bjs.ojp.gov/Home.

CHAPTER 1: MONUMENTAL, UNSATISFYING VICTORIES

1. Lydia Saad, "Concerns About Sexual Harassment Higher Than in 1988," Gallup, November 3, 2017, https://news.gallup.com/poll/221216/concerns-sexual -harassment-higher-1998.aspx.

2. Lydia Saad, "Most in U.S. Back Funding for Sexual Violence Victims," Gallup, March 8, 2013, https://news.gallup.com/poll/161180/back-funding-sexual-violence -victims.aspx.

3. Pew Research Center, "More Than Twice as Many Americans Support Than Oppose the #MeToo Movement," September 29, 2022, https://www.pewresearch.org /social-trends/2022/09/29/more-than-twice-as-many-americans-support-than-oppose -the-metoo-movement.

4. Frank R. Baumgartner and Sarah McAdon, "There's Been a Big Change in How the Media Covers Sexual Assault," *Washington Post*, May 11, 2017, https://www .washingtonpost.com/news/monkey-cage/wp/2017/05/11/theres-been-a-big-change-in -how-the-news-media-cover-sexual-assault.

5. Mary P. Koss, Kevin M. Swartout, Elise C. Lopez, Raina V. Lamade, Elizabeth J. Anderson, Carolyn L. Brennan, and Robert A. Prentky, "The Scope of Rape Victimization and Perpetration Among National Samples of College Students Across 30 Years," *Journal of Interpersonal Violence* 37, nos. 1-2 (2022): NP25-NP47, https://doi .org/10.1177/08862605211050103.

6. US Bureau of Justice Statistics, "National Crime Victimization Survey Dashboard (N-DASH)," last updated April 23, 2024, ncvs.bjs.ojp.gov/Home.

7. US Bureau of Justice Statistics, *Hate Crime Victimization, 2005–2019*, https:// bjs.ojp.gov/press-release/hate-crime-victimization-2005-2019.

8. US Bureau of Justice Statistics, *Criminal Victimizations, 2018*, https://bjs.ojp .gov/content/pub/pdf/cv18.pdf.

9. Ira Glass, "My Lying Eyes: People Staring Squarely at the Truth, and Still Finding It Hard to Believe What They're Seeing," *This American Life*, aired May 6, 2022, https://www.thisamericanlife.org/770/my-lying-eyes.

10. Mary P. Koss, "Hidden, Unacknowledged, Acquaintance, and Date Rape: Looking Back, Looking Forward," *Psychology of Women Quarterly* 35, no. 2 (2011): 348–54, https://doi.org/10.1177/0361684311403856.

11. Koss et al., "The Scope of Rape Victimization and Perpetration Among National Samples of College Students Across 30 Years," NP25-NP47.

12. Association of American Universities, *Report on the AAU Campus Climate Survey on Sexual Assault and Misconduct*, January 17, 2020, https://www.aau.edu/sites /default/files/AAU-Files/Key-Issues/Campus-Safety/Revised%20Aggregate%20report %20%20and%20appendices%201-7_(01-16-2020_FINAL).pdf.

13. US Centers for Disease Control and Prevention, *The National Intimate Partner and Sexual Violence Survey 2016–17*, https://www.cdc.gov/violenceprevention/pdf/nisvs /nisvsreportonsexualviolence.pdf.

14. RaeAnn E. Anderson, Kristin E. Silver, Alyssa M. Ciampaglia, Amanda M. Vitale, and Douglas L. Delahanty, "The Frequency of Sexual Perpetration in College Men: A Systematic Review of Reported Prevalence Rates from 2000 to 2017," *Trauma, Violence, & Abuse* 22, no. 3 (2021): 481–95, https://doi.org/10.1177/1524838 019860619.

15. Audrey Carlsen, "#MeToo Brought Down 201 Powerful Men. Nearly Half of Their Replacements Are Women," *New York Times*, October 29, 2018, https://www .nytimes.com/interactive/2018/10/23/us/metoo-replacements.html.

16. Personal communication from GrantsPolicy@OD.NIH.gov, received April 21, 2023.

17. Stacey H. Hust, Emily G. Marett, Ming Lei, Chunbo Ren, and Wenia Ran, "*Law & Order, CSI,* and *NCIS*: The Association Between Exposure to Crime Drama Franchises, Rape Myth Acceptance, and Sexual Consent Negotiation Among College Students," *Journal of Health Communincation* 20, no. 12 (2015): 1369–81, doi: 10.1080/10810730.2015.1018615, Epub September 29, 2015, PMID: 26418170.

18. Charles E. Cobb Jr., *This Nonviolent Stuff'll Get You Killed: How Guns Made the Civil Rights Movement Possible* (New York: Basic Books, 2015).

19. M. Aziz, "Built with Empty Fists: The Rise and Circulation of Black Power Martial Artistry During the Cold War," PhD diss., University of Michigan, Ann Arbor, 2020.

20. Aziz, "Built with Empty Fists."

21. Wendy L. Rouse, *Her Own Hero: The Origins of the Women's Self-Defense Movement* (New York: NYU Press, 2017), 136.

22. Rouse, *Her Own Hero*, 149.

23. Patricia Searles and Ronald Berger, "The Feminist Self-Defense Movement: A Case Study," *Gender & Society* 1, no. 1 (1987): 61–84, https://doi.org/10.1177/089124387001001004.

24. Martha McCaughey, *Real Knockouts: The Physical Feminism of Women's Self-Defense* (New York: New York University Press, 1997), 178.

CHAPTER 2: THE COST OF FEAR

1. Fiona Vera-Gray, *The Right Amount of Panic: How Women Trade Freedom for Safety* (Bristol, UK: Policy Press, 2018).

2. Carol W. Runyan, Cari Casteel, Kathryn E. Moracco, and Tamera Coyne-Beasley, "US Women's Choices of Strategies to Protect Themselves from Violence," *Injury Prevention* 13, no. 4 (August 2007): 270–75, doi: 10.1136/ip.2006.014415.

3. Shannon K. Jacobsen, "Gendered Responses to Fear of Victimization? A Comparative Study of Students' Precautionary and Avoidance Strategies in Suburban and Urban Contexts," *Violence Against Women* (2024), https://doi.org/10.1177/10778012241228284.

4. Justin McCarthy and Camille Wong, "Majority of U.S. Black Women Don't Feel Safe Walking Alone," *Gallup Blog*, March 8, 2023, https://news.gallup.com/opinion/gallup/471236/majority-black-women-don-feel-safe-walking-alone.aspx.

5. Jennifer Wong and Samantha Balemba, "The Effect of Victim Resistance on Rape Completion: A Meta-Analysis," *Trauma, Violence & Abuse* 19, no. 3 (2018): 352–65, https://doi.org/10.1177/1524838016663934.

6. Jongyeon Tark and Gary Kleck, "Resisting Rape: The Effects of Victim Self-Protection on Rape Completion and Injury," *Violence Against Women* 20, no. 3 (2014): 270–92, doi: 10.1177/1077801214526050.

7. Nicole Bedera and Kristjane Nordmeyer, "'Never Go Out Alone': An Analysis of College Rape Prevention Tips," *Sexuality & Culture* 19 (2015): 533–42, https://doi.org/10.1007/s12119-015-9274-5.

8. Cora Peterson, Sarah DeGue, Curtis Florence, and Colby N. Lokey, "Lifetime Economic Burden of Rape Among U.S. Adults," *American Journal of Preventive Medicine* 52, no. 6 (June 2017): 691–701, doi: 10.1016/j.amepre.2016.11.014. Epub 2017 Jan 30. PMID: 28153649; PMCID: PMC5438753.

9. NBC Boston, "Protesters Confronted by Counter-Protesters Outside Boston Children's Hospital," September 18, 2022, https://www.nbcboston.com/news/local/no-arrests-after-protesters-counter-protesters-gather-outside-boston-childrens-hospital/2837606/.

CHAPTER 3: HOW NOT TO GET STRANGLED BY YOUR PONYTAIL

1. Dan Schilling, *The Power of Awareness: And Other Secrets from the World's Foremost Spies, Detectives, and Special Operators on How to Stay Safe and Save Your Life* (New York: Grand Central, 2021), 39–40.

2. Schilling, *The Power of Awareness*, 40.

3. Empowerment Self-Defense Alliance, "Code of Ethics for Practitioners of Empowerment Self-Defense," https://www.empowermentsd.org/code-of-ethics.

CHAPTER 4: BAD PEOPLE DO BAD THINGS

1. US Centers for Disease Control and Prevention, "Fast Facts: Preventing Child Sexual Abuse," https://www.cdc.gov/violenceprevention/childsexualabuse/fastfact.html.

2. Brendan Nyhan, "Facts and Myths About Misperceptions," *Journal of Economic Perspectives* 34, no. 3 (2020): 220–36, https://www.jstor.org/stable/26923548.

3. Jonas T. Kaplan, Sarah I. Gimbel, and Sam Harris, "Neural Correlates of Maintaining One's Political Beliefs in the Face of Counterevidence," *Scientific Reports* 6 (2106): 39589, doi: 10.1038/srep39589. PMID: 28008965; PMCID: PMC5180221.

4. Drew Westen, Pavel S. Blagov, Keith Harenski, Clint Kilts, and Stephan Hamann, "Neural Bases of Motivated Reasoning: An FMRI Study of Emotional Constraints on Partisan Political Judgment in the 2004 U.S. Presidential Election," *Journal of Cognitive Neuroscience* 18, no. 11 (2006): 1947–58, doi:10.1162/jocn.2006.18.11.1947.

5. Sam Harris, Jonas T. Kaplan, Ashley Curiel, Susan Y. Bookheimer, Marco Iacoboni, and Mark S. Cohen, "The Neural Correlates of Religious and Nonreligious Belief," *PloS One* 4, no. 10 (October 1, 2009), doi:10.1371/journal.pone.0007272.

6. Hugo Mercier and Dan Sperber, *The Enigma of Reason* (Cambridge, MA: Harvard University Press, 2019).

7. Kristen Zgoba and Meghan Mitchell, "The Effectiveness of Sex Offender Registration and Notification: A Meta-Analysis of 25 Years of Findings," *Journal of Experimental Criminology* 19 (2021), doi: 10.1007/s11292-021-09480-z.

8. US Department of Justice, "Legislative History of Sex Offender Registration and Notification," https://smart.ojp.gov/sorna/current-law/legislative-history.

9. National Association for Rational Sex Offense Laws, "NARSOL Calls for End to Sex Offender Registries," October 27, 2022, https://www.narsol.org/2022/10/press-release-narsol-calls-for-end-to-sex-offender-registries.

10. David Patrick Connor and Richard Tewksbury, "Public and Professional Views of Sex Offender Registration and Notification," *Criminology, Criminal Justice, Law and Society* 18, no. 1 (2017): 1–27, https://ccjls.scholasticahq.com.

11. Connor and Tewksbury, "Public and Professional Views of Sex Offender Registration and Notification," 1–27.

12. Andrew Harris and Kelly Socia, "What's in a Name? Evaluating the Effects of the 'Sex Offender' Label on Public Opinions and Beliefs," *Sexual Abuse: A Journal of Research and Treatment*, 28, no. 7 (2014): 1–19, doi: 10.1177/1079063214564391.

13. Joshua C. Cochran, Elisa L. Toman, Ryan T. Shields, and Daniel P. Mears, "A Uniquely Punitive Turn? Sex Offenders and the Persistence of Punitive Sanctioning," *Journal of Research in Crime and Delinquency* 58, no. 1 (2021): 74–118, https://doi.org/10.1177/0022427820941172.

14. "United States Department of Justice: Adult Sex Offender Management," July 2015, https://smart.ojp.gov/sites/g/files/xyckuh231/files/media/document/adultsexoffendermanagement.pdf.

15. "United States Department of Justice: The Prosecution of Child Sexual Abuse: A Partnership to Improve Outcomes," 2019, https://www.ojp.gov/pdffiles1/nij/grants/252768.pdf.

16. Nicole Pittman and Human Rights Watch, *Raised on the Registry: The Irreparable Harm of Placing Children on Sex Offender Registries in the US*, May 1, 2013, https://www.hrw.org/report/2013/05/01/raised-registry/irreparable-harm-placing-children-sex-offender-registries-us.

17. Michael F. Caldwell, "Quantifying the Decline in Juvenile Sexual Recidivism Rates," *Psychology, Public Policy, and Law* 22, no. 4 (2016): 414–26, https://doi.org /10.1037/law0000094.

18. Reuters, "Fact Check: California Bill Does Not Legalize Pedophilia," September 4, 2020, https://www.reuters.com/article/idUSKBN25V21O.

19. Alliance for Safety and Justice, *Crime Survivors Speak: National Survey of Victims' Views on Safety and Justice*, September 2022, https://allianceforsafetyandjustice .org/wp-content/uploads/2022/09/Alliance-for-Safety-and-Justice-Crime-Survivors -Speak-September-2022.pdf.

20. Judith Herman, *Truth and Repair: How Trauma Survivors Envision Justice* (New York: Basic Books, 2023).

21. Herman, *Truth and Repair*, 111.

22. Herman, *Truth and Repair*, 112.

23. Leah Lakshmi Piepzna-Samarasinha and Ejeris Dixon, *Beyond Survival: Strategies and Stories from the Transformative Justice Movement* (Chico: AK Press, 2020).

24. Ejeris Dixon, "Building Community Safety," in Piepzna-Samarasinha and Dixon, *Beyond Survival*, 15–26.

25. Ashley F. Jespersen, Martin L. Lalumière, and Michael C. Seto, "Sexual Abuse History Among Adult Sex Offenders and Non-Sex Offenders: A Meta-Analysis," *Child Abuse & Neglect*, 33, no 3 (2009): 179–92, doi:10.1016/j.chiabu.2008.07.004.

26. Citizens for Juvenile Justice, "Criminal Justice Reform Act of 2018: A Path Forward for Juvenile Justice," https://www.cfjj.org/jjreforms-2018.

27. National Juvenile Justice Network, "Raising the Minimum Age for Prosecuting Children," https://www.njjn.org/our-work/raising-the-minimum-age-for -prosecuting-children.

CHAPTER 5: COMPLIANCE BREEDS ABUSE

1. Steffi Lee, "Ex-Taekwondo Champion Speaks Out Against Banned Olympic Coach from Texas," *Concho Valley*, April 6, 2018, https://www.conchovalleyhomepage .com/news/ex-taekwondo-champion-speaks-out-against-banned-olympic-coach -from-texas/

2. Jeremy Fuchs, "Terror in Taekwondo," *Sports Illustrated*, September 5, 2018, https://www.si.com/olympics/2018/09/05/taekwondo-us-olympics-steven-lopez-jean -lopez-sexual-misconduct-lawsuit.

3. Ronan Farrow, "From Aggressive Overtures to Sexual Assaults: Harvey Weinstein's Victims Tell Their Stories," *New Yorker,* October 10, 2017, https://www.newyorker .com/news/news-desk/from-aggressive-overtures-to-sexual-assault-harvey-weinsteins -accusers-tell-their-stories; Jodi Kantor and Megan Twohey, "Harvey Weinstein Paid Off Sexual Harassment Accusers for Decades," *New York Times*, October 5, 2017, https:// www.nytimes.com/2017/10/05/us/harvey-weinstein-harassment-allegations.html.

4. Dave Hingsburger, *Just Say Know! Understanding and Reducing the Risk of Sexual Victimization* (Richmond Hill, Ontario: Diverse City Press, 1995).

5. Hingsburger, *Just Say Know!*, 80.

6. Amy Judy and Wisconsin's Violence Against Women with Disabilities and Deaf Women Project, "Creating Safety by Asking: What Makes People Vulnerable?" 2011, https://www.disabilityrightswi.org/wp-content/uploads/2018/06/Creating -Safety.pdf.

7. Judy and Wisconsin's Violence Against Women with Disabilities and Deaf Women Project, "Creating Safety by Asking," 3.

8. Judy and Wisconsin's Violence Against Women with Disabilities and Deaf Women Project, "Creating Safety by Asking," 23.

9. Judy and Wisconsin's Violence Against Women with Disabilities and Deaf Women Project, "Creating Safety by Asking," 27.

10. Judy and Wisconsin's Violence Against Women with Disabilities and Deaf Women Project, "Creating Safety by Asking," 17.

11. Judy and Wisconsin's Violence Against Women with Disabilities and Deaf Women Project, "Creating Safety by Asking," 26.

12. Hingsburger, *Just Say Know!*, 80–81.

13. Used and Abused Series Home Page, *New York Times*, https://archive.nytimes.com/www.nytimes.com/interactive/nyregion/abused-and-used-series-page.htm.

14. Dan Barry, "The 'Boys' in the Bunkhouse," *New York Times*, March 9, 2014, https://www.nytimes.com/interactive/2014/03/09/us/the-boys-in-the-bunkhouse.html.

15. Tricia Bruce, *Faithful Revolution: How Voice of the Faithful Is Changing the Church* (New York: Oxford University Press, 2011).

16. RAND Corporation, *Countering Sexual Assault and Sexual Harassment in the U.S. Military: Lessons from RAND Research*, July 19, 2021, https://www.rand.org/pubs/research_reports/RRA1318-1.html.

17. US Department of Defense, "Mental Health Evaluations of Members of the Military Services," https://www.esd.whs.mil/Portals/54/Documents/DD/issuances/dodi/649004p.pdf.

18. Seth Harp, "She Asked the Army to Investigate a Rape Trial. They Fired Her," *Rolling Stone*, January 4, 2022, https://www.rollingstone.com/culture/culture-features/army-rape-trial-special-forces-fort-bragg-1277246.

CHAPTER 6: NOT OVERREACTING

1. National Women's Law Center and Time's Up, *Coming Forward: Key Trends and Data from the Time's Up Legal Defense Fund*, https://nwlc.org/wp-content/uploads/2020/10/NWLC-Intake-Report_FINAL_2020-10-13.pdf.

2. Blair Druhan Bullock, "Uncovering Harassment Retaliation," *Alabama Law Review*, 29, no. 2 (2021): 671–721, https://www.law.ua.edu/lawreview/files/2021/05/1-Bullock-671-721.pdf.

3. Martha E. Thompson, "Empowerment Through Feminist Self-Defense: The IMPACT Lasts," *Violence Against Women* 29, no. 14 (2023): 2915–40, doi:10.1177/10778012231197576.

4. Sara E. Crann, Charlene Y. Senn, H. Lorraine Radtke, and Karen L. Hobden, "'I Felt Powerful and Confident': Women's Use of What They Learned in Feminist Sexual Assault Resistance Education," *Psychology of Women Quarterly* 46, no. 2 (June 2022): 147–61, doi: 10.1177/03616843211043948.

5. Jocelyn A. Hollander, "'I Can Take Care of Myself': The Impact of Self-Defense Training on Women's Lives," *Violence Against Women* 10, no. 3 (2004): 205–35, https://doi.org/10.1177/1077801203256202.

6. Laura Siller, Katie M. Edwards, Leon Leader Charge, Simone Bordeaux, Damon Leader Charge, and Ramona Herrington, "'I Learned That I Am Worth Defending': A Process Evaluation of a Sexual Assault Prevention Program Implemented on

an Indian Reservation," *Journal of Commuity Psychology* 49, no. 7 (September 2021): 2221–37, https://doi.org/10.1002/jcop.22632.

7. Maiya E. Hotchkiss, Lisa Weinberg, and Danielle S. Berke, "Implementation of Empowerment Self-Defense Programming in a University Counseling Center: An Effective Sexual Violence Prevention Delivery Model," *Journal of American College Health* (2022): 1–9. https://doi.org/10.1080/07448481.2022.2115299.

8. Maiya E. Hotchkiss, "Tailoring Evidence-Based Violence Prevention Programming for Trans Women and Trans Femmes: Findings from a Community-Based Clinical Trial," Presentation at Association of Behavioral and Cognitive Therapies, 56th Annual Conference, New York, NY, November 17–20, 2022.

9. Thompson, "Empowerment Through Feminist Self-Defense," 2915–40.

CHAPTER 7: THE EVIDENCE AND ITS DISCONTENTS

1. Jan Hoffman, "College Rape Prevention Program Proves a Rare Success," *New York Times*, June 10, 2015, https://www.nytimes.com/2015/06/12/health/college-rape-prevention-program-proves-a-rare-success.html.

2. Sarah DeGue, Linda Anne Valle, Melissa K. Holt, Greta M. Massetti, Jennifer L. Matjasko, and Andra Teten Tharp, "A Systematic Review of Primary Prevention Strategies for Sexual Violence Perpetration," *Aggression and Violent Behavior* 19, no. 4 (2014): 346–62, doi:10.1016/j.avb.2014.05.004.

3. Eilene Zimmerman, "Campuses Struggle with Approaches for Preventing Sexual Assault," *New York Times*, June 22, 2016, https://www.nytimes.com/2016/06/23/education/campuses-struggle-with-approaches-for-preventing-sexual-assault.html.

4. Charlene Y. Senn, Misha Eliasziw, Paula C. Barata, Wilfreda E. Thurston, Ian R. Newby-Clark, H. Lorraine Radtke, and Karen L. Hobden, "Efficacy of a Sexual Assault Resistance Program for University Women," *New England Journal of Medicine* 372, no. 24 (2015): 2326–35, doi: 10.1056/NEJMsa1411131.

5. Jocelyn A. Hollander and Jeanine Cunningham, "Empowerment Self-Defense Training in a Community Population," *Psychology of Women Quarterly* 44, no. 2 (2020): 187–202, https://doi.org/10.1177/0361684319897937.

6. Jocelyn A. Hollander, "Does Self-Defense Training Prevent Sexual Violence Against Women?" *Violence Against Women* 20, no. 3 (2014): 252–69, doi:10.1177/1077801214526046.

7. Clea Sarnquist, Jake Sinclair, Benjamin Omondi Mboya, Nickson Langat, Lee Paiva, Bonnie Halpern-Felsher, Neville H. Golden, Yvonne A. Maldonado, and Michael T. Baiocchi, "Evidence That Classroom-Based Behavioral Interventions Reduce Pregnancy-Related School Dropout Among Nairobi Adolescents," *Health Education & Behavior* 44, no. 2 (2017): 297–303, doi:10.1177/1090198116657777.

8. Jessica Valenti, "We Need to Stop Rapists, Not Change Who Gets Raped," *The Guardian*, June 12, 2015, https://www.theguardian.com/commentisfree/2015/jun/12/stop-rapists-not-change-who-gets-raped.

9. Gabby Bess, "This Controversial Program Teaches Women to Spot 'Pre-Rape' Warning Signs," *Vice*, October 17, 2017, https://www.vice.com/en/article/a3kpz4/this-controversial-program-teaches-women-to-spot-pre-rape-warning-signs#.

10. Libby Nelson, "Teaching Women to Avoid Rape Works, but It's Controversial," *Vox*, June 15, 2015, https://www.vox.com/2015/6/15/8783171/rape-study-nejm.

11. Jesse Singal, "A Promising New Approach to Fighting Campus Sexual Assault," *The Cut*, June 29, 2015, https://www.thecut.com/2015/06/promising-approach-to -fighting-college-rape.html.

12. Kathleen Basile, "A Comprehensive Approach to Sexual Violence Prevention," *New England Journal of Medicine* 372, no. 24 (2015): 2350–52, doi:10.1056/NEJM e1503952.

13. Charlene Y. Senn, Misha Eliasziw, Karen L. Hobden, Ian R. Newby-Clark, Paula C. Barata, H. Lorraine Radtke, and Wilfreda E. Thurston, "Secondary and 2-Year Outcomes of a Sexual Assault Resistance Program for University Women," *Psychology of Women Quarterly* 41, no. 2 (2017): 147–62, https://doi.org/10.1177 /0361684317690119.

14. Lindsay M. Orchowski, Christine A. Gidycz, and Holly Raffle, "Evaluation of a Sexual Assault Risk Reduction and Self-Defense Program: A Prospective Analysis of a Revised Protocol," *Psychology of Women Quarterly* 32, no. 2 (2008): 204–18, https:// doi.org/10.1111/j.1471-6402.2008.00425.x.

15. Laurie M. Graham, Venita Embry, Belinda-Rose Young, Rebecca J. Macy, Kathryn E. Moracco, Heather Luz McNaughton Reyes, and Sandra L. Martin, "Evaluations of Prevention Programs for Sexual, Dating, and Intimate Partner Violence for Boys and Men: A Systematic Review," *Trauma, Violence & Abuse* 22, no. 3 (2021): 439–65, doi:10.1177/1524838019851158.

16. Rory Newlands and William O'Donohue, "A Critical Review of Sexual Violence Prevention on College Campuses," *Acta Psychopathologica* (2016): 1–13, doi:10.4172/2469-6676.100040.

17. Graham et al., "Evaluations of Prevention Programs for Sexual, Dating, and Intimate Partner Violence for Boys and Men."

18. Lauren A. Wright, Nelson O. O. Zounlome, and Susan C. Whiston, "The Effectiveness of Male-Targeted Sexual Assault Prevention Programs: A Meta-Analysis," *Trauma, Violence & Abuse* 2, no. 5 (2020): 859–69, doi:10.1177/1524838018801330.

19. Gabriela N. Mujal, Meghan E. Taylor, Jessica L. Fry, Tatiana H. Gochez-Kerr, and Nancy L. Weaver, "A Systematic Review of Bystander Interventions for the Prevention of Sexual Violence," *Trauma, Violence & Abuse* 22, no. 2 (2021): 381–96, doi:10.1177/1524838019849587.

20. Nada Elias-Lambert and Beverly M. Black, "Bystander Sexual Violence Prevention Program: Outcomes for High- and Low-Risk University Men," *Journal of Interpersonal Violence* 31, no. 19 (2016): 3211–35, doi:10.1177/0886260515584346.

21. Kelsey Banton, Ronald D. Williams, and Jeff M. Housman, "Systematic Review of College-Based Bystander Interventions to Reduce Sexual Violence," *Health Behavior and Policy Review* 10, no. 2 (March 2023): 1204–17, doi: https://doi.org /10.14485/HBPR.10.2.2.

22. Jennifer Katz and Christine E. Merrilees, "White Female Bystanders' Responses to a Black Woman at Risk for Sexual Assault: Positive Effects of Intergroup Contact," *Violence and Victims* 33, no. 4 (2018): 739–45, doi:10. 1891/0886-6708.VV -D-17-00062.

23. Ann L. Coker, Bonnie S. Fisher, Heather M. Bush, Suzanne C. Swan, Corrine M. Williams, Emily R. Clear, and Sarah DeGue, "Evaluation of the Green Dot Bystander Intervention to Reduce Interpersonal Violence Among College Students

Across Three Campuses," *Violence Against Women* 21, no. 12 (December 2015): 1507–27, doi: 10.1177/1077801214545284.

24. Newlands and O'Donohue, "A Critical Review of Sexual Violence Prevention on College Campuses."

25. Lindsay M. Orchowski, Christine A. Gidycz, and Kathryn Kraft, "Resisting Unwanted Sexual and Social Advances: Perspectives of College Women and Men," *Journal of Interpersonal Violence* 36, no. 7–8 (2021): NP4049–NP4073, doi:10.1177 /0886260518781805.

26. Lindsay M. Orchowski, Daniel W. Oesterle, and Michelle Haikalis, "What Stops Unwanted Sexual and Social Advances Made by Heavy Drinking College Men?" *Journal of Interpersonal Violence* 37, no. 23–24 (2022): NP22250–NP22272, doi:10.1177/08862605211072157.

27. Bruce Taylor and Nan D. Stein, *Shifting Boundaries: Final Report on an Experimental Evaluation of a Youth Dating Violence Prevention Program in New York City Middle Schools*, US Department of Justice, October 16, 2011, https://www.ojp.gov /pdffiles1/nij/grants/236175.pdf.

28. Ann L. Coker, Heather M. Bush, Patricia G. Cook-Craig, Sarah A. DeGue, Emily R. Clear, Candace J. Brancato, Bonnie S. Fisher, and Eileen A. Recktenwald, "RCT Testing Bystander Effectiveness to Reduce Violence," *American Journal of Preventive Medicine* 52, no. 5 (2017): 566–78, doi:10.1016/j.amepre.2017.01.020.

29. Katie M. Edwards, Victoria L Banyard, Emily A. Waterman, Kimberly J. Mitchell, Lisa M. Jones, Laura M. Mercer Kollar, Skyler Hopfauf, and Briana Simon, "Evaluating the Impact of a Youth-Led Sexual Violence Prevention Program: Youth Leadership Retreat Outcomes," *Prevention Science: The Official Journal of the Society for Prevention Research* 23, no. 8 (2022): 1379–93, doi:10.1007/s11121-022-01343-x.

30. US Centers for Disease Control and Prevention, *STOP SV: A Technical Package to Prevent Sexual Violence, 2016*, https://stacks.cdc.gov/view/cdc/39126.

31. Melanie S. Dove, Douglas W. Dockery, Murray A. Mittleman, Joel Schwartz, Eileen M. Sullivan, Lois Keithly, and Thomas Land, "The Impact of Massachusetts' Smoke-Free Workplace Laws on Acute Myocardial Infarction Deaths," *American Journal of Public Health* 100, no. 11 (2010): 2206–12, doi:10.2105/AJPH.2009.189662.

32. James C. Fell and Robert B. Voas, "Mothers Against Drunk Driving (MADD): The First 25 Years," *Traffic Injury Prevention* 7, no. 3 (2006): 195–212, doi:10.1080 /15389580600727705.

33. Todd S. Purdum, "St. Paul's Before and After the Owen Labrie Rape Trial," *Vanity Fair*, March 1, 2016, https://www.vanityfair.com/news/2016/03/st-pauls-owen -labrie-rape-trial.

34. Danny Hakim and Vivian Wang, "Eric Schneiderman Resigns as New York Attorney General Amid Assault Claims by 4 Women," *New York Times*, May 17, 2018, https://www.nytimes.com/2018/05/07/nyregion/new-york-attorney-general-eric -schneiderman-abuse.html.

35. US Centers for Disease Control and Prevention, "Violence Prevention: Funded Research," https://www.cdc.gov/violenceprevention/fundinghub/funded programs/research-awards.html.

36. Elizabeth Miller, Kelley A. Jones, Alison J. Culyba, Taylor Paglisotti, Namita Dwarakanath, Michael Massof, Zoe Feinstein, Katie A. Ports, Dorothy Espelage,

Julie Pulerwitz, Aapta Garg, Jane Kato-Wallace, and Kaleab Z. Abebe, "Effect of a Community-Based Gender Norms Program on Sexual Violence Perpetration by Adolescent Boys and Young Men: A Cluster Randomized Clinical Trial," *JAMA Network Open* 3, no. 12 (December 2020): e2028499, doi:10.1001/jamanetworkopen.2020.28499.

37. Alison J. Culyba, Barbara Fuhrman, Gary Barker, Kaleab Z. Abebe, and Elizabeth Miller, "Primary Versus Secondary Prevention Effects of a Gender-Transformative Sexual Violence Prevention Program Among Male Youth: A Planned Secondary Analysis of a Randomized Clinical Trial," *Journal of Interpersonal Violence* 38, no. 19 e202849920 (2023): 11220–242, doi:10.1177/08862605231179717.

38. Randall Waechter and Van Ma, "Sexual Violence in America: Public Funding and Social Priority," *American Journal of Public Health* 105, no. 12 (2015): 2430–37, doi:10.2105/AJPH.2015.302860.

39. Jennifer S. Hirsch and Claude A. Mellins, *Sexual Health Initiative to Foster Transformation (SHIFT) Final Report*, March 2019, https://sexualrespect.columbia.edu/sites/default/files/content/Images/shift_final_report_4-11-19_1.pdf.

40. Jennifer S. Hirsch and Shamus Khan, *Sexual Citizens: Sex, Power, and Assault on Campus* (New York: W. W. Norton, 2020).

41. Hirsch and Khan, *Sexual Citizens*, 266.

42. Hirsch and Khan, *Sexual Citizens*, 266.

43. Charlene Y. Senn, Jocelyn A. Hollander, and Christine A. Gidycz, "What Works? Critical Components of Effective Sexual Violence Interventions for Women on College and University Campuses," in *Sexual Assault Risk Reducton and Resistance*, ed. Lindsay Orchowski and Christine A. Gidycz (Cambridge: Elsevier, 2018).

44. Leanne R. Brecklin and Rena K. Middendorf, "The Group Dynamics of Women's Self-Defense Training," *Violence Against Women* 20, no. 3 (2014): 326–42, doi:10.1177/1077801214526044.

45. Caitlin M. Pincotti and Holly K. Orcutt, "Rape Aggression Defense: Unique Self-Efficacy Benefits for Survivors of Sexual Trauma," *Violence Against Women* 24, no. 5 (2018): 528–44, https://doi.org/10.1177/1077801217708885.

46. Darcy Shannon Cox, "An Analysis of Two Forms of Self-Defense Training and Their Impact on Women's Sense of Personal Safety Self-Efficacy," PsyD diss., Old Dominion University, 1999, doi: 10.25777/pb25-y427.

47. Elizabeth Ozer and Alfred Bandura, "Mechanisms Governing Empowerment Effects: A Self-Efficacy Analysis," *Journal of Personality and Social Psychology* 58, no. 3 (1990): 472–86, doi:10.1037//0022-3514.58.3.472.

48. *Framingham Heart Study*, https://www.framinghamheartstudy.org.

CHAPTER 8: RESISTING RACISM

1. "Marissa Alexander: Survived and Punished," https://bcrw.barnard.edu/videos/marissa-alexander-survived-and-punished.

2. Christine Hauser, "Florida Woman Whose 'Stand Your Ground' Defense Was Rejected Is Released," *New York Times*, February 7, 2017, https://www.nytimes.com/2017/02/07/us/marissa-alexander-released-stand-your-ground.html.

3. "Free Marissa Now," http://www.freemarissanow.org.

4. Mariame Kaba, *No Selves to Defend: The Legacy of Criminalizing Women of Color for Self-Defense*, https://noselves2defend.files.wordpress.com/2016/09/noselvestodefend_v5.pdf.

5. Emily Thuma, *All Our Trials: Prisons, Policing, and the Feminist Fight to End Violence* (Urbana: University of Illinois Press, 2019).

6. Nancy Matthews, *Confronting Rape: The Feminist Anti-Rape Movement and the State* (New York: Routledge, 1994).

7. Matthews, *Confronting Rape*, 153.

8. Matthews, *Confronting Rape*, 149.

9. Beth E. Richie, *Arrested Justice: Black Women, Violence, and America's Prison Nation* (New York: NYU Press, 2012), 65.

10. Richie, *Arrested Justice*, 94–95.

11. Mimi E. Kim, "The Carceral Creep: Gender-Based Violence, Race, and the Expansion of the Punitive State, 1973–1983," *Social Problems* 67, no. 2 (May 2020): 251–69, https://doi.org/10.1093/socpro/spz013.

12. Thuma, *All Our Trials*.

13. Alisa Bierria and Colby Lenz, *Defending Self-Defense: A Call to Action by Survived & Punished*, March 2022, https://csw.ucla.edu/wp-content/uploads/2022/03/DSD-Report-Mar-21-final.pdf.

14. John Roman, *Race, Justifiable Homicide, and Stand Your Ground Laws: Analysis of FBI Supplementary Homicide Report Data*, July 2013, https://www.urban.org/sites/default/files/publication/23856/412873-Race-Justifiable-Homicide-and-Stand-Your-Ground-Laws.PDF.

15. Mariame Kaba and Colby Lenz, "Bresha Meadows Returns Home After Collective Organizing Efforts," *Teen Vogue*, February 5, 2018, https://www.teenvogue.com/story/bresha-meadows-returns-home-after-collective-organizing-efforts.

CHAPTER 9: STRENGTHENING ACTIVISM

1. Sasha Khokha, "Before #MeToo, Women Janitors Rallied to Fight Workplace Harassment," *USA Today*, January 30, 2018, https://www.usatoday.com/story/news/nation/2018/01/30/women-janitors-fight-harassment/1077897001.

2. "Rape on the Night Shift," *Frontline*, PBS, 2015, https://www.pbs.org/wgbh/frontline/documentary/rape-on-the-night-shift/ 2015.

3. Lilia Garcia-Brower, "Bold Moves to End Sexual Violence: Self-Defense and Self-Empowerment for Women Workers," *Ms.*, August 1, 2018, https://msmagazine.com/2018/08/01/yo-soy-alguien.

CHAPTER 10: EMBRACING RESISTANCE

1. Gloucester Stage, "Conflict Resolution Path," https://gloucesterstage.com/_website/wp-content/uploads/2022/04/Conflict-Resolution-Path-22.pdf.

2. IMPACT Boston, *Line Drawn Summit and Survey Report*, https://cdn.ymaws.com/www.stagesource.org/resource/resmgr/files/line_drawn_summits_1_and_2_n.pdf.

3. Not in Our House, *Chicago Theatre Standards*, 2017, https://notinourhouseorg.files.wordpress.com/2022/03/chicago-theatre-standards-12-11-17-2.pdf.

4. Chelsea Pace, with contributions from Laura Rikard, *Staging Sex: Best Practices, Tools, and Techniques for Theatrical Intimacy* (New York: Routledge, 2020).

5. Bill Marx, "By Request: Out of the Past—Sexual Harassment Trouble at the Gloucester Stage Company," *The Arts Fuse*, November 2, 2018, https://artsfuse.org/165002/by-request-out-of-the-past-sexual-harassment-trouble-at-the-gloucester-stage

-company. Originally published in the *Boston Phoenix* in 1993 but not available online from the *Phoenix*.

6. Jessica Bennett, "Nine Women Accuse Israel Horovitz, Playwright and Mentor, of Sexual Misconduct, *New York Times*, November 30, 2017, https://www.nytimes.com /2017/11/30/theater/israel-horovitz-sexual-misconduct.html.

7. Center for Institutional Courage, https://www.institutionalcourage.org/the -call-to-courage.

8. Alec M. Smidt, Alexis A. Adams-Clark, and Jennifer J. Freyd, "Institutional Courage Buffers Against Institutional Betrayal, Protects Employee Health, and Fosters Organizational Commitment Following Workplace Sexual Harassment," *PloS One* 18, no. 1 (2023): e0278830, doi:10.1371/journal.pone.0278830.

9. Aguilar Shank, "Beyond Firing: How Do We Create Community-Wide Accountability for Sexual Harassment in Our Movements?" *Medium*, November 25, 2017, https://medium.com/@amashaoo/beyond-firing-how-do-we-create-community -wide-accountability-for-sexual-harassment-in-our-fb6b1259a24d.

10. Gloucester Stage, "In Memoriam: Passing of Israel Horovitz," 2020, https:// gloucesterstage.com/memoriam-horovitz.

CONCLUSION: SO, WHAT SHOULD I DO?
WHAT SHOULD I TELL MY DAUGHTER?

1. Lauren A. Leotti, Sheena S. Iyengar, and Kevin N. Ochsner, "Born to Choose: The Origins and Value of the Need for Control," *Trends in Cognitive Sciences* 14, no. 10 (2010): 457–63, https://doi.org/10.1016/j.tics.2010.08.001.

2. Jennifer S. Wong and Samantha Balemba, "The Effect of Victim Resistance on Rape Completion: A Meta-Analysis," *Trauma, Violence, & Abuse* 19, no. 3 (2018): 352–65, https://doi.org/10.1177/1524838016663934.

3. Nadia Telsey and Lauren R. Taylor, *Get Empowered: A Practical Guide to Thrive, Heal, and Embrace Your Confidence in a Sexist World* (New York: Penguin Random House, 2023), 45.

4. Gary Kleck and Jongyeon Tark, *Draft Final Technical Report: The Impact of Victim Self Protection on Rape Completion and Injury for United States Department of Justice*, 2005, https://www.ojp.gov/pdffiles1/nij/grants/211201.pdf.